THE *GAWAIN*-POET

GARLAND REFERENCE LIBRARY
OF THE HUMANITIES
(VOL. 129)

THE *GAWAIN*-POET
An Annotated Bibliography
1839–1977

Malcolm Andrew

GARLAND PUBLISHING, INC. • NEW YORK & LONDON
1979

Library of Congress Cataloging in Publication Data

Andrew, Malcolm.
　The Gawain-poet.

　(Garland reference library of the humanities ; v. 129)
　Includes indexes.
　1. English poetry—Middle English, 1100–1500—
Bibliography.　2. Pearl (Middle English poem)—
Bibliography.　3. Cleanness (Middle English poem)—
Bibliography.　4. Patience (Middle English poem)—
Bibliography.　5. Gawain and the Grene Knight—
Bibliography.　I. Title.
Z2014.P7A55　[PR1972.G35]　016.821′1　78-68243
ISBN 0-8240-9815-3

Printed on acid-free, 250-year-life paper
Manufactured in the United States of America

CONTENTS

v

ACKNOWLEDGMENTS

It is a pleasure to acknowledge the help I have received from many people during the preparation of this book.

I am grateful above all to Eiichi Suzuki, who provided references for much of the Japanese material, and supplied me with the information on which the notes for most of these items are based.

Another Japanese scholar, Toshiyuki Takamiya, read and provided notes for items 474, 570, 1209, and 1210. My wife, Lena, read materials written in Scandinavian languages, and helped me with German from time to time. Many friends and colleagues have cooperated by offering suggestions, checking references, and sending photocopies. My thanks are due especially to Carl T. Berkhout, A.S.G. Edwards, and Clifford Peterson, and also to Robert W. Ackerman, J.J. Anderson, J.B. Bamborough, Richard Beadle, Diane Bornstein, Gloria Cigman, David Farley-Hills, Manfred Görlach, Ralph Hanna, Avril Henry, Robert E. Lewis, Charlotte C. Morse, George B. Pace, Derek Pearsall, and Ronald Waldron. The editors of two journals obligingly supplied me with photocopies of articles which I had been unable to see: my thanks to Albert M. Gessman, editor of *Language Quarterly*, and Thomas H. Seiler, managing editor of publications of the Medieval Institute, Western Michigan University.

I am also grateful to the staffs of the libraries in which I have worked—the Cambridge University Library; the Bodleian Library, Oxford; the British Library, London; and the library of my own university, the University of East Anglia, Norwich. The inter-library-loan staff at the University of East Anglia, Ann Wood and her assistant Jean Eslick, have been particularly helpful in ordering many obscure items on my behalf. A number of American librarians were kind enough to answer specific

vii

queries: my thanks to Stephen A. Hanson of the University of
Southern California, Norma Hovden of the University of Minnesota, Joseph A. LoSchiavo of Fordham University, and the
inter-library-loan staff of Cornell University.

Finally, I am grateful to the University of East Anglia, Norwich, for providing me with the time and facilities for research.

INTRODUCTION

The outstanding quality of the four poems preserved in British Library MS Cotton Nero A.x.—*Pearl*, *Cleanness* (or *Purity*), *Patience*, and *Sir Gawain and the Green Knight*—has long been acknowledged. Their common survival in a unique manuscript, taken together with various similarities of style, theme, and outlook, has led a majority of scholars to conclude that they are the work of a single author, commonly referred to as "the *Gawain*-Poet" or "the *Pearl*-Poet." The same hypothetical author has sometimes been credited with another contemporary poem, *St. Erkenwald*—but this attribution is based on altogether less substantial grounds. In compiling a bibliography of writings on the four Cotton Nero poems, but excluding material purely on *St. Erkenwald*, I have been guided by the current critical consensus. Thus, for instance, the authors of the three most recent books on "the *Gawain*-Poet" (items 159, 330, and 358 in this bibliography) have all endorsed or taken for granted the common authorship of *Pearl*, *Cleanness*, *Patience*, and *Sir Gawain*, but none has included *St. Erkenwald* in the poet's canon. The name "the *Gawain*-Poet" in the title of this book has been used basically for the sake of clarity and convenience, and is not intended to signify support for the theory of common authorship.[1] Indeed, such a concern would seem entirely inappropriate in a book of this kind, the essential function of which is to record and summarize the views of others.

Since the publication of Madden's edition of *Sir Gawain* (item 97) in 1839, editors, translators, scholars, and critics have produced a substantial body of work on the four poems of MS Cotton Nero A.x. The object of this book is to provide a reasonably comprehensive yet reasonably compact bibliographical guide to these writings. Clearly such an intention requires more specific definition. The question of compactness is mainly con-

sidered below, in the comments on annotation (though certain of
my observations in this paragraph will also have some bearing on
the matter). The question of comprehensiveness is, of course,
fundamental to any bibliographical work. I therefore wish to
specify clearly the criteria on which material has been incorpo-
rated in this book or omitted from it. My intention has been to
include all editions and translations of any of the four poems,
and all books, articles, and notes specifically about one or more
of them.[2] This much is unproblematic; but dealing with various
other kinds of material—such as adaptations of the poems, or
brief but relevant comments contained in works mainly on some
other subject—is less straightforward. An item of the latter kind
has normally been included only if it provides at least two pages
of sustained relevant discussion. Though this criterion has been
used merely as a guide, and has not been rigidly adhered to, it
has provided a rational basis for the exclusion of many brief
passages from such works as encyclopedias and general literary
histories which could otherwise have cluttered the bibliography
with material of little relevance to the serious study of the
poems. Conversely, interesting or significant items, however
short and from whatever source, have been included. Adaptations, such as plays or children's books, have been omitted, and
discussions of the manuscript are included only if they have a
direct bearing on the poems themselves. There has been no
attempt to cover records, tapes, or films.

Reviews are listed under the more significant items: major
editions and translations, and critical works entirely or substan-
tially on the poet or on one or more of the poems. The listing of
reviews is selective (indeed, any attempt at comprehensive
coverage would seem both pointless and impractical). Further-
more, the number of reviews cited in any given case is intended
to reflect the relative importance of the work in question. These
proportions can, of course, be no more than approximate (since
the number of reviews available varies greatly from one work to
another) and cannot apply to recently published items (for
which adequate numbers of reviews have yet to appear). I have
attempted to select what seem to me the most significant and

interesting reviews and, wherever possible, to represent American, British, and European opinion.

It has been my intention to cite all relevant doctoral dissertations, together with selected theses for lower research degrees (B.Litt, M.A., M.Phil) at British universities.[3]

Items have been included in Section III (Reference) only if they contain a chapter or part of a chapter specifically devoted to the poet or to one or more of the poems. I am, nevertheless, glad to take this opportunity of acknowledging my indebtedness to various annual bibliographies—in particular those of the MLA and the M.H.R.A., *The Year's Work in English Studies*, and the "Bibliography of Critical Arthurian Literature" (1922–63)—as well as major reference works such as the *National Union Catalog* and the *British Museum General Catalogue of Printed Books*.

This bibliography is intended to cover the years 1839 to 1977. While the former date has some inherent significance, in that it marks the publication of the first edition of one of the poems, the latter is dictated merely by expediency. I have therefore felt free to include the three relevant books published during 1978 (items 1, 159, and 614).

It had been my intention to read every item contained in this bibliography, with the exception of the Japanese material read on my behalf by Professor Suzuki and Mr. Takamiya (see Acknowledgments, p. vii). This has—unfortunately, but, I suppose, inevitably—not proved possible, and a few items which I have not actually seen are therefore included.[4] In all such cases, I have made every effort to verify the reference, and have marked the entry "not seen." Untraceable items have generally been assumed to be "ghosts."

Arrangement of Material

The material has been divided and grouped as follows:[5]

    I. Editions and Translations:
        A. of more than one poem;
        B. of *Pearl*;
        C. of *Cleanness*;

    D. of *Patience*;
    E. of *Sir Gawain*.[6]
  II. Critical Writings:
    A. on more than one poem;
    B. on *Pearl*;
    C. on *Cleanness*;
    D. on *Patience*;
    E. on *Sir Gawain*.
  III. Reference.[7]

More detailed principles of arrangements and organization are specified in the following notes:

1. In order to locate all the material on a particular poem, it is necessary to check sections I.A and II.A as well as the sections specifically devoted to the poem in question.
2. All items on the identity of the poet, irrespective of title, are placed in section I.A. If the title of such an item might lead one to expect it to be located elsewhere, a cross-reference is supplied.
3. Cross-references are provided in cases of potential uncertainty, and for works involving more than one author, editor, or translator.
4. The concordance to the poems and facsimiles of the manuscript are included in section I.A.
5. Within each section, the sequence of items is alphabetical by name of author, editor, or translator (the letters *ä, ö, ø*, and *ü* being treated as *ae, oe, oe*, and *ue* respectively). If two or more items by the same author occur in a particular section, these are placed in chronological order. If two or more such items share the same year of publication, and no other logical order exists (as it does, for example, in the cases of items 539–40 and 931–32), then these are ordered alphabetically by title.
6. Authors' names are given exactly as they appear

on the title page of the work listed. In cases of potential confusion, or when the name appears elsewhere in a fuller form, the remainder of the full name is supplied within square brackets. A similar procedure is followed when it has been possible to establish the identity of an author whose name is represented by initials. The alphabetical position of such items is that of the full name, with cross-reference under the initials.

7. Where reviews are cited, they are arranged in alphabetical sequence of reviewers' names.

8. When a book has exactly the same title as the dissertation on which it is based, the two are combined in a single entry. If there are differences, they are listed as separate items.

9. The wording of titles is reproduced exactly, though excessively long subtitles are not recorded in full. Style in titles is normalized to MLA usage.

10. Titles originally in Japanese have been translated into English. Titles in other foreign languages are not translated.

11. Full bibliographical details are usually provided, but reprints are listed only if revision or a change of publisher has taken place. In cases where an item of relatively minor importance has a long and complex bibliographical history, listing of such details may be selective.

Annotation

Each published item is followed by a note on its contents. I have taken a pragmatic approach to the writing of these notes, for it seems to me that their function is essentially utilitarian. Since one of the main aims of this book is to provide a bibliographical guide of compact dimensions, the quantity of annotation has been strictly limited.[8] The length of each entry is approximately proportionate to that of the item it summarizes.

In my notes I have felt free to use the forms and terms I prefer (e.g., *Cleanness*, fitt), and—in cases of potential confusion or actual error—have normalized line numbers and spellings to those of the editions I take to be standard: Gordon's *Pearl*, Anderson's *Cleanness* and *Patience*, and Davis's revised version of Tolkien and Gordon's *Sir Gawain* (items 44, 58, 65, and 111).

Some notes include cross-references to related items. It has been my intention always to supply references to the components of specific critical debates, but beyond this, the choice of connections is a personal one, and is not intended to be objective, systematic, or exhaustive.[9]

Annotation is not provided for dissertations and theses, except in the form of a brief note to explain why a particular item has been included if this is not apparent from the title. References to abstracts of dissertations, where such exist and are known to me, are provided.

NOTES

1. It would, however, be disingenuous not to admit my own conviction: that a single poet wrote the four Cotton Nero poems, but was probably not responsible for *St. Erkenwald*.

2. I do, of course, acknowledge that I will have omitted some material inadvertently, and apologize for any inconvenience such omissions may cause.

3. In case this policy arouses suspicions of chauvinism on my part, I should like to point out that it was adopted at the suggestion of the publishers (and, incidentally, resulted in the exclusion of my own M.A. thesis).

4. These amount to less than one per cent of the total number of items in the bibliography.

5. Arranging a compilation of varied writings, each of which may deal with anything from one to four of the poems, presents considerable problems of organization. After experimenting with a number of different arrangements, I concluded that none provided the ideal blend of ease of reference and freedom from ambiguity, but that the arrangement adopted here was the least unsatisfactory.

6. The order *Pearl, Cleanness, Patience, Sir Gawain*, is that of the poems in the manuscript. It may well be merely accidental, but is followed since it is the only sequence which has authority of any kind.

7. It has also been necessary to place a few items (details of which were not available when the bulk of the entries was numbered) in a supplement. This supplementary list follows the same principles of organization and presentation as the main list.

8. It is, of course, impossible to do justice in a brief note to subtle or complex arguments. My aim has been to provide enough information to give a general impression of the subject of a particular item, and thus enable the reader to judge whether or not it is relevant to his interests.

9. In cases where I wish to provide a considerable number of references, these are not all listed under each relevant item. Instead, the complete list is supplied under one item, with a cross-reference under each of the others. Thus, for instance, all the material to which I refer the reader on the subject of the role of Morgan in *Gawain* is listed under item 696, while other relevant items are supplied with a note in the form: "cf. items 696, etc." Cross-references are not provided in cases where it is possible to locate material by using the line-number index (e.g., discussions of the name *Bertilak*, which occurs only in *Gawain*, line 2445).

ABBREVIATIONS

In the bibliographical entries, extensive use is made of abbreviations. The guiding principle has been to save space without making the material unduly difficult to read.

Abbreviations are listed below under four headings: 1. the poems; 2. journals and series; 3. collections, festschriften, and reference books; 4. general.

1. The Poems

Cl	*Cleanness* (cf. *Pur*)
Erk	*Erkenwald* (cf. *StE*)
G	Gawain (character)
G	*Gawain* (cf. *SG*, *SGGK*)
	(and in related titles: e.g., *The Turk and G* = *The Turk and Gawain*)
The GK	The Green Knight (character)
The GK	*The Green Knight* (poem in the Percy MS)
Pat	*Patience*
Pe	*Pearl* (cf. *The Pe*)
The Pe	*The Pearl* (cf. *Pe*)
Pur	*Purity* (cf. *Cl*)
SG	Sir Gawain (character)
SG	*Sir Gawain* (cf. *G*, *SGGK*)
SGGK	*Sir Gawain and the Green Knight* (cf. *G*, *SG*)
StE	*St. Erkenwald* (cf. *Erk*)

Note: Entries in the bibliography employ whichever of the variant abbreviations (*Cl* or *Pur*; *Erk* or *StE*; *Pe* or *The Pe*; *G*, *SG*, or *SGGK*) corresponds with the usage in the relevant item. In cases where an author uses a form not listed above (e.g., *Perle, Syr Gawayne*), it is left unabbreviated.

2. Journals and Series

ABR	American Benedictine Review
Academy	The Academy
Acme	Acme (Milan)
AF	Anglistische Forschungen
AION-SG	Annali Istituto Universitario Orientale di Napoli, Sezione Germanica
AN&Q	American Notes and Queries
AnglB	Anglia Beiblatt
AnM	Annuale Medievale (Duquesne University)
Archiv	Archiv für das Studium der neueren Sprachen und Literaturen
ARFAL	Annual Report of the Faculty of Arts and Letters (Tohoku University)
ArL	Archivum Linguisticum
Athen	The Athenaeum
AUSB	Annales Universitatis Scientiarum Budapestinensis de Rolando Eötvös nominatae, sectio philologica moderna
BBA	Bonner Beiträge zur Anglistik
BBCA	Baghdad Bulletin of the College of Arts
BBSIA	Bulletin Bibliographique de la Société Internationale Arthurienne
BDENU	Bulletin of the Department of Education of Nagasaki University
BFLA	Bulletin of the Faculty of Liberal Arts (Utsunomiya University)
BHB	Bulletin of Hiroshima Bunkyo Women's University
Bibelot	The Bibelot (Portland, Me.)
BK	Bulletin of Kocki Women's University
BKK	Bulletin of Kobe Kaisei Women's University
BR	Bunken Ronshu (Senshu University, Graduate School)
BRMMLA	Bulletin of the Rocky Mountain Modern Language Association
BSC	Bulletin of Seisen College
BSEP	Bonner Studien zur englischen Philologie
BTGU	Bulletin of the Tokyo Gakugei University
BTIT	Bulletin of the Tohoku Institute of Technology
BYU	Bulletin of the Yamagota University (Cultural Science)
C&L	Christianity and Literature

CathW	*Catholic World*
CE	*College English*
CEA	*CEA Critic*
ChauR	*Chaucer Review*
Cithara	*Cithara* (St. Bonaventure University)
CJL	*Canadian Journal of Linguistics*
CL	*Comparative Literature*
ClioI	*Clio: An Interdisciplinary Journal of Literature, History, and the Philosophy of History*
Comitatus	*Comitatus: Studies in Old and Middle English Literature*
Criticism	*Criticism* (Wayne State University)
CritQ	*Critical Quarterly*
DA	*Dissertation Abstracts* (continued as *DAI*)
DAI	*Dissertation Abstracts International* (continuation of *DA*)
DBGÜ	*Deutsche Beiträge zur Geistigen Überlieferung*
DelN	*Delaware Notes*
DQR	*Dutch Quarterly Review*
DUB	*Dacca University Bulletin*
DUJ	*Durham University Journal*
EA	*Etudes Anglaises*
EALit	*English and American Literature* (Japan)
E&S	*Essays and Studies by Members of the English Association*
EASG	*English and American Studies in German: Summaries of Theses and Monographs*
EBS	*Eigo Bungaku Sekai*
EGS	*English and Germanic Studies*
EIC	*Essays in Criticism*
EigoS	*Eigo Seinen* ("The Rising Generation")
ELH	*ELH: A Journal of English Literary History*
ELN	*English Language Notes*
EM	*English Miscellany*
EngR	*English Record*
EngS	*English Studies* (Tokyo Gakugei University)
EQ	*English Quarterly* (Japan)
ES	*English Studies*
ESA	*English Studies in Africa*
ESC	*English Studies in Canada*
ESELL	*Essays and Studies in English Language and Literature* (Tohoku Gakuin University)

ESQ	*Emerson Society Quarterly*
EStn	*Englische Studien*
Expl	*The Explicator*
F-L	*Folk-Lore*
FMLS	*Forum for Modern Language Studies* (University of St. Andrews)
ForL	*Foreign Literature* (Utsunomiya University)
GeibunK	*The Geibun Kenkyu*
Genre	*Genre* (University of Illinois at Chicago Circle)
GGP	Grundriss der germanischen Philologie
GHÅ	*Göteborgs Högskolas Årsskrift*
GothSE	Gothenburg Studies in English
GRM	*Germanisch-Romanische Monatsschrift*
HSELL	*Hiroshima Studies in English Language and Literature*
Interpretations	*Interpretations: Studies in Language and Literature*
Ivy	*Ivy: The Nagoya Review of English Studies*
JAE	*Journal of Aesthetic Education*
JAF	*Journal of American Folklore*
JAsiat	*Journal Asiatique*
JCulS	*Journal of Cultural Science* (Kobe University of Commerce)
JEGP	*Journal of English and Germanic Philology*
JEI	*Journal of the English Institute* (Tohoku Gakuin University)
JFA	*Journal of the Faculty of Arts* (University of Malta)
JFFL	*Journal of the Faculty of Foreign Languages* (Komazawa University)
JFLit	*Journal of Foreign Literature* (Komazawa University)
JLDS	*Journal of the Lancashire Dialect Society*
JNT	*Journal of Narrative Technique*
JPC	*Journal of Popular Culture* (Bowling Green University)
KenK	*Kenkyu-Kiyo* (Keisen Women's Junior College)
KSELL	*Kagoshima Studies in English Language and Literature*
L&P	*Literature and Psychology* (Fairleigh Dickinson University)
Lang	*Language: Journal of the Linguistic Society of America*
Lang&S	*Language and Style: An International Journal*
LangQ	*Language Quarterly* (University of South Florida)
LanM	*Les Langues Modernes*

LAR	*The Liberal Arts Review* (Tohoku University)
LeedsSE	*Leeds Studies in English and Kindred Languages* (Old Series); *Leeds Studies in English* (New Series)
LfGRP	*Literaturblatt für germanische und romanische Philologie*
LHR	*The Lock Haven Review* (Lock Haven State College, Pa.)
Library	*The Library*
LingS	*Linguistic Science* (Kyushu University)
LMS	*London Mediaeval Studies*
LT	*Levende Talen*
LundSE	Lund Studies in English
MAE	*Medium AEvum*
M&H	*Medievalia et Humanistica* (North Texas State University)
MCR	*Melbourne Critical Review*
MEB	*Missouri English Bulletin*
Mimesis	*Mimesis* (Tezukayama Gakuin University)
MLN	*Modern Language Notes*
MLQ	*Modern Language Quarterly* (Seattle)
MLQ (Lon)	*Modern Language Quarterly* (London)
MLR	*Modern Language Review*
MM	*The Mariner's Mirror: the Journal of The Society for Nautical Research*
Month	*The Month*
MP	*Modern Philology*
MS	*Mediaeval Studies* (Toronto)
MSE	*Massachusetts Studies in English*
MSpr	*Moderna Språk*
MTJ	*Mark Twain Journal*
Names	*Names: Journal of the American Name Society*
N&Q	*Notes and Queries*
NDEJ	*Notre Dame English Journal*
Neophil	*Neophilologus*
NM	*Neuphilologische Mitteilungen*
NMS	*Nottingham Mediaeval Studies*
NS	*Die Neueren Sprache*
NSM	*Nuovi studi medievali*
OL	*Orbis Litterarum*
OSR	*The Okayama Shodai Ronso*

Palaestra	Palaestra (Lisbon)
PAPA	*Publications of the Arkansas Philological Association*
PAPS	*Proceedings of the American Philosophical Society*
Parergon	*Parergon: Bulletin of the Australian and New Zealand Association for Medieval and Renaissance Studies*
Parnassus	*Parnassus: Poetry in Review*
PBA	*Proceedings of the British Academy*
PELL	*Papers on English Language and Literature* (continued as *PLL*)
PLL	*Papers on Language and Literature* (continuation of *PELL*)
PMASAL	*Papers of the Michigan Academy of Science, Arts, and Letters*
PMLA	*Publications of the Modern Language Association of America*
PMLC	*Papers of the Manchester Literary Club*
Poetica	*Poetica: International Journal of Linguistic-Literary Studies* (Tokyo)
PP	*Philologica Pragensia*
PQ	*Philological Quarterly*
PRPSG	*Proceedings of the Royal Philosophical Society of Glasgow*
QF	Quellen und Forschungen zur Sprach- und Kulturgeschichte der germanischen Völker
RBPH	*Revue Belge de Philologie et d'Histoire*
RES	*Review of English Studies*
RH	*Roczniki Humanistyczne*
RikR	*The Rikkyo Review* (Japan)
RKHS	*Register of the Kentucky Historical Society*
RLC	*Revue de Littérature Comparée*
RPh	*Romance Philology*
RR	*Romanic Review*
RUO	*Revue de l'Université d'Ottawa*
SA	*The Scottish Antiquary or Northern Notes and Queries*
Saga-Book	*Saga-Book of the Viking Club*
SB	*Studies in Bibliography*
SBK	*Seiyo Bungaku Kenkyu* (Tokyo University of Education)
ScA	*The Scottish Antiquary*
ScR	*Scottish Review*

ScS	*Scottish Studies*
SDAP	*Studies in Descriptive and Applied Linguistics* (Japan)
SEEP	Select Early English Poems
SELing	*Studies in English Linguistics* (Japan)
SELit	*Studies in English Literature* (Japan)
SELL	*Studies in English Language and Literature* (Fukuoka, Japan)
SEP	Studien zur englische Philologic
SETG	*Studies and Essays of Tezukayama Gakuin University Faculty*
Shiron	*Shiron* (Tohoku University)
ShoR	*The Shodai Ronshu* (Kobe University of Commerce)
SHumD	*Studies in the Humanities* (Doshisha University)
SHumF	*Studies in the Humanities* (Fukuoka Women's University)
SHumO	*Studies in the Humanities* (Osaka City University)
SHumS	*Studies in the Humanities* (Shizuoka University)
SLitI	*Studies in the Literary Imagination* (Georgia State College)
SLUS	*St. Louis University Studies*
SMC	*Studies in Medieval Culture* (Western Michigan University)
SML	*Statistical Methods in Linguistics* (Stockholm)
SN	*Studia Neophilologica*
SoQ	*The Southern Quarterly* (University of Southern Mississippi)
SoRA	*Southern Review* (Adelaide)
SP	*Studies in Philology*
SPR	*St. Paul's Review* (Tokyo)
StEng	*Studies in English* (University of Cape Town)
StG	*Studi Germanici*
StI	*Studia Islandica*
StLit	*Studies in Literature* (Kyushu University, Faculty of Literature)
Style	*Style* (University of Arkansas)
TC	*The Twentieth Century*
TGAS	*Transactions of the Glasgow Archaeological Society*
Theoria	*Theoria: A Journal of Studies in the Arts, Humanities and Social Sciences*
THES	*The Times Higher Education Supplement* (London)

Times	*The Times* (London)
TkR	*Tamkang Review*
TLS	*The Times Literary Supplement* (London)
Tohoku	*Tohoku* (Tohoku Gakuin University Graduate School)
TPB	*Tennessee Philological Bulletin*
TPS	*Transactions of the Philological Society*
Trivium	*Trivium* (St. David's College, Lampeter)
TSE	*Tulane Studies in English*
TYDS	*Transactions of the Yorkshire Dialect Society*
UCS	*University of Colorado Studies*
UE	*Use of English*
UES	*Unisa English Studies*
UpsalaE&S	English Institute in the University of Upsala: Essays and Studies in English Language and Literature
UTQ	*University of Toronto Quarterly*
UWPE	*University of Washington Publications in English*
Viator	*Viator: Medieval and Renaissance Studies*
W&R	*The Wind and the Rain*
WBEP	Weiner Beiträge zur englischen Philologie
WUSt	*Washington University Studies, Humanistic Series*
WVUPP	*West Virginia University Bulletin: Philological Papers*
XUS	*Xavier University Studies*
YAPS	*Yearbook of the American Philosophical Society*
YES	*Yearbook of English Studies*
YSE	Yale Studies in English
YWES	*Year's Work in English Studies*
ZAA	*Zeitschrift für Anglistik und Amerikanistik* (East Berlin)

3. Collections, Festschriften, and Reference Books

Abrams	*The Norton Anthology of English Literature.* Ed. M.H. Abrams, et al. New York: Norton, 1962; rev. eds., 1968, 1975.
Chambers	*Chambers's Cyclopaedia of English Literature*, I. London and Edinburgh: Chambers, 1901.
Daiches/Thorlby	*The Medieval World. Literature and Western Civilization.* Ed. David Daiches and Anthony Thorlby. London: Aldus Books, 1973.
DNB	*The Dictionary of National Biography*
Enc. Brit.	*The Encyclopaedia Britannica*, 11th ed.
Ford	*The Age of Chaucer. The Pelican Guide to English Literature*, I. Ed. Boris Ford. Harmondsworth and Baltimore: Penguin, 1954; rev. eds., 1959, 1969.
Frappier	*Mélanges de Langue et de Littérature du Moyen Age et de la Renaissance Offerts à Jean Frappier . . . par ses collègues, ses élèves et ses amis.* 2 vols. Publications Romanes et Françaises, 112. Genève: Droz, 1970.
Frost	*The Age of Chaucer.* Ed. William Frost. *English Masterpieces: An Anthology of Imaginative Literature from Chaucer to T.S. Eliot*, I. Gen. ed. Maynard Mack. New York: Prentice-Hall, 1950; 2nd ed., Englewood Cliffs, N.J., 1961.
Hornstein	*Medieval Studies in Honor of Lillian Herlands Hornstein.* Ed. Jess B. Bessinger, Jr., and Robert R. Raymo. New York: New York UP, 1976.
Kuranaga	Kuranaga, Makoto. *English Literature and Christianity.* Tokyo: Kenkusha, 1965.
Loomis/Loomis	*Medieval Romances.* Ed. Roger Sherman Loomis and Laura Hibbard Loomis. The Mod. Lib. New York: Random House, 1957.
Loomis/Willard	*Medieval English Verse and Prose in Modernized Versions.* Ed. Roger Sherman Loomis and Rudolph Willard. New York: Appleton, 1948.
MED	*The Middle English Dictionary*

Newstead	*Chaucer and His Contemporaries: Essays on Medieval Literature and Thought.* Ed. Helaine Newstead. Greenwich, Conn.: Fawcett, 1968.
OED	*The Oxford English Dictionary*
Oiji	*Chaucer and His Contemporaries.* Ed. Takero Oiji. Tokyo: Bunrishoin, 1968.
Robbins	*Chaucer and Middle English Studies in Honor of Rossell Hope Robbins.* Ed. Beryl Rowland. Kent, Ohio: Kent State UP; London: Allen and Unwin, 1974.
Schlauch	*Studies in Language and Literature in Honour of Margaret Schlauch.* Warszawa: Panstwowe Wydawnictwo Naukowe, 1966; New York: Russell and Russell, 1971.
Severs/Hartung	Severs, Jonathan Burke, and Albert E. Hartung, ed. *A Manual of the Writings in Middle English 1050–1500.* New Haven: Connecticut Academy of Arts and Sciences, 1967–.
Willard	*Studies in Language, Literature, and Culture of the Middle Ages and Later: Studies in Honor of Rudolph Willard.* Ed. E. Bagby Atwood and Archibald A. Hill. Austin: Univ. of Texas, 1969.
Witherspoon	*The College Survey of English Literature.* Shorter, rev. ed. Ed. Alexander M. Witherspoon, et al. New York: Harcourt, 1951.
Zesmer	Zesmer, David M. *Guide to English Literature: From "Beowulf" through Chaucer and Medieval Drama.* College Outline ser., 53. New York: Barnes and Noble, 1961.

4. General

abst.	abstract
AN	Anglo-Norman
anon.	anonymous
art.	article
AS	Anglo-Saxon
bibliog.	bibliographical
cf.	compare
chap.	chapter
col.	column
comp.	compiler(s), compiled by
cont.	continued
corr.	correction, corrected
CT	*The Canterbury Tales*, in *The Works of Geoffrey Chaucer*, ed. F.N. Robinson, 2nd ed., Boston: Houghton, 1957.
diss.	dissertation
ed.	edition, editor(s), edited by
enl.	enlarged
ES	Extra Series
et al.	and others
fasc.	fascicle
gen.	general
hist.	history
lang.	language
lib.	library
ME	Middle English
MLA	Modern Language Association of America
mod.	modern
ModE	Modern English
MS	Manuscript
n.d.	no date
no.	number
n.p.	no place
NS	New Series
NW	North-West(ern)
OE	Old English
OF	Old French
ON	Old Norse
OS	Original Series

OT	Old Testament
p., pp.	page, pages
para.	paragraph
p.b.	paperback
pr.	printed
pt.	part
pub.	published, publisher
rev.	revision, revised (by)
rpt.	reprint(ed)
sect.	section
ser.	series
soc.	society
Sr.	Sister
sum.	summary
supp.	supplement(ary)
tr.	translation, translated by
univ.	university
UP	University Press
vol.	volume

ANNOTATED BIBLIOGRAPHY

I. EDITIONS AND TRANSLATIONS

A. Editions and Translations of More Than One Poem

*   Anderson, J.J.   See item 5.

1.   Andrew, Malcolm, and Ronald Waldron, ed. *The Poems of the "Pe" MS:* *"Pe," "Cl," "Pat," "SGGK"*. York Medieval Texts, 2nd ser. London: Arnold, 1978.

   Contains ME texts, with textual and explanatory notes below, followed by a full glossary. Major biblical sources (Vulgate text) are printed in the appendix. The introduction provides discussion of the alliterative revival and general critical comments on each poem, with emphasis on the relationship between the narrative and didactic intent in *Pat*, and on that between theme and structure in *Cl*; on formal unity and the development of the Dreamer in *Pe*; and on the subtlety, ambiguity, and avoidance of didacticism in *G*. Includes an extensive bibliography. Cf. item 18.

2.   Brandl, A., and O. Zippel, ed. *Mittelenglische Sprach- und Literaturproben: Ersatz für Mätzners Altenglische Sprachproben*. Berlin: Weidmann, 1917; 2nd ed., subtitled *Neuausgabe von Mätzners...*, 1927; tr. as *ME Literature*, New York: Chelsea, 1947.

   Includes text of *G* 491–535 and 730–1125, and of *Pe* 1–360 (pp. 58–66, 140–44).

3.   Burrow, John [A.], ed. *English Verse 1300–1500*. Longman Annotated Anthologies of English Verse, 1. London and New York: Longman, 1977.

   Provides partially modernized texts of *Pat* 61–296, *Pe* 121–360, and *G* 1998–2530 (pp. 48–61, 63–76, 78–104), with commentary and glosses at the foot of the page. Each text is preceded by a brief note on themes, sources, and critical

writings. The general introduction provides comments on
alliterative verse and on the stanza forms of *G* and *Pe*.

*   Byrnes, Edward T. See item 7.

4.   Cawley, A.C., ed. *"Pe"* [;] *"SGGK"*. Everyman's Library.
        London: Dent; New York: Dutton, 1962; p.b., 1972.

        An edition of *Pe* and *G*, with partially modernized spell-
        ing, marginal glosses of obscure words, and translations
        of difficult lines at the foot of the page. The intro-
        duction offers brief comments on the alliterative reviv-
        al, and summaries and general critical readings of each
        poem. Also provides a select bibliography, and appen-
        dixes on spelling, grammar, and metre.

5.   ———, and J.J. Anderson, ed. *"Pe*[,]*" "Cl*[,]*" "Pat*[,]*"*
        [*and*] *"SGGK"*. Everyman's Library. London: Dent; New
        York: Dutton, 1976.

        An expanded version of item 4. Adds texts of *Cl* and *Pat*
        (treated similarly to those of *Pe* and *G*). Brief sec-
        tions, offering general critical readings of *Cl* and *Pat*,
        are added to the introduction.

        Reviews: G.C. Britton, *N&Q*, 222 (1977), 282–83.
                 Derek Pearsall, *RES*, NS 29 (1978), 69–70.

6.   Cook, Albert Stanburrough, ed. *A Literary ME Reader*.
        Boston, New York, etc.: Ginn, 1915; rpt. Folcroft, Pa.:
        Folcroft, 1974 (limited ed.).

        Fully glossed text of *G* 130–249, 2212–478 and of *Pe*
        (based on item 56) 37–300, 385–420 (pp. 53–70, 441–53).

7.   Dunn, Charles W., and Edward T. Byrnes, ed. *ME Litera-
        ture*. New York, Chicago, etc.: Harcourt, 1973.

        Complete, partially modernized texts of *Pe* and *G* (pp.
        339–459), with marginal glosses and brief introductions.
        The general introduction includes critical comments and
        notes on verse-form (pp. 30, 33).

8.   Gardner, John, tr. *The Complete Works of the "G"-Poet:
        In a Modern English Version with a Critical Introduction*.
        Chicago, London, and Amsterdam: Univ. of Chicago Press,
        1965; p.b., Carbondale and Edwardsville: Southern Illi-
        nois UP; London and Amsterdam: Feffer and Simons, 1970;
        Univ. of Chicago Press, 1975.

Contains translations of the four poems (and *Erk*), in
verse which stays fairly close to the originals. Quatrains are used for *Pat* but not for *Cl*. The long introduction includes discussion of the following topics: the
poet; the alliterative revival; number symbolism; the
use of sources and conventions; four-level exegesis; the
poet's view of nature and his dramatic sense. Goes on
to provide general critical accounts of each poem, sometimes applying four-level interpretation, and arguing
that all deal with the discrepancy between earthly and
heavenly values. Cf. item 32.

Reviews: Larry D. Benson, *JEGP*, 65 (1966), 580-83.
Cecily Clark, *MAE*, 36 (1967), 285-87.
Donald R. Howard, *Speculum*, 42 (1967), 149-52.
Dieter Mehl, *Anglia*, 85 (1967), 82-90.

9. Gerould, Gordon Hall, tr. *"Beowulf" and "SGGK": Poems
of Two Great Eras with Certain Contemporary Pieces.* New
York: Ronald, 1929.

Includes a prose translation of *G* and a verse translation of *Pe* 1-180, with brief introduction and notes.
Cf. item 10.

10. ————, tr. *OE and Medieval Literature.* Nelson's English ser. New York: Nelson, 1929; rev. eds., 1933, 1935,
1937. Rev. as *Beowulf to Shakespeare*, New York: Nelson,
1938; rev. ed., New York: Ronald, 1945; rpt., St. Clair
Shores, Mich.: Scholarly Press, 1972.

Contains the same material as item 9.

11. Gollancz, I[srael], ed. *"Pe," "Cl," "Pat," and "SG":
Reproduced in facsimile from the unique MS. Cotton Nero
A.x in the British Museum.* EETS, OS 162. London, New
York, and Toronto: Oxford UP, 1923.

A facsimile of the entire MS, including illustrations.
The introduction provides discussion of the history of
the MS and its illustrations, and a list of scribal errors and suggested emendations. Cf. item 17.

Review: W.W. Greg, *MLR*, 19 (1924), 223-28.

12. Hartley, Dorothy, tr. *The Old Book: A Medieval Anthology.* London and New York: Knopf, 1930.

Includes loose, and somewhat contracted, translations of
Pat 247-300 (p. 128) and 437-507 (pp. 265-66), and of *Cl*
297-540 (pp. 183-89).

13. Haskell, Ann S., ed. *A ME Anthology*. Garden City,
     N.Y.: Doubleday, 1969.

     Contains complete ME texts of *G* (pp. 1–138) and *Pe* (pp.
     278–341), with partially modernized spelling and glosses
     on the facing page. Also provides bibliographies of
     editions and translations (pp. 525, 527).

14. Kaiser, Rolf, ed. *Alt- und Mittelenglische Anthologie*.
     Berlin: privately pr., 1954; 2nd ed., 1955; 3rd ed., rev.
     and tr. as *Medieval English: An OE and ME Anthology*.
     Berlin: privately pr., 1958; rev., 1961; rpt., St. Clair
     Shores, Mich.: Scholarly Press, 1971.

     Includes texts of *Pe* 1–192, 229–88, 409–20, 961–96, 1093–
     1188, 1201–12, and *G* 691–927, 1690–1732, 1998–2068, 2479–
     503 (pp. 297–304 and 417–24 in English ed.).

15. Kluge, Friedrich, ed. *Mittelenglisches Lesebuch*. With
     glossary by Arthur Kölbing. Halle a.S.: Niemeyer,
     1904; 2nd ed., 1912.

     Contains texts (based on items 99 and 19) of *G* 491–535
     and *Pat* 61–244 (pp. 115–19).

*   Kölbing, Arthur. See item 15.

16. Kottler, Barnet, and Alan M. Markman, comp. *A Concord-
     ance to Five ME Poems: "Cl," "StE," "SGGK," "Pat," "Pe"*.
     Pittsburgh: University of Pittsburgh Press, 1966.

     A computer concordance. The preface specifies texts and
     principles, and is followed by lists of omitted words
     and variant readings. The appendixes list words partial-
     ly concorded, and head-words in order of frequency.
     (See item 253).

     Reviews: Larry D. Benson, *Speculum*, 42 (1967), 382–84.
              Norman Davis, *MAE*, 37 (1968), 324–28.
              Charles Moorman, *ChauR*, 3 (1969), 304–08.
              Eiichi Suzuki, *ESELL*, 51–52 (1967), 352–56.

*   Markman, Alan M. See item 16.

17. MLA. Collection of Photographic Facsimiles, no. 2. New
     York: MLA, ?1923.

     A facsimile of the MS. Not seen.

18. Moorman, Charles, ed. *The Works of the "G"-Poet*. Jack-
     son: UP of Mississippi, 1977.

An unpunctuated ME text of the four poems, with textual
and explanatory notes at the foot of the page, followed
by a limited glossary. The introduction provides discussion of: editorial principles; the MS; the alliterative revival; authorship, date, and place of composition;
sources and analogues; the literary art of each poem;
and general themes. It ends with a brief review of the
poet's language, and is followed by an extensive bibliography. Cf. item 1.

Review: M. Stokes, *RES*, NS 29 (1978), 334-35.

19. Morris, Richard, ed. *Early English Alliterative Poems
in the West-Midland Dialect of the Fourteenth Century*.
EETS, OS 1. London, New York, and Toronto: Oxford UP,
1864; rev. ed., 1869. Extract from preface rpt. in item
397.

The first edition of *Pe*, *Cl*, and *Pat*. Texts are printed
with plot summary and textual notes in the margins, and
are followed by explanatory notes and glossary. The preface argues that the poems were written in the West Midland dialect, suggests that the poet may also be the
author of the *Destruction of Troy*, summarizes each poem,
and provides a review of dialect and language.

20. ———, R[ichard], ed. *Specimens of Early English: Selected from the Chief English Authors*. Clarendon Press
ser. Oxford: Clarendon, 1867.

Contains texts of *Cl* 235-544, 947-72, 1009-51, and of *G*
1-490, with notes and glossary. Cf. item 63.

21. Mossé, Fernand, ed. *Manuel de l'Anglais du Moyen Age
des Origines au XIVe Siècle*. Editions Montaigne. Paris:
Aubier, 1949. The 2nd pt. tr. by James A. Walker as *A
Handbook of ME*. Baltimore: Johns Hopkins, 1952.

Excerpts from *G* (713-62, 1126-1401) and *Pe* (985-1093),
with introductory comments and extensive notes.

22. Neilson, W.A., and K.G.T. Webster, ed. *Chief British
Poets of the Fourteenth and Fifteenth Centuries: Selected
Poems*. The Chief Poets ser. Boston: Houghton; London:
Harrap, 1916.

Contains prose translations of *Pe* and *G* (pp. 7-18, 21-
47), together with the ME text of *Pe* 1-72 and *G* 1-84.
Cf. item 115.

23. Sampson, George, ed. *The Cambridge Book of Prose and Verse in Illustration of English Literature from the Beginnings to the Cycles of Romance*. Cambridge: UP, 1924.

   Includes (pp. 318-39): comments on the MS; *Pe* 37-48, 61-96, 157-252, 985-1032, 1045-56, 1093-1116, 1177-88 (based on item 43) with linking summaries, followed by a translation of the same lines (based on item 36); a summary of *Cl*; *Pat* 137-76 (based on item 68); *G* 130-78, 203-31, 279-300, 390-459 (based on item 100 [rev. ed.]) with linking summaries. All ME texts are partially modernized.

24. Sisam, Celia and Kenneth, ed. *The Oxford Book of Medieval English Verse*. Oxford: Clarendon, 1970; corr. rpt., 1973.

   Contains *Pe* 1-180, *Pat* 137-240, and *G* 1178-1318, 1372-1401, in partially modernized texts with parallel translation.

25. Sisam, Kenneth, ed. *Fourteenth Century Verse and Prose*. Oxford: Clarendon, 1921; corr. eds., 1937, 1955.

   Provides ME text of *G* 2069-428 and *Pe* 361-612 (pp. 44-56, 57-67), with brief prefatory comments, textual and explanatory notes, and glossary (by J.R.R. Tolkien).

26. Spearing, A.C. and J.E., ed. *Poetry of the Age of Chaucer*. London: Arnold, 1974.

   Contains (pp. 80-135) partially modernized texts of *G* 37-490 and *Pat* 61-352, with notes and glosses on the facing page. Individual introductions provide plot summaries and general critical accounts. The general introduction includes comments on dialect (pp. 21-22) and the genres of romance and sermon (pp. 27-28, 30-32), as well as numerous passing references to both poems.

* Spearing, J.E. See item 26.

27. Stone, Brian, tr. *Medieval English Verse*. Harmondsworth and Baltimore: Penguin, 1964.

   Includes (pp. 118-74) translations (which stay fairly close to the verse forms of the originals) of *Pat* and *Pe*, each preceded by a brief general introduction on themes and sources.

28. Tolkien, J.R.R., tr. *"SGGK," "Pe," and "Sir Orfeo."*
London: Allen and Unwin; Boston: Houghton, 1975.

Contains (pp. 25-122) complete translations, which imi-
tate the original verse forms, of *G* and *Pe*, followed by
a glossary of archaic words (pp. 138-41). The introduction provides brief comments on the poet, and general
critical observations on both poems (pp. 13-23).

Review: Roger Sale, *Parnassus*, 4, ii (1976), 183-91.

* ————. Soo aloo item 25.

* Waldron, Ronald. See item 1.

* Walker, James A. See item 21.

29. Warren, Kate M., ed. and tr. *A Treasury of English Literature (From the Beginning to the Eighteenth Century).*
London: Constable, 1906. The relevant pt. also pub.
separately as *Twelfth Century to Age of Elizabeth.* London: Constable, 1908.

Texts, with translations at the foot of the page, and
linking summaries, of *G* 232-49, 301-42, 740-47; *Pe* 49-
72, 157-72; *Cl* 529-39, 947-72; *Pat* 437-81 (pp. 162-71 in
1st ed.).

* Webster, K.G.T. See item 22.

30. Weston, Jessie L., tr. *Romance, Vision and Satire: English Alliterative Poems of the Fourteenth Century.* Boston and New York: Houghton; London: Nutt, 1912; rpt.
Gloucester, Mass.: Smith, 1965.

Includes translations, which stay fairly close to the
original verse forms, of *G* and *Pe* (complete), *Cl* 1357-
1812, and *Pat* 61-344, followed by brief notes.

31. Williams, Margaret, tr. "Pe-Poetry," in her *Glee-Wood:
Passages from ME Literature from the Eleventh Century to
the Fifteenth.* New York: Sheed and Ward, 1949. Pp. 360-
418.

Sections on each poem, containing introductory comments,
followed by verse translations of selected passages, with
linking summaries. The lines translated are: *G* 25-59,
85-106, 130-78, 417-51, 500-35, 713-66, 785-810, 842-63,
1105-25, 1180-1207, 1383-89, 1690-98, 1846-59, 1998-2024,

2171-238, 2299-330, 2345-68, 2513-30; *Cl* 601-44, 781-
812, 941-68, 1805-12; *Pat* 61-116, 129-60, 181-96, 221-
28, 245-76, 301-20, 325-28, 337-48, 524-27; *Pe* 1-12, 25-
84, 109-20, 157-216, 229-76, 409-68, 481-92, 637-48,
745-68, 793-804, 841-52, 961-84, 1045-56, 1069-80, 1093-
1116, 1129-1212.

32.   ————, R.S.C.J., tr. *The "Pe"-Poet: His Complete Works.*
New York: Random House, 1967; p.b., Vintage, 1970.

Contains translations of the four poems and *Erk*, in
verse which stays close to the originals (using quatrains for *Pat* and *Cl*). Additional material includes
appendixes on the MS, language, and prosody, a substantial bibliography, and charts illustrating the structure
of each poem. The extensive introduction provides background information on the alliterative revival and the
poet's cultural and intellectual milieu (including rhetorical and exegetical traditions), and general critical
comments. Particular topics covered include: the homiletic intent and handling of scriptural sources in *Pat*
and *Cl*; sources, *cortaysye*, various critical approaches,
and the moral theme in *G*; the debate, the influence of
Dante and Boccaccio, elegiac and allegorical interpretations, and lapidary symbolism in *Pe*. Cf. item 8.

*   Zippel, O. See item 2.

                 B. Editions and Translations of *Pearl*

*   Andrews, Alice E. See item 53.

*   Balfour, Dale Elliman. See item 39.

*   Blaustein, Donna Rosenbaum. See item 39.

33.   Borroff, Marie, tr. *"Pe": A New Verse Translation.* New
York: Norton; Toronto: McLeod, 1977.

A line-by-line translation which reproduces the schemes
of "rhyme, repetition, and concatenation" of the original. The introduction offers general critical comments
and a plot summary. Appendices deal with the metrical
form and provide specimen scansions.

Review: Denton Fox, *N&Q*, 223 (1978), 74.

34. Bowdoin College, Members of the Chaucer Course, ed.
     "The Pe": *The Text of the Fourteenth Century English*
     Poem. Boston: Humphries, 1932; London: Daniel, 1933.

     Provides a ME text and glossary. The appendix consists
     of a note on the treatment of the text, a list of tex-
     tual variants, a note on the language, and a bibliogra-
     phy. Foreword by S.P. C[hase].

     Reviews: Dorothy Everett, *RES*, 9 (1933), 467–69.
              Karl Hammerle, *Archiv*, 165 (1934), 94–99.
              Clark S. Northup, *JEGP*, 33 (1934), 116–17.

35. Chase, Stanley Perkins, tr. *"The Pe"*: *The Fourteenth*
     Century English Poem Rendered in Modern Verse. New York
     and London: Oxford UP, 1932.

     A translation which follows the metre and rhyme of the
     original. The extensive introduction provides basic in-
     formation on the language and authorship; a summary of
     the poem's argument; a summary of elegiac and allegori-
     cal interpretations (with endorsement of the latter);
     and comments on form and metre.

     Reviews: Everett and Hammerle, cited under item 34.

*   ———. See also item 34.

36. Coulton, G.G., tr. *"Pe"*: *A Fourteenth-Century Poem,*
     rendered into Modern English. London: Nutt, 1906; 2nd
     ed., 1907; 3rd ed., Methuen's English Classics ser.,
     London: Methuen, 1921.

     A line-for-line translation which follows the original
     metre and rhyme-scheme. Includes a brief introduction.
     Cf. item 400.

     Reviews: Clark S. Northup, *MLN*, 22 (1907), 21–22 (item
              512).
              H.T. Price, *AnglB*, 17 (1906), 290–91.

37. Crawford, John F., and Andrew Hoyem, tr. *"The Pe."* San
     Francisco: Grabhorn-Hoyem, 1967.

     Consists of a translation with the ME text printed in-
     terlinearly. Not seen.

*   Davidov, Myrna. See item 39.

38. Decker, Otto, tr. *"Die Perle"*: *Das mittelenglische Ge-*
     dicht in freier metrischer Übertragung. Beilage zum

Jahresbericht des Grossherzoglichen Realgymnasiums zu
Schwerin). Schwerin: Sengebusch, 1916.

A verse translation in German. Includes a brief general
introduction.

39. deFord, Sara, ed. and tr. *Anonymous: "The Pe."* Crofts
    Classics. New York: Appleton; p.b., Northbrook, Ill.:
    AHM, 1967.

    Provides a ME text, with notes at the foot of the page,
    a brief introduction, and a select bibliography--all by
    deFord. The verse translation, printed facing the text,
    is credited to deFord with Dale Elliman Balfour, Donna
    Rosenbaum Blaustein, Myrna Davidov, Clarinda Harriss
    Lott, and Evelyn Dyke Schroedl. See item 407.

40. Farnham, Anthony E., ed. *A Sourcebook in the History of
    English.* New York, etc.: Holt, 1969.

    Following brief introductory comments, provides ME text
    of *Pe* 61-120 (leaving scribal abbreviations unexpanded)
    with parallel translation.

41. Gollancz, Israel, ed. and tr. *"Pe": An English Poem of
    the Fourteenth Century. With a Modern Rendering.* Lon-
    don: Nutt, 1891; rev. ed., London: privately pr., 1897.

    A text with parallel translation in blank verse, explan-
    atory notes, and a fairly basic glossary. The introduc-
    tion provides: general observations on *Pe*; comments on
    Cl and *Pat*, with text and translation of *Cl* 361-70, 381-
    83, 414-24, 1110-32, and of *Pat* 137-56, 268-81, 289-302;
    translation only of *Cl* 551-56; text and translation of
    G 740-62, with a summary and discussion of the poem; a
    review of the authorship question, a hypothetical bio-
    graphy, and the suggestion that the author was Ralph
    Strode (cf. items 185, etc.).

    Reviews: Anon., *Athen*, 8 Aug. 1891, p. 184.
               Thomas P. Harrison, *MLN*, 7 (1892), 186-89.
               F. Holthausen, *Archiv*, 90 (1893), 144-48 (item
                 461).
               E. Kölbing, *EStn*, 16 (1892), 268-73 (item 472).
               R. Morris, *Academy*, 39 (1891), 602-03 (item
                 496).

42. ————, tr. *"Pe": An English Poem of the Fourteenth
    Century.* British Red Cross ed. London: Jones, 1918.

A revised version of the translation which is included
in item 41, preceded by a brief general introduction.

43.   ————, Sir Israel, ed. and tr. *"Pe"*: *an English Poem
       of the XIVth Century: with modern rendering, together
       with Boccaccio's "Olympia."* The Medieval Library. Lon-
       don: Chatto and Windus, 1921. Also in a limited ed.,
       SEEP, 8. London: Milford, Oxford UP, 1921.

       A ME text, with parallel verse translation, followed by
       textual notes, extensive explanatory notes, and full
       glossary. The introduction includes a plot summary, an
       imaginary biography of the poet, and a bibliographical
       note. Also provides comments on the following: the MS;
       metre, diction, and style; sources; links with the other
       three poems; the Huchown controversy; Strode. An appen-
       dix contains texts, with parallel translations, of Bocca-
       ccio's *Olympia* and his letters to Petrarch and Martin
       da Signa.

       Reviews: Anon., *TLS*, 18 May 1922, p. 319 (item 125).
                F. Holthausen, *ES*, 5 (1923), 133-36.
                J.R. Hulbert, *MP*, 25 (1927), 118-19.
                Aldo Ricci, *NSM*, 2 (?1925), 186-93.
                (See also item 415).

44.   Gordon, E.V., ed. *Pe*. Oxford: Clarendon; Toronto, New
       York: Oxford UP, 1953.

       Contains a ME text, with textual notes at the foot of
       the page, followed by explanatory notes and a full
       glossary. Appendixes deal with metre, spelling, phono-
       logy, Scandinavian and French elements, and accidence.
       The introduction has sections on the following: the MS;
       form and purpose (including support for the elegiac in-
       terpretation and comments on the fictional first person);
       the doctrinal theme (asserting the poet's orthodoxy);
       the symbolism of the pearl; sources, analogues, and tra-
       ditions; verse and style; the poet; date; and dialect
       (with sections on rhymes and vocabulary). Includes a
       bibliography. In the preface, Ida L. Gordon explains
       that this edition represents her revision of her late
       husband's work.

       Reviews: D.S. Brewer, *RES*, NS 6 (1955), 189-91.
                Norman Davis, *MAE*, 23 (1954), 96-100.
                Marie P. Hamilton, *JEGP*, 54 (1955), 123-26.
                E.A. Horsman, *DUJ*, 46 (1953), 33-35.
                L. Le Grelle, *EA*, 7 (1954), 316-18.

        Bogislav von Lindheim, *Anglia*, 72 (1954), 473-74.
        A.A. Prins, *ES*, 35 (1954), 264-66.
        D.W. Robertson, Jr., *Speculum*, 30 (1955), 107-08.
        H.L. Savage, *MLN*, 71 (1956), 124-29.
        B.J. Timmer, *YWES*, 34 (1953), 79-80.

*   Gordon, Ida L. See item 44.

45. Guidi, Augusto, ed. and tr. "Il meglio de *Pe*," *AION-SG*,
     9 (1966), 199-223.

     A text of *Pe* 1-240, based on item 44 (but with lines in-
     correctly numbered), followed by an Italian prose trans-
     lation (based on item 54), and glossarial notes. The
     brief introduction concentrates on the relationship be-
     tween form and content.

46. Hillmann, Sr. Mary Vincent, ed. and tr. "Text and Liter-
     al Translation of *The Pe*, with Explanatory Notes and In-
     terpretation." Diss., Fordham, 1941. Abst.: *Disserta-*
     tions accepted for higher degrees in the graduate school
     [Fordham Univ.], 8 (1942), 27-32. (Cf. item 47).

47. ————. *"The Pe"*: *Mediaeval Text with a Literal Transla-*
     tion and Interpretation. Convent Station, N.J.: College
     of Saint Elizabeth Press, Univ. Publishers, 1961; 2nd,
     rev. ed., with introduction and additional bibliography
     by Edward Vasta, Notre Dame and London: Univ. of Notre
     Dame Press, 1967.

     A conservatively edited ME text, with a facing verse
     translation, followed by textual notes, extensive explan-
     atory notes, bibliography, and full glossary. Introduc-
     tory material is restricted to a brief preface, and an
     "interpretation," in which the pearl is taken to stand
     for the Dreamer's soul. In the revised edition, Vasta
     contributes a general introduction (which includes a re-
     view of critical approaches) and updates the bibliography.
     Cf. item 46.

     Reviews: *1st ed.*: I.L. Gordon, *RES*, NS 13 (1962), 398-99.
              Henry L. Savage, *Speculum*, 39 (1964), 155-59.
           2nd ed.: G.C. Britton, *YWES*, 48 (1967), 75.

*   Hoyem, Andrew. See item 37.

48. Jewett, Sophie, tr. *"The Pe"*: *A Modern Version in the Metre*
     of the Original. New York: Crowell, 1908: rpt. in *Loomis/*
     Willard.

The translation follows the rhyme and metre of the original. Includes a brief general introduction.

49. Kalma, D., tr. *"De Pearel": in Visioen ut it Middel-Ingelsk oerbrocht yn it Nij-Frysk*. Dokkum: Kamminga, 1938.

    A Frisian verse translation (based on item 43). Includes a brief introduction.

    Review: F.P. Magoun, Jr., *MLN*, 60 (1945), 353-54.

50. Kirtlan, Ernest J.B., tr. *"Pe": A Poem of Consolation. Rendered into Modern English Verse*. London: Kelly, 1918.

    A verse translation in the original metre. The introduction offers a summary, a discussion of the poet's theology, and an account of alliterative poetry.

* Lott, Clarinda Harriss. See item 39.

51. Mead, Marian, tr. *"The Pe": an English Vision-Poem of the Fourteenth Century Done into Modern Verse*. Portland, Me.: Mosher, 1908.

    Follows the metrical form of the original. Includes a general introduction, brief notes, and a bibliography.

52. Mitchell, S. Weir, tr. *"Pe": Rendered into Modern English Verse*. New York: Century, 1906. Rpt., *Bibelot*, 14, vii (1908); *Century Readings in English Literature*, ed. J.W. Cunliffe et al., New York: Century, 1910; 5th ed., New York and London: Appleton, 1940.

    Translates stanzas 1-11, 13-22, 25-27, 29, 31-37, 40-46, 48, and 97-101 in rhyming verse. Preceded by a brief, general introduction.

    Review: Clark S. Northup, *MLN*, 22 (1907), 21-22 (item 512).

* Miyata, Takeshi. See item 1292.

* Naruse, Masaiku. See item 1293.

53. Newcomer, Alphonso Gerald, and Alice E. Andrews, tr. *Twelve Centuries of English Poetry and Prose*. Chicago: Scott, 1910; rev. ed., 1928.

    Includes ME text of *Pe* 1-12, and a verse translation of *Pe* 1-24, 37-72, 97-120, 145-68, 181-204, 229-64.

54. Olivero, Federico, tr. *"La Perla"*: *Poemetto Inglese del Secolo XIV.* Torino: Treves, 1926.

A verse translation, based on item 56, with explanatory notes. The brief introduction includes a review of critical writings on *Pe*.

Review: H.S.V. Jones, *JEGP*, 28 (1929), 287-88.

55. ————, ed. and tr. *"La Perla"*: *Poemetto in "ME."* Bologna: Zanichelli, 1936.

A ME text (based in item 56) with facing verse translation in Italian, and explanatory notes. The introduction provides: a survey of interpretations; a bibliography; and some general critical discussion, in which *Pe* is related to the mystical tradition, and seen as evidence of the approach of the Renaissance.

56. Osgood, Charles G., Jr., ed. *"The Pe"*: *A ME Poem.* The Belles-Lettres ser., sect. 2: ME Literature. Boston and London: Heath, 1906.

A ME text, with textual notes, extensive explanatory notes, list of biblical quotations and allusions, bibliography, and full glossary. In the substantial introduction, Osgood comments on the MS, date of composition, dialect, metre, and the alliterative revival. Considers a parallel with Chaucer's *Book of the Duchess*, and the influence of Boccaccio and Dante, and the traditions of chivalry, dream-vision, homily, and debate. While recognizing allegorical elements, sees the poem primarily as an elegy. Discusses the poet's theology, reviews the authorship question (emphatically supporting common authorship of the four poems), and speculates about the poet's life.

Reviews: F. Holthausen, *Archiv*, 123 (1909), 241-45.
        J.R. Hulbert, *MP*, 18 (1921), 499-503.
        (See also item 569).

57. ————, tr. *"The Pe"*: *an Anonymous English Poem of the Fourteenth Century, Rendered in Prose.* Princeton: privately pr., 1907.

A prose translation, preceded by a brief general introduction.

Review: A.M., *MLR*, 4 (1908), 132.

*   Schroedl, Evelyn Dyke. See item 39.

*   Sekigawa, Sakyo.   See item 1294.

*   Terasawa, Yoshio.   See item 1295.

*   Vasta, Edward.   See item 47.

   C. Editions and Translations of *Cleanness*

58. Anderson, J.J., ed.   *Cl*.   Old and ME Texts.   Manchester:
     UP; New York: Barnes and Noble, 1977.

     A ME text, arranged in quatrains, with textual notes be-
     low, followed by substantial explanatory notes, an appen-
     dix on language and versification, and a full glossary.
     The brief introduction provides discussion of the MS,
     authorship, theme, and structure.   Includes an extensive
     bibliography.

     Review: A.C. Spearing, *THES*, 9 Sept. 1977, p. 16.

*   Brewer, D.S.   See item 61.

59. Gollancz, Sir Israel, ed.   *"Cl": An Alliterative Tripar-*
     tite Poem on the Deluge, the Destruction of Sodom, and
     the Death of Belshazzar, by the Poet of "Pe."   SEEP,
     7.   London: Milford, Oxford UP, 1921.

     Contains a ME text arranged in quatrains, followed by
     textual notes (emendations and notes on the MS, and sug-
     gested metrical emendations), explanatory notes, and an
     index of words and phrases discussed in the notes and
     preface.   The preface provides consideration of the MS,
     the quatrain arrangement, relations with the other three
     poems, date and place of composition, structure, and use
     of sources (biblical and non-biblical).   The edition is
     completed by item 60.

     Reviews: Anon., *TLS*, 18 May 1922, p. 319 (item 125).
               Robert J. Menner, *MLN*, 37 (1922), 355-62 (item
               610).

60. ————.   *"Cl": Glossary and Illustrative Texts*.   SEEP,
     9.   London: Milford, Oxford UP, 1933.

     Contains a glossary to item 59, and texts of biblical
     sources and non-biblical material which Gollancz regarded
     as sources (extracts from *Le Livre du Chevalier de la*
     Tour Landry, *Cursor Mundi*, and the French *Mandeville*).

Reviews: Dorothy Everett, YWES, 14 (1933), 130.
        Robert J. Menner, MLN, 50 (1935), 336-38 (item
        611).

61. ———. "Cl": An Alliterative Tripartite Poem ... With
     new English translation by D.S. Brewer. Cambridge: Brew-
     er; Totowa, N.J.: Rowman and Littlefield, 1974.

     Reprints items 59 and 60 in one volume, together with a
     parallel prose translation.

     Review: R.W. McTurk and D.J. Williams, YWES, 55 (1974),
        103.

*   ———. See also item 41.

62. Menner, Robert J., ed. "Pur": a ME Poem. YSE, 61. New
     Haven: Yale UP; London: Milford, Oxford UP, 1920; rpt.,
     Hamden, Conn.: Archon, 1970. Diss., Yale, 1918.

     Contains a ME text (not arranged in quatrains), textual
     notes, explanatory notes, full glossary, and selective
     bibliography. The extensive introduction provides dis-
     cussion of the following: the MS and the scribe; parallels
     between Cl and the other three poems; the alliterative
     revival; parallels between Cl and various alliterative
     poems; evidence for dating; sources; literary art (empha-
     sizing structure, theme, treatment of biblical sources,
     and style); metre and alliteration; language and dialect.
     The appendix contains the Vulgate texts of the longer
     biblical passages adapted by the poet.

     Reviews: Gustav Binz, LfGRP, 42 (1921), cols. 376-79.
        Oliver Farrar Emerson, JEGP, 20 (1921), 229-41
           (item 598).
        F. Holthausen, AnglB, 34 (1923), 136-38.

63. Morris, Richard, and Walter W. Skeat, ed. From Robert of
     Gloucester to Gower, A.D. 1298-A.D. 1393. Specimens
     of Early English: A New and Revised Edition, pt. 2. Claren-
     don Press ser. Oxford: Clarendon, 1872; rev. ed., 1894.

     Includes text of Cl 235-544, 947-72, 1009-51, with notes
     and glossary. Cf. item 20.

*   Skeat, Walter W. See item 63.

64. Stone, Brian, tr. The Owl and the Nightingale--Cl--StE.
     Harmondsworth and Baltimore: Penguin, 1971.

A translation in unrhymed alliterative lines, arranged in
quatrains, with a few explanatory notes at the foot of
the page. The introduction provides a detailed summary,
and comments on theme, tone, structure, and descriptive
power.

D. Editions and Translations of *Patience*

65. Anderson, J.J., ed. "An Edition with Full Critical Ap-
    paratus of the ME Poem *Pat*." Diss., Adelaide, 1965.

    Cf. item 66.

66. ⸺. *Pat*. Old and ME Texts. Manchester: UP; New
    York: Barnes and Noble, 1969.

    A ME text (arranged in quatrains), with textual notes be-
    low, followed by extensive explanatory notes and a full
    glossary. Appendixes contain the Vulgate text of the
    Book of Jonah and Matt. 5:3-10, and a review of the lan-
    guage. The introduction provides discussion of: the MS;
    relations with the other three poems; sources; theme and
    structure; versification; dialect. Includes an extensive
    bibliography.

    Reviews: G.C. Britton and W.A. Davenport, *YWES*, 50 (1969),
    92.
    A.C. Spearing, *MAE*, 39 (1970), 347-48.
    R.M. Wilson, *MLR*, 65 (1970), 594-96.

67. Bateson, Hartley, ed. *"Pat": A West Midland Poem of the
    Fourteenth Century*. University of Manchester Pubs., 70;
    English ser., 3. Manchester: UP, 1912; 2nd, rev., ed., Man-
    chester: UP; London, New York, Bombay: Longman, 1918.

    A ME text (not arranged in quatrains), with textual notes,
    extensive explanatory notes, and full glossary. The in-
    troduction contains discussion of: the relationship with
    the other three poems and probable order of composition;
    evidence for dating; dialect and language; the MS; themes
    and treatment; sources (including the *De Jona*). Con-
    cludes with a hypothetical sketch of the author, appen-
    dixes on the relation of *De Sodomas* to *Cl* and of *Piers
    Plowman* to *Pat*, and a selective bibliography.

    The second edition reflects extensive revision to text,
    notes, glossary, and introduction. The sketch of the

author and the appendixes are omitted, and replaced by
new appendixes, providing (1) a discussion of the relationship between *Piers Plowman* and *Pat* and *Cl*, and (2)
texts of sources (the *De Jona* and the Vulgate text of
the book of Jonah and Matt. 5:3-10).

Reviews: *1st ed.*: Anon., *Athen*, 26 Oct. 1912, p. 477.
        Eilert Ekwall, *AnglB*, 24 (1913), 133-36 (item
          640).
        Oliver Farrar Emerson, *MLN*, 28 (1913), 171-80,
          232 (item 645).
        S.B. Liljegren, *EStn*, 49 (1915), 142-43.
        G.C. Macauley, *MLR*, 8 (1913), 396-98.
        2nd ed.: Oliver Farrar Emerson, *JEGP*, 18 (1919),
          638-40.

*   Del Lungo, Gabriella. See item 634.

*   Eichler, Albert. See item 74.

68. Gollancz, I[srael], ed. *"Pat": An Alliterative Version
     of "Jonah" by the Poet of "Pe."* SEEP, 1. London: Mil-
     ford, Oxford UP, 1913; 2nd, rev., ed., 1924.

Contains a ME text (arranged in quatrains) with extensive
notes and a full glossary. Also prints the Vulgate text
of the Book of Jonah and Matt. 5:3-10, and an extract
from the *De Jona*. In the preface, Gollancz describes the
MS, expresses support for the quatrain arrangement and
the theory of common authorship, and discusses the place
and date of composition. The revised edition adds textual notes, listing (a) scribal errors and (b) emendations suggested on metrical grounds.

Reviews: *1st ed.*: Anon., *Athen*, 18 July 1914, p. 71.
        Karl Brunner, *Archiv*, 132 (1914), 184-85.
        Eilert Ekwall, *EStn*, 49 (1915), 144-46 (item
          641).
        J.H.G. Grattan, *MLR*, 9 (1914), 403-05.
        2nd ed.: Eilert Ekwall, *AnglB*, 36 (1925), 268-70.

*   ————. See also item 41.

*   Lungo, Gabriella Del. See Del Lungo, Gabriella.

69. MacLean, George Edwin, ed. *An Old and ME Reader on the
     Basis of Professor Julius Zupitza's "Alt- und Mitteleng-
     lisches Übungsbuch."* New York and London: Macmillan,
     1893.

Provides text of 61-156, based on item 19. (Cf. item 74).

* Schipper, J. See item 74.

70. Sweeney, Margaret, ed. "A Critical Edition of *Pat*, a ME Poem in the West Midland Dialect of the Fourteenth Century." Diss., Yale, 1901.

71. Ushigaki, Hiroto, tr. "*Pat* (a Japanese Version)," *KSELL*, no. 7 (1976), 53-72.

    A complete Japanese translation.

72. Vantuono, William, ed. "*Pat*: An Edition," Diss., New York, 1969. Abst.: *DAI*, 30 (1969), 2502A.

73. Wülcker, Richard Paul, ed. *Die zeit von 1350-1500 umfassend. Altenglisches lesebuch: Zum gebrauche bei vorlesungen und zum selbstunterricht*, II. Halle a.S.: Lippert, 1879.

    Prints text of 137-236, based on item 19.

74. Zupitza, Julius. *Altenglisches Übungsbuch zum Gebrauche bei Universitäts-vorlesungen*. Wien: Braumüller, 1874; 2nd, rev., ed., *Alt- und Mittelenglisches Übungsbuch* ..., 1882; 5th ed., rev. J. Schipper, Wien und Leipzig: Braumüller, 1897; 13th ed., rev. Albert Eichler, 1928.

    Provides text (based on item 19) of lines 61-100, 109-14, 129-56 in the 1st ed.; thereafter, lines 61-156. (Cf. item 69).

E. Editions and Translations of *Sir Gawain and the Green Knight*

75. Anderson, George K., tr. *SGGK*. *The Literature of England*. Ed. George B. Woods et al. Chicago: Scott, 1936; 5th ed., ed. George K. Anderson and William E. Buckler, Glenview, Ill.: Scott, 1968. Abridged ed., Chicago: Scott, 1953; rev. George K. Anderson and William E. Buckler, Glenview, Ill., 1967.

    A prose translation of *G*, with a few notes at the foot of the page and a very brief introduction.

76. Andrew, S.O., tr. *"SGGK"*: *A Modern Version of the XIV Century Alliterative Poem in the Original Metre*. London, etc.: Dent; New York: Dutton, 1929. School ed.: London: Dent, 1931.

    Attempts to preserve the original metre. Retains some archaic words (glossed at the foot of the page, and in the concise glossary). Includes a brief general introduction.

    Reviews: Dorothy Everett, *YWES*, 10 (1929), 126–28.
    Frank E. Farley, *Speculum*, 5 (1930), 222–24.
    R.W. King, *RES*, 6 (1930), 457–60.

77. Banks, Theodore Howard, Jr., tr. *SGGK*. New York: Appleton, 1929. Rpt. in *Frost*, *Loomis/Willard*, and *Witherspoon*, and in items 106 and 109.

    A verse translation (from item 111). Retains the stanza form and much alliteration. Also provides a brief general introduction.

    Reviews: Everett and Farley, cited under item 76.

78. Barron, W.R.J., ed. and tr. *SGGK*. Manchester Medieval Classics. Manchester: UP; New York: Barnes and Noble, 1974.

    Provides a ME text, with textual notes beneath and a prose translation on the facing page, followed by explanatory notes. The introduction offers some comments on romance tradition, a detailed plot summary incorporating a good deal of critical comment, and a brief bibliography.

    Reviews: Avril Henry, *MAE*, 45 (1976), 344–46.
    Derek Pearsall, *RES*, NS 26 (1975), 329–31.
    R.A. Waldron, *N&Q*, 220 (1975), 77–78.

79. Berry, Francis, ed. "Anonymous: *Sir Gawayne and the Grene Knight*." *Ford*, pp. 349–428.

    A complete, partially modernized, ME text, with difficult words glossed at the foot of the page.

80. Berti, I., tr. "Traduzione e introduzione al poemetto medio-inglese *Ser Galvano e il Cavaliere Verde*." Diss., Pisa, 1974.

81. Borroff, Marie, tr. *"SGGK"*: *a new verse translation*. New York: Norton; Toronto: McLeod, 1967; London: Longman, 1968. Rpt. in *Abrams*, 2nd and 3rd eds.

A verse translation which retains the verse form and alliteration of the original. Preceded by an introduction
on theme, style, and translation; followed by a note on
metre.

Review: G.C. Britton, *YWES*, 48 (1967), 72.

82. Brunner, Karl, and Rudolf Hittmair, ed. *Mittelenglisches
Lesebuch für Anfänger*. Heidelberg: Winter, 1929.

Contains text of *G* 640-69, 1421-75, and 2069-90, and a
brief introduction (pp. 30-35). The anthology includes a
limited glossary.

83. Burrow, J[ohn] A., ed. *SGGK*. Penguin English Poets.
Harmondsworth and Baltimore: Penguin, 1972.

Provides a ME text with partially modernized spelling,
explanatory notes, textual notes, and glossary. The introduction consists of a note on spelling and vocabulary,
and a brief bibliography.

84. Cebesoy, Ayse, tr. *Sir Gawain ve Yesil Sövalye*. İngiliz
Klâsikleri, 53. İstanbul: Millî Eğitim Basîmevi, 1947.

A Turkish prose translation. Not seen.

85. Como, Frank Thomas, ed. "*SGGK*: A Normalized and Glossed
Text." Diss., Arizona, 1969. Abst.: *DAI*, 30 (1969),
2512A.

86. Cox, John Harrington, tr. *SGGK*. *Knighthood in Germ and
Flower: The Anglo-Saxon Epic, "Beowulf," and the Arthurian Tale "SGGK."* Boston: Little, 1910. Rpt. separately as *SGGK*, All-Time Tales ser., London: Harrap,
n.d. [?1913].

A rather loose translation, designed for the general
reader.

*   Davis, Norman. See item 111.

*   Day, Mabel. See item 88.

87. Frey, Leonard H., ed. and tr. *Readings in Early English
Language History*. Indianapolis and New York: Bobbs-
Merrill, Odyssey, 1966.

Includes text and prose translation of *G* 619-69.

*   Gerould, Gordon Hall. See items 9 and 10.

*   Goldbeck, Karl. See item 98.

88. Gollancz, Sir Israel, ed. *"SGGK": Re-edited from MS.*
     Cotton Nero, A.x., in the British Museum. EETS, OS 210.
     London, New York, and Toronto: Oxford UP, 1940; p.b., 1957.

     A ME text, with textual notes at the foot of the page and
     marginal summaries, followed by extensive explanatory
     notes and a full glossary.

     Mabel Day's introduction provides discussion of the MS
     and the poet, of the relation of *G* to the other three
     poems and the *Wars of Alexander*, and of the sources and
     theories thereon.

     Mary S. Serjeantson's essay on "The Dialect of MS. Cotton
     Nero A.x." provides a thorough review of language and di-
     alect.

     Reviews: Anon., *TLS*, 25 Jan. 1941, p. 46.
             E.G. Bowen and Gwyn Jones, *MAE*, 13 (1944), 58–
               65 (item 720).
             Angus Macdonald, *MLR*, 36 (1941), 517–18.
             Henry Savage, *MLN*, 59 (1944), 342–50 (item 1140).
             Gladys Doidge Willcock, *YWES*, 21 (1940), 75–77.

*   ————. See also items 41, 100.

*   Gordon, E.V. See item 111.

89. Greenwood, Ormerod, tr. *"SGGK," a Fourteenth-Century Al-*
     literative Poem Now Attributed to Hugh Mascy. London:
     Lion and Unicorn Press, 1956.

     A translation which follows the original metre. The in-
     troduction provides general critical comment on *G* and
     reference to the other poems. Goes on to argue that the
     poet was Hugh Mascy, providing some evidence about his
     family. Emphasizes numerical symbolism. (On Mascy, cf.
     items 275, etc.).

90. Guidi, A., ed. and tr. *Galvano e il Cavaliere Verde.*
     Edizione Fussi. Firenze: Sansoni, 1958.

     A ME text, with parallel prose translation in Italian,
     and textual notes. In the brief introduction, Guidi dis-
     cusses sources, metre, and themes, and argues that the
     poet of *G* did not write *Pe.*

91. ————, tr. "Un brano del *Galvano* inglese." *Studi in*
     onore di Angelo Monteverdi. Modena: Società Tipografica
     Editrice Modenese, 1959. I, 313–17.

A translation of *G* 498-535 in Italian verse, together
with brief introductory comments.

92. Hare, Kenneth, tr. *"Sir Gawayne and the Green Knight"*:
     A Fourteenth-Century Poem Done into Modern English.
     Stratford-upon-Avon: Shakespeare Head, 1918; 2nd ed., with
     introduction, notes and a bibliog. by R.M. Wilson, London:
     Eyre and Spottiswoode, 1948.

     A translation in Spenserian stanzas. The second edition
     adds a general introduction, notes, and bibliography, all
     brief, and an appendix which provides the ME text of
     lines 2047-102.

     Reviews: A. Macdonald, *RES*, 25 (1949), 350-51.
              Henry L. Savage, *MLN*, 66 (1951), 489-91.

93. Hemon, Roparz, tr. *Gaovan Hag an den Gwen.* Brezhoneg
     Eeun, 2. La Baule: La Mouette, n.d.

     A somewhat abbreviated prose translation in Breton. No
     introduction or notes.

*   Hittmair, Rudolf. See item 82.

*   Isaacs, Neil D. See item 104.

94. Jones, Gwyn, tr. *"SGGK"*: *a prose translation.* [London]:
     Golden Cockrell Press, 1952.

     A prose translation, followed by a brief glossary of dif-
     ficult words. The introduction discusses theme and
     sources, and compares *G* to the *Carl of Carlisle.*

     Review: Anon., *TLS*, 20 Feb. 1953, p. 118.

95. Jones, R.T., ed. *"Sir Gawain and the Grene Gome"*: *A reg-
     ularized text.* Pietermaritzburg: Univ. of Natal Press,
     1960; rev. ed., Pietermaritzburg: Univ. of Natal Press;
     London: Heinemann; New York: Barnes and Noble, 1972.

     A regularized ME text, with difficult words glossed on
     the facing page; no notes and minimal glossary. Brief
     interpretative introduction.

96. Kirtlan, Ernest J.B., tr. *"SGGK,"* *rendered literally in-
     to modern English from the alliterative romance poem of
     A.D. 1360.* London: Kelly, n.d. [?1912].

     Not seen.

     Review: P.G. Thomas, *EStn*, 47 (1913), 250-56.

*   Kreuzer, James R. See item 107.

97. Madden, Sir Frederic, ed. *"Syr Gawayn and the Grene Knyჳt."* *Syr Gawayne; A Collection of Ancient Romance-Poems by Scotish [sic] and English Authors, relating to that celebrated Knight of the Round Table.* Bannatyne Club, 61. London: Taylor, 1839. Rpt. New York: AMS Press, 1971.

    The first edition of *G*. Provides a text, with notes and a rather limited glossary. The introduction discusses sources and origins, and the treatment of G in earlier romances, both prose and verse.

    Review: Thomas A. Knott, *MLN*, 30 (1915), 102-08 (item 936).

98. Mätzner, Eduard, with the assistance of Karl Goldbeck, ed. *Altenglische Sprachproben nebst einem Wörterbuche*, I. Berlin: Weidmann, 1867.

    Text of *G* 232-465, with notes and introduction (pp. 311-20).

99. Miyata, Takeshi, tr. *"SGGK": A Japanese Translation.* Kobe: Konan Univ. Bungaku-kai, 1957.

    A complete Japanese translation.

100. Morris, Richard, ed. *"Sir Gawayne and The Green Knight":* *an Alliterative Romance-Poem, (ab. 1320-30 A.D.) by the Author of "The Early English Alliterative Poems."* EETS, OS 4. London, New York, and Toronto: Oxford UP, 1864; rev. ed., 1869. Rev. I. Gollancz, 1897; rev. ed., 1912.

    The first separate edition of *G*. Contains full ME text, brief notes, and a fairly basic glossary. The introduction consists mainly of a plot-summary.

    Reviews: T.G. F[oster], *MLQ* (Lon), 1 (1897), 53-55 (item 826).
    Thomas A. Knott, *MLN*, 30 (1915), 102-08 (item 936).

*   Neilson, W.A. See item 115.

101. Nicholson, Hilary, tr. *SGGK*. *Argosy*, Jan. 1950, pp. 63-80.

    An abridged and rather free translation in prose.

102. Pace, George B., tr. *SGGK*. *English Literature: A College Anthology*. Ed. Donald B. Clark et al. New York: Macmillan, 1960.

A slightly abbreviated prose translation with an introductory note (pp. 35-54).

103. Pons, Emile, ed. and tr. *"Sire Gauvain et le Chevalier
      Vert": Poème Anglais du XIVe Siècle.* Bibliothèque de
      Philologie Germanique, 9. Paris: Aubier, Editions Mon-
      taigne, 1946.

      Provides a ME text with parallel translation in French
      verse and a few brief notes at the foot of the page.
      The extensive introduction covers the following topics:
      the nature descriptions; the handling of courtly mate-
      rial; the comic element; the meaning of *capados* (186,
      etc.); the founding of the Order of the Carter; the
      other three poems; the theory of common authorship
      (which Pons questions); Arthurian themes; the history of
      scholarship on *G*; sources; myth and symbol; the pent-
      angle; the character of G; the temptation scenes; the
      quest motif. Also provides a bibliography.

      Reviews: A.A. Prins, *ES*, 28 (1947), 19-20.
               Henry L. Savage, *JEGP*, 47 (1948), 44-52 (item
               1144).
               H.M. Smyser, *Speculum*, 22 (1947), 92-95.
               Beatrice White, *MLR*, 43 (1948), 253-55.

104. Raffel, Burton, tr. *SGGK.* Afterword by Neil D. Isaacs.
      New York and Toronto: Mentor, New American Library; Lon-
      don: New English Library, 1970.

      A verse translation, which stays fairly close to the
      original. The introduction provides discussion of the
      poet, language, and verse form; praise for the vitality
      of the poem; a general discussion of theme and tone; an
      acid review of critical writings; a brief bibliography,
      annotated with similar acidity.

      The "Afterword" begins with the assertion that the gir-
      dle is not magic, and goes on to provide general liter-
      ary-historical comments, a review of criticism, and
      praise for Raffel's translation.

      Review: Robert J. Blanch, *Archiv*, 210 (1973), 185-89.

105. Ridley, M.R., tr. *The Story of "SGGK" in modern English.*
      Leicester: Ward, 1944; rev. ed., 1950. Rpt. in *Loomis/
      Loomis*.

      A prose translation with general introduction and some
      brief notes at the foot of the page.

106. Robertson, D.W., Jr., ed. *The Literature of Medieval England.* New York, etc.: McGraw-Hill, 1970.

Reprints Banks's translation (item 77), with new notes and a brief introduction (pp. 366-408).

107. Rosenberg, James L., tr., and James R. Kreuzer, ed. *SGGK.* Rinehart Editions, 97. New York and Toronto: Rinehart, 1959.

An alliterative verse translation in the metre of the original. Rosenberg comments on the translation in a note (pp. lxxv-lxxxiii).

The substantial introduction by Kreuzer contains the following: plot summary with comments on sources; stanza-by-stanza commentary; critical observations on characterization; discussion of the alliterative revival (with lines 516-35 quoted in ME); plot summary of *Pe*, with critical comments; brief comments on *Cl*, *Pat*, and *Erk*; general discussion of romance and courtly love; bibliographical note. See item 1056.

*   Serjeantson, Mary S. See item 88.

108. Silverstein, Theodore, tr. *"SGGK": A Comedy for Christmas.* Chicago and London: Univ. of Chicago Press, 1974.

An illustrated verse translation.

109. Spencer, Hazelton, ed. *From "Beowulf" to Sheridan. British Literature*, I. Boston: Heath, 1952; 2nd ed., 1963.

Contains Banks's translation (item 77), with a new introductory note (pp. 80-109). Also prints a reproduction of one of the MS illustrations (between pp. 128 and 129).

110. Stone, Brian, tr. *SGGK.* Harmondsworth and Baltimore: Penguin, 1959; rev. ed., 1974, rpt. in item 112.

A verse translation, which retains some alliteration and the original stanza form. Provides a few footnotes to the text. Appendixes offer comment on the following: the MS, theories of authorship, G, Arthur, Camelot, the pentangle, Morgan, and Merlin; and extracts from the ME text (lines 179-202, 713-39, 1208-40). The introduction provides discussion of sources, structure, and themes, and is followed by a note on the translation.

In the second edition, the translation is extensively
revised. Other revisions include: a new introduction
(containing information on relevant traditions, and general critical comments); explanatory notes, following
the text (replacing footnotes); "Notes on Arthurian Matters" (replacing appendixes); three new essays ("The
Common Enemy of Man" on the role of the GK, "G's Eternal
Jewel" on the moral theme, and "The Poem as a Play" on
a dramatization); and bibliographical notes.

Reviews: 1st ed.: Guy Bourquin, *EA*, (1961), 51-52.
          (See also item 1056).
     rev. ed.: R.W. McTurk and D.J. Williams,
          YWES, 55 (1974), 97-98.

111. Tolkein, J.R.R., and E.V. Gordon, ed. *SGGK*. Oxford:
      Clarendon, 1925; corr. rpt., 1930; 2nd. ed., rev. Norman
      Davis, Oxford: Clarendon; New York: Oxford UP, 1967;
      p.b. 1968.

      A ME text with textual notes. Followed by extensive ex-
      planatory notes, notes on metre (with sections on the
      alliterative long line, rhyming lines, and alliteration)
      and language (with sections on spelling, phonology, the
      Scandinavian and French elements, and grammar), and a
      full glossary. The introduction provides comments on
      the MS; a plot summary; discussion of sources, the auth-
      orship question, date, and dialect; and a selective bib-
      liography.

      Davis's revised edition follows much the same format,
      but contains extensive and substantial revisions through-
      out.

      Reviews: 1st ed.: Anon., *N&Q*, 148 (1925), 396.
                Cyril Brett, *MLR*, 22 (1927), 451-58 (item 726).
                Oliver Farrar Emerson, *JEGP*, 26 (1927), 248-58.
                Dorothy Everett, *YWES*, 6 (1925), 96-97.
                J.H.G. Grattan, *RES*, 1 (1925), 484-87 (item
                  843).
                F. Holthausen, *AnglB*, 36 (1925), 162-63.
                J.R. Hulbert, *MP*, 23 (1925), 246-49.
                Robert J. Menner, *MLN*, 41 (1926), 397-400 (item
                  1017).
                (See also items 988, 989).
                2nd ed.: G.C. Britton, *YWES*, 48 (1969), 71-72.
                Juliette De Caluwé-Dor, *RBPH*, 47 (1969), 279-
                  81.
                A.R. Heiserman, *Speculum*, 44 (1969), 176-77.
                Sylvia Wallace Holton, *SN*, 41 (1969), 179-80.
                S.S. Hussey, *N&Q*, 213 (1968), 189-90.

John MacQueen, *RES*, NS 20 (1969), 70-71.
Belinda Vaughan, *AUMLA*, 30 (1968), 237-38.
R.M. Wilson, *MLR*, 64 (1969), 854.

112. Trapp, J.B., ed. "Medieval English Literature." *The
      Middle Ages through the Eighteenth Century. The Oxford
      Anthology of English Literature*, I. Ed. Frank Kermode
      and John Hollander. New York, London, and Toronto: Ox-
      ford UP, 1973.

      Contains the revised version of Stone's translation
      (item 110), with new explanatory notes at the foot of
      the page, and a brief general introduction (pp. 284-
      348).

113. Tsuchiya, Tadayuki, ed. *"SGGK" Annotated by "OED" and
      "MED."* Tokyo: privately printed, 1976.

      Provides a complete text, based on Davis's revision of
      Tolkien and Gordon (item 111), but with partially mod-
      ernized spelling. Words are glossed from the *OED* and
      MED (which the author credits appropriately). Does not
      include textual or explanatory notes.

114. Waldron, R.A., ed. *SGGK.* York Medieval Texts. London:
      Arnold; Evanston, Ill.: Northwestern UP, 1970.

      A ME text with partially modernized spelling, textual
      notes and extensive explanatory notes at the foot of the
      page, and a glossary. The substantial critical intro-
      duction provides a plot summary and discussion of ro-
      mance convention, narrative and dramatic qualities, ten-
      sions between Christian and secular aspects of chivalry,
      and the poet's use of ambiguity and avoidance of di-
      dacticism. Also contains a note on language and metre,
      and a select bibliography.

      Reviews: G.C. Britton and W.A. Davenport, *YWES*, 51
              (1970), 82-83.
            T.A. Shippey, *MLR*, 66 (1971), 850-51.
            J.R. Simon, *EA*, 25 (1972), 82.

115. Webster, K.G.T., and W.A. Neilson, tr. and ed. *"SGGK"*
      [;] *"Piers the Ploughman."* Riverside Literature ser.
      Boston: Houghton; London: Harrap, 1917.

      Contains a prose translation of *G*, together with a brief
      general introduction and the ME text of lines 1-84. Cf.
      item 22.

116. Weston, Jessie L., tr. *"SGGK": A ME Arthurian Romance
     Retold in Modern Prose.* Arthurian Romances Unrepresented
     in Malory's *Morte d'Arthur,* 1. London: Nutt, 1898; 2nd
     ed., 1900; rpt., in a limited ed., New York: New Amster-
     dam Books, 1905; rpt. New York: AMS, 1970. Also rpt.
     in *Ideas and Forms in English and American Literature,*
     ed. H.A. Watt and J.B. Munn, Chicago, Atlanta, etc.:
     Scott, 1925.

     Somewhat abbreviated prose translation with short
     general introduction and brief notes.

117. Whiting, B.J., tr. *SGGK. The College Survey of English
     Literature,* I. Ed. B.J. Whiting et al. New York:
     Harcourt, 1942.

     A prose translation.

*   Wilson, R.M. See item 92.

II. CRITICAL WRITINGS

A. Critical Writings on More Than One Poem

118. A., L.E. "*SGGK* and *Pe.*" *N&Q*, 170 (1936), 27.

     Asks whether *Pe* and *G* are still believed to be by the same author.

119. Ackerman, Robert W. "'Pared out of Paper': *G* 802 and *Pur* 1408." *JEGP*, 56 (1957), 410-17.

     Argues that the reference is not to "subtleties" but to earlier table ornaments, comparing the *Parson's Tale* (*CT* X) 444. Cf. items 945, 1162.

120. ————. "ME Literature to 1400." *The Medieval Literature of Western Europe: A Review of Research, Mainly 1930-1960.* Ed. John H. Fisher. New York: New York UP for the MLA; London: Univ. of London Press, 1966.

     Includes discussion of writings on *Pe* and *G* (pp. 91-93 and 100).

121. Allen, Judson Boyce. *The Friar as Critic: Literary Attitudes in the Later Middle Ages.* Nashville, Tenn.: Vanderbilt UP, 1971.

     Applies the allegory of the spiritual sense to *Pe* (pp. 11, 137-39) and *G* (pp. 145-49).

122. Amours, F.J. "Introduction" to his ed. of *Scottish Alliterative Poems In Riming Stanzas*, I. Scottish Text Soc., 27. Edinburgh and London: Blackwood, 1892.

     In a discussion of the Huchown controversy, summarizes the opinions expressed in items 19, 97, and 342.

123. Anderson, George K. "Old and ME Literature from the Beginnings to 1485." *A History of English Literature.*

Ed. Hardin Craig. New York: Oxford UP, 1950; corr.
rpt., Toronto: Crowell-Collier; New York: Macmillan,
1962. Also pub. separately, New York: Collier, 1962.

Contains general comments on the poet and all four poems,
and a bibliography (pp. 140-43, 631 in the 1st ed.).

124.   Andrew, S.O. "The Preterite in North-Western Dialects."
       RES, 5 (1929), 431-36.

       Reviews forms of strong verb preterites in the NW dia-
       lect, using examples from all four poems.

125.   Anon. "*Pe* and *Pur*." *TLS*, 18 May 1922, p. 319.

       A review of items 43 and 59. Comments on *Pe* 462, 568,
       755, and *Cl* 491. (Cf. items 190, 191).

126.   Bailey, Richard N. "The Development of English."
       Daiches/Thorlby, pp. 127-62.

       Contains comments on the poet's language and dialect
       (pp. 154-55).

127.   Baldwin, Charles Sears. *An Introduction to English Me-
       dieval Literature*. New York, etc.: Longmans, Green,
       1914.

       Praises the vividness and variety of *G* and the formal
       beauty of *Pe* (pp. 154-61, 174-77).

128.   ———. *Three Medieval Centuries of Literature in Eng-
       land* [:] *1100-1400*. Boston: Little, 1932; rpt., New
       York: Phaeton Press, 1968.

       Includes a summary of *G*, together with general critical
       comments, and discussion of form and meaning in *Pe* (pp.
       127-32, 170-73). Also provides bibliographical notes on
       all four poems (pp. 257-58, 262-63).

129.   Baugh, Albert C. *The ME Period (1100-1500)*. *A Liter-
       ary History of England*, ed. Albert C. Baugh, I, pt. 2.
       New York: Appleton; London: Routledge, 1948; 2nd ed.,
       New York: Meredith; London: Routledge, 1967.

       A general account of all four poems; cautiously supports
       common authorship (pp. 233-38).

130.   Benson, Larry D. "The Authorship of *StE*." *JEGP*, 64
       (1965), 393-405.

Argues--mainly from evidence of style, vocabulary, and phraseology--that the author of the four poems did not write *StE*. Cf. items 192, etc.

131. Blamires, Harry. *A Short History of English Literature.* New York: Barnes and Noble; London: Methuen, 1974.

Includes summaries and brief critical evaluations of *G* and *Pe* (pp. 13-16).

132. Blanch, Robert J., ed. *"SGGK" and "Pe": Critical Essays.* Bloomington and London: Indiana UP, 1966.

Contains the following items: 375, 443, 478, 560, 574, 739, 829, 846, 887, 997, 1033.

Review: R.M. Wilson, *MLR*, 65 (1970), 368-69.

133. Bloomfield, Morton W. "Some Notes on *SGGK* (Lines 374, 546, 752, 1236) and *Pe* (Lines 1-12, 61, 775-76, 968)." *Willard*, pp. 300-02.

Interpretative notes on the lines specified.

* Boyson, V.F. See item 237.

134. Bradley, Henry. "The English *G*-Poet and *The Wars of Alexander.*" *Academy*, 33 (1888), 27.

Suggests common authorship for the *Wars* and the four poems. (Cf. item 200).

135. Brandl, Alois. "Mittelenglische Literatur (1100-1500)." *GGP*, 2, i. Strassburg: Trübner, 1893. Pp. 609-718.

Includes a general account of the four poems and *Erk* (pp. 661-65).

* ———. See also item 140.

136. Brett, Cyril. "Notes on *Cl* and *SG*." *MLR*, 10 (1915), 188-95.

Notes on: *bougounz* (*Cl* 1416), *scholes* (*G* 160), *grayn* (*G* 211), *schale* (*G* 1240), *devaye* (*G* 1497).

137. Brewer, Derek [S.]. *Chaucer in his Time.* London: Nelson, 1963.

Discusses the audience of *Pe* and *G* (p. 225), and descriptions of court life in *G* (pp. 89-91, 177-78, 180); various passing references.

138.   ————, D[erek] S. "Courtesy and the *G*-Poet." *Patterns of Love and Courtesy: Essays in Memory of C.S. Lewis.* Ed. John Lawlor. London: Arnold; Evanston: Northwestern UP, 1966. Pp. 54-85. Rpt. in *Newstead*.

Contains an account of each poem, with emphasis on the significance of "courtesy." Suggests that the poet understands "courtesy" to include many qualities (e.g., truth, honor, moderation, cleanliness, chastity), and that he asserts its value in social, personal, and spiritual contexts. Cf. items 169, 256, 931.

139.   ————. "The *G*-Poet; A General Appreciation of Four Poems." *EIC*, 17 (1967), 130-42.

Sees the controlling of selfish desire as a recurring theme. Argues that the poet's vision is essentially affirmative. Cf. item 1124.

140.   Brink, Bernhard ten. *Bis zu Wiclifs Auftreten. Geschichte der Englische Literatur*, I. Berlin: Oppenheim, 1877; 2nd ed., rev. Alois Brandl, Strassburg: Trübner, 1899. 1st ed., tr. Horace M. Kennedy as *Early English Literature (to Wiclif)*. London: Bell, 1883.

Provides a detailed summary of *G*, and a translation of lines 491-535. Offers a hypothetical biography of the poet (cf. item 41). Briefly summarizes *Pe*, *Cl*, and *Pat* (pp. 336-51 in the English ed.).

141.   Brown, Arthur C.L. "On the Origin of Stanza-Linking in English Alliterative Verse." *RR*, 7 (1916), 271-83.

Suggests that the devices discussed in item 258 may reflect Welsh influence.

142.   Brown, Carleton F. "The Author of *The Pe*, Considered in the Light of his Theological Opinions." *PMLA*, 19 (1904), 115-45. Also pub. separately, Baltimore: MLA, 1904.

Reviews the Huchown controversy. Discusses the handling of biblical narrative in *Cl*. Suggests that *Pe* reflects the contemporary theological debate about the relative importance of grace and merit in the scheme of salvation. Observes that the poet's assertion of the equality of heavenly reward is at odds with contemporary orthodoxy. Cf. items 539, etc. (Items 385 and 593 are printed as continuations of this article).

Review: Clark S. Northup, *MLN*, 22 (1907), 21-22 (item 512).

143. Brown, J.T.T. "The Poems of David Rate, Confessor of King James the First of Scotland." *ScA* , 12 (1897), 5-12.

Questions the evidence on which the four poems were assigned to Strode (see items 41 and 185), and suggests that they could be the work of David Rate.

144. ————. *Huchown of the Awle Ryale and His Poems: Examined in the Light of Recent Criticism.* Glasgow: no pub., 1902. Abst. in *PRPSG*, 33 (1901-2), 315-16.

A critique of item 274. Points out the danger of attempting to establish authorsnip from parallel passages in alliterative poetry. Nevertheless supports the theory of common authorship for the four poems. Cf. item 274, etc.

145. Burgess, Valerie Mary. "The Treatment of Character Types and Methods of Character Portrayal in *Pat* and *Pur*, considered with reference to other literature of the late fourteenth and early fifteenth century, including drama." M.Phil. thesis, London, 1976.

146. Burrow, J[ohn] A. *Ricardian Poetry: Chaucer, Gower, Langland and the "G" Poet.* London: Routledge; New Haven: Yale UP, 1971.

Includes many passing references to all four poems. Provides more sustained discussion of the following matters: the MS and early editions (pp. 4-5); alliterative tradition and style (pp. 24-28, 41-42); the narrator's voice (pp. 40-41); form, structure, and narrative framing (pp. 58, 60, 64-65); "pointing" in *G* (pp. 69, 72-73); exemplification in *Pat*, *Cl*, and *G* (pp. 85-87); the unheroic view of man (pp. 95-96, 101-03); the penitential (pp. 107-08); ironic humor (pp. 113-14, 127-29); similes (pp. 133-35, 140).

Reviews: Morton W. Bloomfield, *Speculum*, 48·(1973), 345-47.
        D. Farley-Hills, *RES*, NS 23 (1972), 325-27.
        M.C. Seymour, *ES*, 54 (1973), 274-75.

147. Cargill, Oscar, and Margaret Schlauch. "*The Pe* and its Jeweller." *PMLA*, 43 (1928), 105-23.

Speculates that *Pe* is an elegy for Margaret, daughter
of the Earl of Pembroke and Margaret, daughter of Edward
III; that *G* may reflect Pembroke connections with Ire-
land; and that either John Donne or John Prat (both
clerks in the Pembroke household) could be the poet.
Cf. item 534.

148. Chapman, Coolidge Otis. "The Musical Training of the
      Pe Poet." *PMLA*, 46 (1931), 177-81.

      Argues that *Pe*, *G*, and *Cl* provide evidence of the poet's
      knowledge of music. Cf. item 395.

149. ———. "The Authorship of the *Pe*." *PMLA*, 47 (1932),
      346-53.

      Suggests that the four poems were written by John of
      Erghome, an Augustinian Friar of York, author of the
      Latin poem *Prophecy of John of Bridlington*. Cf. item
      797.

150. ———. "Virgil and the *G*-Poet." *PMLA*, 60 (1945), 16-
      23.

      Presents evidence that the poet knew the *Aeneid*.

*   ———. See also item 756.

151. Clark, John Williams. "The Authorship of *SGGK*, *Pe*, *Cl*,
      Pat, and *Erk* in the Light of the Vocabulary." Diss.,
      Minnesota, 1941. Abst.: *Summaries of Ph.D. Theses, Univ.
      of Minnesota*, 4 (1949), 107-12.

152. ———. John W[illiams]. "Observations on Certain Dif-
      ferences in Vocabulary between *Cl* and *SGGK*." *PQ*, 28
      (1949), 261-73.

      Specifies differences between *G* and *Cl* in vocabulary and
      usage; concludes that the two poems are not by the same
      poet.

153. ———. "'The *G*-Poet' and the Substantival Adjective."
      JEGP, 49 (1950), 60-66.

      Contends that Oakden's list (item 279, pp. 394-95) of
      substantival adjectives in the four poems and *Erk* is
      evidence against rather than for common authorship.

154. ———. "Paraphrases for 'God' in the Poems Attributed
      to 'the *G*-Poet.'" *MLN*, 65 (1950), 232-36.

Lists periphrases for "God" in the four poems and *Erk*; argues that their distribution suggests multiple authorship.

155. ————. "On Certain 'Alliterative' and 'Poetic' Words in the Poems Attributed to 'The *G*-Poet.'" *MLQ*, 12 (1951), 387–98.

Argues against common authorship, on the basis of differences between the poems in the use of vocabulary.

* Coulson, J. See item 237.

156. Cuffe, Edwin Dodge, S.J. "An Interpretation of *Pat*, *Cl*, and *The Pe*, from the Viewpoint of Imagery." Diss., North Carolina, 1951.

157. Daiches, David. *A Critical History of English Literature*, I. London: Secker and Warburg; New York: Ronald, 1960.

Includes general accounts of *G* and *Pe* (pp. 60–62, 83–84).

158. Dale, Edmund. *National Life and Character in the Mirror of Early English Literature*. Cambridge: UP, 1907.

Uses various passages in *G* to illustrate courtly life; cites *Pe* as an example of parental feeling (pp. 202–08, 287–88).

159. Davenport, W.A. *The Art of the "G"-Poet*. London: Athlone; New Jersey: Humanities Press, 1978.

1. An introductory statement; supports common authorship.
2. *Pe*: Provides a critical reading, suggesting division into emotional, didactic, and sacramental stages. Considers the use of dream conventions, structural patterns, and wordplay; argues that the poem combines literal and allegorical modes. Concludes by emphasizing tensions between feeling and form.
3. Sees *Cl* as lacking unity (though containing much fine poetry), and as characterized by conflict between narrative and didactic impulses. Discusses the adaptation of biblical sources (stressing differences in the treatment of the various narratives); the use of homiletic material in bridging passages; and thematic links.

   4. *Pat*: Analyzes the treatment of the Vulgate Book of
      Jonah. Argues that the poem is more complex, equi-
      vocal, and ironic than it is usually taken to be.
   5. *G*: Considers the interweaving of plot-strands and the
      combination of romantic and realistic modes. Ana-
      lyzes the roles and functions of G's adversaries fitt
      by fitt, pointing out the recurring sense of ambi-
      guity. Emphasizes the poet's interest in the anti-
      thesis of opposites and in interplay between the
      ideal and the actual.
   6. Conclusion: Argues that the poet's art is one of an-
      tithesis and conflict. Suggests that the order of
      the poems in the MS is the order of their composition.

   Review: J.A. Burrow, *TLS*, 10 Nov. 1978, p. 1320.

160. Day, Mabel. "The Weak Verb in the Works of the *G*-Poet."
      MLR, 14 (1919), 413-15.

      Discusses the omission of final *-d* in the preterites and
      past participles of weak verbs. Cf. item 437.

161. ————. "Strophic Division in ME Alliterative Verse."
      EStn, 66 (1931), 245-48.

      Argues that a number of alliterative poems, including
      Pat and *Cl*, were written in quatrains. Cf. items 68,
      164, 212, 218, 292, 610, 647, 678.

162. Dobson, E.J. "The Etymology and Meaning of *Boy*." *MAE*,
      9 (1940), 121-54.

      Includes comments on usage in *Pe* 806 (pp. 133, 151) and
      Cl 878 (pp. 134, 147).

163. Döll, Helene. *Mittelenglische Kleidernamen im Spiegel
      literarischer Denkmäler des 14. Jahrhunderts*. Giessen:
      Glasgow, 1932. Diss., Giessen, 1932.

      Contains references to words for clothing and material
      in all four poems.

164. Duggan, Hoyt N. "Strophic Patterns in ME Alliterative
      Poetry." *MP*, 74 (1977), 223-47.

      Includes consideration of the quatrain theory with ref-
      erence to *Pat* and *Cl* (pp. 223-26). Cf. items 161, etc.

   *   Dunstan, A.C. See item 219.

165. Ebbs, John Dale. "Stylistic Mannerisms of the *G*-Poet."
     JEGP, 57 (1958), 522-25.

     Discusses stylistic mannerisms as evidence of common
     authorship. Cf. item 348.

166. Elliott, Ralph W.V. "Landscape and Rhetoric in ME Al-
     literative Poetry." *MCR*, 4 (1961), 65-76.

     Includes discussion of the nature descriptions in *G* and
     the portrayal of the garden in *Pe*. Cf. items 264, 289,
     354, 446, 524, 806, 902, 1240.

167. Emerson, Oliver Farrar. "Imperfect Lines in *Pe* and the
     Rimed Parts of *SGGK*." *MP*, 19 (1921), 131-41.

     Considers the emendations needed to regularize these ir-
     regular lines. Cf. item 569.

168. ————. "Shakespearean and Other Feasts." *SP*, 22
     (1925), 161-83.

     Comments on conventions of feasting reflected in *G* and
     Cl (pp. 175, 178, 181).

A   Ende, Frederick Albert Chaffey Von. See Von Ende.

169. Evans, W.O. "*Cortaysye* in ME." *MS*, 29 (1967), 143-57.

     Argues that *cortaysye* usually refers to a virtue, often
     specifically Christian; uses examples from all four po-
     ems. Cf. items 138, etc.

170. Everett, Dorothy. *Essays on ME Literature*. Ed. Patricia
     Kean. Oxford: Clarendon; New York: Oxford UP, 1955. Ex-
     tract on *Pc* rpt. in *Newstead*; extract on *G* rpt. in item
     827.

     Makes brief comments on the poet. Emphasizes the homi-
     letic character and narrative vitality of *Pat* and *Cl*.
     Discusses the metre of *G*, the moral theme, and nar-
     rative and descriptive technique. Compares *Pe* to *Lyci-
     das*, and comments on form, the pearl symbol, and the use
     of the Bible (pp. 68-96).

171. Farley-Hills, David. "The *Roman de la Rose* and the Po-
     ems of MS Cotton Nero Ax, 4." *JFA*, 2 (1964), 229-35.

     Suggests that the treatment of the relationship between
     sexuality and Christian morals in *Cl* and *G* may reflect
     the influence of the *Roman*. Cf. item 532.

172. ———. Letter. *RES*, NS 26 (1975), 451.

Rejects the views expressed by Turville-Petre in item 347.

*   ———. See also item 275.

173. Finlayson, John. "Rhetorical *Descriptio* of Place in the Alliterative *Morte Arthure*." *MP*, 61 (1963), 1-11.

Makes a number of comparisons with *G* and *Pe* (pp. 5, 6, 8-9, 10-11).

174. Fischer, Joseph. *Die Stabende Langzeile in den Werken des Gawaindichters.* Darmstadt: Otto, 1900; rpt. in BBA, 11, Bonn: Hanstein, 1901, pp. 1-64. Diss., Bonn, 1900.

Sets out to apply Trautmann's seven-stress theory (see item 1234) to the four poems and *Erk*. Includes *Erk* among the poet's works on the authority of items 227 and 343. Provides a review of the poet's language and a list of editorial emendations (mostly by Morris).

Review: Karl Luick, *AnglB*, 12 (1901), 33-49.

175. ———, and Franz Mennicken. "Zur Mittelenglischen Stabzeile." BBA, 11. Bonn: Hanstein, 1901. Pp. 139-54.

A reply to Luick's review (cited under item 174).

176. Fisher, John H. "Wyclif, Langland, Gower, and the *Pe* Poet on the subject of Aristocracy." *Studies in Medieval Literature: In Honor of Professor Albert Croll Baugh.* Ed. MacEdward Leach. Philadelphia: Univ. of Pennsylvania Press, 1961. Pp. 139-57.

Sees the poet as a supporter of hierarchy which could be mystically resolved into equality.

177. Fuhrmann, Johannes. *Die alliterierenden Sprachformeln in Morris' "Early English Alliterative Poems" und im "Sir Gawayne and the Green Knight."* Hamburg: Hintel, 1886. Diss., Kiel, 1886.

Provides references to parallels in other alliterative works to the alliterative formulaic phrases found in the four poems. Entries are grouped according to type, and arranged alphabetically within these sections.

* G., A. See Gibb, Anthony.

178. Gardner, John. *The Life and Times of Chaucer.* New York: Knopf; London: Cape, 1977.

Refers to the poet as John Massey (see item 275, etc.). Includes a general discussion of the four poems, and numerous passing comments.

179. Garnett, Richard. *From the Beginnings to the Age of Henry VIII. English Literature: an Illustrated Record,* I. London: Heinemann; New York: Macmillan, 1903.

General comments on all four poems (pp. 119-23).

180. Gerould, Gordon Hall. "The *G* Poet and Dante: A Conjecture." *PMLA,* 51 (1936), 31-36.

Suggests that the poet's use of dialect may have been inspired by a passage in Dante's *Il Convivio.*

181. G[ibb], A[nthony]. "The *G* Poet." *Britain and the Commonwealth. The Penguin Companion to Literature,* I. Ed. David Daiches. Harmondsworth and Baltimore: Penguin, 1971. Pp. 205-06.

General comments on all four poems, together with a brief bibliography.

182. Gioia, Louis L. "The *Pe* Group: A Study in Thematic Continuity." Diss., Pittsburgh, 1970. Abst.: *DAI,* 31 (1970), 2343A.

Material on *Pe, Cl,* and *Pat.*

183. Glunz, Hans H. *Die Literarästhetik des europäischen Mittelalters: Wolfram--"Rosenroman"--Chaucer--Dante.* Bochum-Langendreer: Pöppinghaus, 1937; rpt. Frankfurt a.M.: Klostermann, 1963.

Describes *Cl* and *Pat* as biblical paraphrases (pp. 329-30). Discusses *Pe* in relation to various poets and conventions (Dante, Boccaccio, the mystics; allegory and dream); terms it an abbreviated *Divina Commedia* (pp. 507-20).

184. Goldbeck, Helen Janne. "The *G* Puzzle: A Study of MS. Cotton Nero A.x." Diss., Oklahoma, 1972. Abst.: *DAI,* 33 (1972), 1142A.

185.   Gollancz, Israel. "Ralph Strode." *DNB*, vol. 55, pp. 57–59.

       Suggests that Strode was the author of the four poems: cf. items 41, 43, 143, 190, 208, 259, 385, 438.

186.   ————. "On Puzzling Words and Passages in the Alliterative Poems—*Pat*, *Cl*, and *Gawain and the Grene Knyght*." *Athen*, 10 Nov. 1894, p. 646.

       (Report of a paper read to the Philological Soc.). Glossarial notes on *Pat* 39, 159, 167, 188; *Cl* 231, 411, 620, 819, 1410, 1634; *G* 154, 632.

187.   ————. "Recent Theories concerning Huchoun and Others." *Athen*, 23 Nov. 1901, p. 705.

       (Report of a paper read to the Philological Soc.). Denies Huchown's authorship of *Pe* and *G*. Cf. items 274, etc.

188.   ————. Untitled report of papers read by Gollancz. *Athen*, 12 Mar. 1904, p. 343.

       Comments on *Ragnel* (*Pat* 188) and *allyt* (*Cl* 599).

189.   ————, I[srael]. "*Pe*, *Cl*, *Pat*, and *Sir Gawayne*." *The Cambridge History of English Literature*. Ed. A.W. Ward and A.R. Waller. Cambridge: UP; New York: Putnam's, 1907. I, 320–34.

       Provides brief critical accounts of each poem and a slightly modified version of the hypothetical biography of the poet contained in item 41.

190.   ————. "*Pe* and *Pur*." *TLS*, 25 May 1922, p. 343.

       A response to item 125. The reviewer's reply is appended. Cf. item 191.

191.   ————. "*Pe* and *Pur*." *TLS*, 1 June 1922, p. 364.

       A further response to item 125. Cf. item 190.

192.   ————, Sir Israel. "Preface" to his ed. of *StE: An Alliterative Poem*. SEEP, 4. London: Milford, Oxford UP, 1932.

       Maintains that *StE* is probably by the author of the four poems (cf. items 130, 207, 227, 266, 279, 290, 292, 310, 343) and that he may have been Ralph Strode (cf. items 185, etc.). (Pp. lvi–lxii).

193. Gradon, Pamela. *Form and Style in Early English Literature.* London: Methuen, 1971.

Includes: an account of the theme and structure of *Cl* (pp. 119-24); discussion of the poet's manipulation of conventional material (e.g., pearl and garden symbolism) in *Pe* (pp. 194-211); comparisons of structuring and nature descriptions in *G* and *Beowulf* (pp. 131-39, 173-74); comments on the use of perspective in *G* and *Pat* (pp. 289-92). Also contains many passing references to all four poems.

* ———. See item 221.

194. Grant, William M. "*Pur* and *Pat*: a History of Scholarship and a Critical Analysis." Diss., Brown, 1968. Abst.: *DAI*, 30 (1969), 280A.

195. Greg, W.W. "A Bibliographical Paradox." *Library*, 4th ser., 13 (1932), 188-91.

Questions Oakden's hypothesis concerning scribal transmission (see item 276, pp. 261-63).

196. Groom, Bernard. *A Literary History of England.* London, New York, Toronto: Longmans, Green, 1929.

General comments on *G* and *Pe* (pp. 18-21).

197. Hanna, Ralph, III. "Introduction" to his ed. of *The Awntyrs off Arthure at the Terne Wathelyn.* Old and ME Texts. Manchester: UP; New York: Barnes and Noble, 1974.

Compares the verse-form of *The Awntyrs* with that of *G* and *Pe* (pp. 14-16); discusses parallels of phrasing and subject matter between *The Awntyrs* and *G* (pp. 38-39, 44-48). Cf. items 504, 1009.

198. Heath, H. Frank. *Social England*, II. Ed. H.D. Traill. London, Paris, and Melbourne: Cassell, 1894.

Includes general comments on all four poems (pp. 205-06).

199. Heather, P.J. "Precious Stones in the ME Verse of the Fourteenth Century." *F-L*, 42 (1931), 217-64, 345-404.

Enumerates, without particular comment, references to precious stones in *Pe*, *Cl*, and *G* (pp. 233, 241, 260, 353-54, 364, 374, 386).

200. Henneman, John Bell. *Untersuchungen über das Mittel-englische Gedicht "Wars of Alexander."* Berlin: Bernstein, 1889. Diss., Berlin, 1889.

Argues against Bradley's suggestion (item 134) that the author of the four poems also wrote the *Wars of Alexander* (pp. 30-36).

201. Heuser, W. "Offenes und geschlossenes *ee* im Westmittelländischen dialekt." *Anglia*, 19 (1897), 451-59.

Includes discussion of examples in *Pe* and *G*.

202. Hieatt, A. Kent. "Symbolic and Narrative Patterns in *Pe*, *Cl*, *Pat*, and *G*." *ESC*, 2 (1976), 125-43.

Considers images and narrative patterns which connect the four poems, emphasizing the motifs of clothing, vessels, beryl, and pearl. Links the woodbine in *Pat* with the lace in *G*. Also discusses numerical structure. Cf. items 206, etc.

203. Hill, John M. "ME Poets and the World: Notes Toward an Appraisal of Linguistic Consciousness." *Criticism*, 16 (1974), 153-69.

Includes discussion of the awareness of the inadequacy of language in *Pe*, and the use of linguistic ambiguity in *Pe* and *G*.

204. Hill, Ordelle Gerhard. "*Pat*: Style, Background, Meaning, and Relationship to *Cl*." Diss., Illinois, 1965. Abst.: *DA*, 26 (1966), 7297.

* Hills, David Farley. See Farley-Hills, David.

205. Hoffman, Donald L. "*Renischche Renkes* and *Runisch Sauez*." *N&Q*, 215 (1970), 447-49.

Argues that *runisch* and *renisch* are two distinct words, referring in detail to usage in *G*, *Cl*, and *Pat*. (Cf. item 334).

206. Hopper, Vincent Foster. *Medieval Number Symbolism: Its Sources, Meaning, and Influence on Thought and Expression.* Columbia Univ. Studies in English and Comparative Literature, 132. New York: Columbia UP, 1958.

Briefly mentions the pentangle in *G* and the New Jerusalem in *Pe* (pp. 124-26). Cf. items 202, 394, 424, 467, 510, 544, 876, 919.

207. Horstmann, C. "Inhalt" to his ed. of *"De Erkenwalde."*
      Altenglische Legenden: Neue Folge. Heilbronn: Henniger,
      1881.

      Advocates the common authorship of *Erk* and the four po-
      ems. Cf. items 192, etc.

208. ————. "Introduction" to his ed., *Yorkshire Writ-
      ers: Richard Rolle of Hampole and his Followers*, II.
      Lib. of Early Writers, 2. London: Swan Sonnenschein;
      New York: Macmillan, 1896.

      Claims to have been the originator of the idea that
      Strode was the author of *Pe* and *G* (p. 18, footnote 3).
      Cf. items 41, 185, 192.

209. Hoshiya, Goishi. *"SG* and *Pe." EigoS*, 97 (1951), 391-
      93, 439-41.

      Discusses the descriptions of nature in *G* and *Pe*. Cf.
      items 166, etc.

210. Huchon, René. *De la Conquête normande à l'introduction
      de l'imprimerie (1066-1475). Histoire de la Langue Ang-
      laise*, II. Paris: Colin, 1930.

      Includes a review of the dialect of the four poems (pp.
      235-43).

211. Hulbert, James Root. "The 'West Midland' of the Ro-
      mances." *MP*, 19 (1921), 1-16.

      Argues that Morris's view (items 19 and 100), that the
      dialect of the four poems is West Midland, has been ac-
      cepted uncritically, and that the evidence does not jus-
      tify localization in the West. (Cf. item 1015).

212. ————, J[ames] R[oot]. "Quatrains in ME Alliterative
      Poems." *MP*, 48 (1950), 73-81.

      Includes support for the view that *Pat* and *Cl* were writ-
      ten in quatrains (cf. items 161, etc.)

   * Irvine, Helen Douglas. See item 236.

   * J., G.P. See item 906.

213. Jacobs, Nicolas. "Alliterative Storms: A Topos in ME.'
      Speculum, 47 (1972), 695-719.

Discusses sources and development of the topos, and compares examples in ME alliterative poetry, including *Pat*
129-64, *Cl* 363-72, 947-72, and *G* 1998-2005. Cf. items
223, 264, 334.

*   Johnson, Hamish. See item 297.

214.   Johnson, Lynn Staley. "Poetic Structure and Christian
      Doctrine: A Reinterpretation of the Works of the *G*-
      Poet." Diss., Princeton, 1973. Abst.: *DAI*, 34 (1974),
      6592A-93A.

215.   Jones, Charles. *An Introduction to ME*. New York, etc.:
      Holt, 1972.

      Reviews dialect; suggests composition in North Stafford-
      shire (pp. 188-89, 214-17). Cf. items 88, 217, 247,
      318, 1015.

216.   Jusserand, J.J. *Des Origines à la Renaissance. Hist-
      oire Littéraire du Peuple Anglais*, I. Paris: Firmin-
      Didot, 1894; 2nd, rev. ed., 1896. Tr. as *From the Ori-
      gins to the Renaissance. A Literary History of the Eng-
      lish People*, I. London: Fisher Unwin; New York: Put-
      nam's, 1895; rev. eds., 1906, 1925.

      Summarizes and praises *Pe* and *G* (pp. 348-52 in the Eng-
      lish ed.).

217.   Kaiser, Rolf. *Zur Geographie des mittelenglischen Wort-
      schatzes*. Palaestra, 205. Leipzig: Mayer und Müller,
      1937.

      Locates composition of the four poems and *Erk* in North-
      East Lancashire, Westmoreland, or Cumberland. Cf. items
      215, etc.

218.   Kaluza, Max. "Strophische gliederung in der mitteleng-
      lischen rein alliterirenden dichtung." *EStn*, 16 (1892),
      169-80.

      Suggests that *Pat* consists of 22 strophes of 24 lines
      each (513-15 taken as an interpolation), and *Cl* of 30
      strophes of 60 lines each (though with some irregulari-
      ties). Cf. items 161, etc.

219.   ————. *Englische Metrik in historischer Entwicklung*.
      Normannia, 1. Berlin: Felber, 1909. Tr. A.C. Dun-
      stan as *A Short History of English Versification from*

the Earliest Times to the Present Day. London: Allen; New York: Macmillan, 1911.

Discusses ME alliterative verse (rhythmical structure, alliteration, stanza forms, and concatenation), with reference to the four poems in sections 156-60, 163, 166, and 173.

*   Kean, Patricia. See item 170.

220.   Keiser, Elizabeth Bassett. "Perfection and Experience: The Celebration of Divine Order and Human Sensibility in *Cl* and *Pat*." Diss., Yale, 1972. Abst.: *DAI*, 34 (1973), 277A.

*   Kennedy, Arthur G. See item 333.

*   Kennedy, Horace M. See item 140.

221.   Ker, W.P. *English Literature* [:] *Medieval*. The Home Univ. Lib. of Mod. Knowledge. London: Williams and Norgate; New York: Holt, 1912; reset ed., with supp. note by R.W. Chambers, London, New York, Toronto: Milford, Oxford UP, 1945. Rpt. as *Medieval English Literature*, with bibliog. note by Pamela Gradon, London, Oxford, New York: Oxford UP, 1969.

Assigns the four poems to Huchown. Offers general comments, mainly on *G* (pp. 75-78, 105-06 in 1969 ed.).

222.   Kirk, Elizabeth D. "Chaucer and His English Contemporaries." *Chaucer: a collection of original articles*. Ed. George D. Economou. New York: McGraw-Hill, 1975. Pp. 111-27.

Considers the poems in the context of the alliterative tradition (pp. 118-23).

223.   Kissack, Robert Ashton, Jr. "The Sea in Anglo-Saxon and ME Poetry." *WUSt*, 13 (1926), 371-89.

Discusses briefly the descriptions of the storm in *Pat* and the Flood in *Cl* (pp. 384-85). Cf. items 213, etc.

224.   Kjellmer, Göran. *Context and Meaning: A Study of Distributional and Semantic Relations in a Group of ME Words*. GothSE, 22. Göteborg, 1971. Diss., Göteborg, 1971.

An analysis of the context and meaning of six ME words meaning "people" (*folk*, *leod*, *man*, *nation*, *people*, and

þeod) in 108 texts, including the four poems.   (Cf.
item 225).

225. ———. *ME Words for "People."* GothSE, 27. Stockholm:
Almqvist och Wiksell, 1973.

Contains further analysis of the material in item 224.
Makes special reference to the four poems on pp. 29, 93,
167-68, 172-73, 287, 290. Expresses doubt about the
theory of common authorship on p. 93: cf. item 226.

226. ———. *Did the '"Pe" Poet' Write "Pe"?* GothSE, 30.
Göteborg, 1975.

Reviews the debate on the authorship of the four poems
and *Erk*, and discusses various methods for establishing
authorship. Specifies his own method: essentially that
of setting up norms for a group of texts and observing
individual deviations. Reports that the following "linguistic dimensions" were used: lexical frequency, clause
length, sentence length, clause-linkage types, subordinate types, passive forms, alliteration; that *Pe* proved
to be the deviant text; and that it remained so both
when *Winner and Waster* was added to the group and when
Erk was removed. Concludes that *Pe* is not by the "*Pe*
Poet." Includes many tables.

Reviews: Rima Handley, *N&Q*, 221 (1976), 480.
           R.W. McTurk and D.J. Williams, *YWES*, 56 (1975),
           86-87.

227. Knigge, Friedrich. *Die Sprache des Dichters von "SGGK,"
der sogenannten "Early English Alliterative Poems" und
"De Erkenwalde,"* I. *Lautlehre.* Marburg: Elwert, 1886.
Diss., Marburg, 1885.

Sets out to prove that *Erk* was written by the author of
the four poems. Analyzes the occurrence of sounds in
the group of five poems under the following headings:
A. Germanic sounds: 1. OE: (a) vowels, (b) consonants;
2. ON: (a) vowels, (b) consonants; B. Romance sounds:
OF: (a) vowels, (b) consonants. Announces plans to pub-
lish this work along with a further volume of texts. Cf.
items 192, etc.

228. Körting, Gustav. *Grundriss der Geschichte der Englischen Litteratur von ihren Anfängen bis zur Gegenwart.*
Sammlung von Kompendien für das Studium und die Praxis,
ser. I, vol. 1. Münster i.W.: Schöningh, 1887; 5th ed.,
1910.

Provides basic information on all four poems, together
with a brief bibliographical guide (sects. 105-08 in
5th ed.).

229. Koziol, Herbert. "Zur Frage der Verfasserschaft einiger
mittelenglischer Stabreimdichtungen." *EStn*, 67 (1932),
165-73.

Argues for the common authorship of the four poems.
Also assigns *Erk* to the poet.

230. ——— Grundzüge der Syntax der mittelenglischen Stabreimdichtungen. WBEP, 58. Wien und Leipzig: Braumüller, 1932.

A study of the syntax of ME alliterative verse; makes
extensive use of examples from all four poems. Includes
surveys of nouns of specific gender and of the pronoun
of address in each poem (pp. 16-21, 55-57).

* Kuriyagawa, Fumio. See item 1296.

* Kuruma, Norio. See item 1297.

231. Lang, Andrew. *History of English Literature from "Beowulf" to Swinburne.* London, etc.: Longmans, Green,
1912; 2nd, rev., ed., 1912; 3rd ed., 1913.

General comments on *G* and *Pe*, and passing reference to
Pat and *Cl* (pp. 72-75).

232. Lasater, Alice Elizabeth. "Hispano-Arabic Relationships to the Works of the *G*-Poet." Diss., Tennessee,
1971. Abst.: *DAI*, 32 (1972), 4570A-71A. Cf. item 233.

233. ———, Alice E[lizabeth]. *Spain to England: A Comparative Study of Arabic, European, and English Literature
of the Middle Ages.* Jackson: UP of Mississippi, 1974.

(Cf. item 232). Includes sections on *Pe* (pp. 69-95),
Cl (pp. 120-23), and *G* (pp. 168-96), as well as many
passing references.

Pe: Reviews the major critical debates. Suggests that
the Maiden reflects the influence of Islamic escha-
tological tradition (cf. pp. 67-69); emphasizes the
combination of elegiac and eschatological elements
within a dream vision. (Cf. item 484).

Cl: Detects Islamic influence in lines 697-708.

G: Reviews critical approaches. Suggests that the exchange of winnings motif reflects the influence of an
Arabic fabliau, and that the GK's closest literary
predecessor is the legendary Persian figure al-Khadir.

234.   Lawrence, John. "Vowel Alliteration in the Fourteenth
       Century compared with that of *Beowulf*." *Chapters on Al-
       literative Verse*. London: Frowde, 1893. Pp. 54-113.

       Compares vowel alliteration in *Beowulf* with that of a
       number of fourteenth-century alliterative poems, includ-
       ing *G*, *Cl*, and *Pat*. Occurrences are tabulated (pp. 89-
       93). General observations on vowel alliteration in the
       three poems follow (pp. 93-99).

235.   Lee, Jennifer Ann. "MS Cotton Nero A.x.: A Study of the
       Illustrator and Translator as Primary Critics of the ME
       Pe, *Cl*, *Pat* and *SGGK*." Diss., New York (Stony Brook),
       1974. Abst.: *DAI*, 35 (1974), 407A.

236.   Legouis, Emile. *Le Moyen Age et la Renaissance (650-
       1660)*. *Histoire de la Littérature Anglais*, I. Paris:
       Hachette, 1924; rev. eds., 1939, 1949. Tr. Helen
       Douglas Irvine as *The Middle Ages and the Renascence
       (650-1660)*. *A History of English Literature*, I. London
       and Toronto: Dent; New York: Macmillan, 1926; rev. eds.,
       1929, 1933, 1937.

       Brief comments on all four poems and summaries of *G* and
       Pe (pp. 67-71 in English ed.).

237.   ———. *A Short History of English Literature*. Tr.
       V.F. Boyson and J. Coulson. Oxford: Clarendon, 1934.

       Brief comments on *G* and *Pe* (pp. 35-36).

238.   Leonard, William Ellery. "The Scansion of ME Allitera-
       tive Verse." *Studies by Members of the Department of
       English*. Univ. of Wisconsin Studies in Language and Lit-
       erature, 11. Madison, 1920. Pp. 58-104.

       Applies the four-accent theory to ME alliterative verse.
       Discusses lines from *G* and *Cl* (pp. 63, 75-76).

239.   Levy, Bernard Sidney. "Style and Purpose: A Reconsidera-
       tion of the Poems in Cotton Nero A.x." Diss., Califor-
       nia (Berkeley), 1962.

240.   Lowell, Patricia. "The Two Voices in English Medieval
       Literature." *Lit*, 7 (1966), 70-73.

       Includes references to *Pe* and *G*. Not seen.

241. Luick, K[arl]. "Die englische stabreimzeille im XIV.,
XV., und XVI. jahrhundert." *Anglia*, 11 (1889), 392-
443, 553-618.

Contains a section on the works of the G-Poet, among
which he includes *Erk*. Presents evidence on language
and metre, taking most of his examples from *G* (pp. 572-
85).

242. ――――, Karl. "Der mittelenglische Stabreimvers." GGP,
2, ii. Strassburg: Trübner, 1905.

Reviews theories of alliterative rhythm; specifics stanza forms. Includes references to *G* and *Pe* (pp. 160-79).

243. ――――. "Über die Betonung der französischen Lehnwörter
im Mittelenglischen." *GRM*, 9 (1921), 14-19.

Includes discussion of the treatment of OF *-é* in the
poems. Cf. item 260.

244. Luttrell, C.A. "The *G* Group. Cruxes, Etymologies, Interpretations." *Neophil*, 39 (1955), 207-17; 40 (1956),
290-301.

Deals with: 1. *bale* (*Cl* 980), *bele* (*Pe* 18), *carye* (*G*
734), *raged* (*G* 745), *rout* (*G* 457), *scarre* (*Cl* 598, etc.),
skyly (*Cl* 62), *skylly skyualde* (*Cl* 529), *skue* (*Cl* 483,
etc., *G* 2167), *sour* (*Cl* 192), *wawe* (*Pe* 287, etc., *Cl*
382, etc., *Pat* 142).
2. *sweȝe* (*G* 1796), *nay* (*Cl* 805, *G* 1836), *barbe* (*G* 2310),
dumpe (*Pat* 362), *lauce* (*-se*) (*Cl* 668, etc., *Pat* 350, *G*
526, etc.), *swey* (*Cl* 87, etc., *Pat* 72, etc., *G* 1429,
etc.), *skly(l)y* (again).

245. ――――. "A *G* Group Miscellany." *N&Q*, 207 (1962), 447-
50.

Notes on *dayly* (*Pe* 313), *freles* (*Pe* 431), *þrad* (*Cl* 751),
child-gered (*G* 86), and *G* 977.

246. MacCracken, Henry Noble. "Concerning Huchown." *PMLA*,
25 (1910), 507-34.

A review of the Huchown controversy; mentions the poems
in passing. Cf. items 274, etc.

247. McIntosh, Angus. "A New Approach to ME Dialectology."
ES, 44 (1963), 1-11.

Localizes *G* in South-East Cheshire or North-East Staffordshire (pp. 5-6). Cf. items 215, etc.

248. Mackenzie, Agnes Mure. *An Historical Survey of Scottish Literature to 1714*. London: MacLehose, 1933.

Brief comments on all four poems, which are attributed to Hucheone [sic]. Suggests that the Scottish Chaucerians were indebted to *Pe* (pp. 29-38). Cf. items 274, etc.

249. McLaughlin, John Cameron. "A Graphemic-Phonemic Study of a ME Manuscript: MS. Cotton Nero A.x." Diss., Indiana, 1961. Abst.: *DA* , 22 (1961), 1617-18.

Cf. item 250.

250. ———, John C[ameron]. *A Graphemic-Phonemic Study of a ME Manuscript*. The Hague: Mouton, 1963.

Specifies intentions as: (a) to present a complete description of the "writing system" of the MS; and (b) to reconstruct a phoemic system of the language. Chapters on: 1. MS and dialect; 2. graphemic theory and terminology; 3. the graphemic system; 4. the phonological significance of the graphemic system; part i, the vocalic nuclei; 5. the same, part ii, the consonants; 6. the graphonemic system. Appendixes: A. OE and ModE phonemic systems; B. transcription of f.39^r (the beginning of *Pe*); C. index of citations from the MS. Includes a bibliography.

Reviews: Jane Crawford, *ES*, 50 (1969), lxxix-lxxxii.
Elliott V.K. Dobbie, *Lang*, 41 (1965), 151-54.
Angus McIntosh, *ArL*, 16 (1964), 78-80.
H.H. Meier, *LT*, 246 (1968), 237-38.

251. McNamara, John Francis. "Responses to Ockhamist Theory in the Poetry of the *Pe*-Poet, Langland, and Chaucer." Diss., Louisiana State, 1968. Abst. in *DA*, 29 (1968), 3148A-49A.

252. McNeil, Geo[rge] P. "Huchown of the Awle Ryale." *ScR*, April 1888, pp. 266-88.

Ascribes the four poems to Huchown, whom he identifies with Sir Hugh of Eglinton. Provides summaries and brief critical comments. Cf. items 274, etc.

253. Markman, Alan. "A Computer Concordance to ME Texts." *SB*, 17 (1964), 55-75.

An account of the processes, textual and technical, involved in the preparation of item 16.

254. Markus, Manfred. *Moderne Erzählperspektive in den Werk-
      en des "G"-Autors.* Sprache und Literatur: Regensburger
      Arbeiten zur Anglistik und Amerikanstik, 3. Regensburg:
      Carl, 1971. Diss., Regensburg, 1971. Abst.: *EASG,*
      1971, pp. 56-58.

      Investigates the handling of narrative perspective in
      the four poems.

      1. Examines the poet's use of tenses in order to ascer-
         tain the effect this has on the temporal relation-
         ship between the narrator and what he describes.
      2. Argues that the poet employs a technique equivalent
         to cinematographic zooming in order to vary perspec-
         tive.
      3. Discusses the use of passages narrated from the pro-
         tagonist's point-of-view, and observes that these are
         often alternated with passages in which the protago-
         nist is seen more objectively.
      4. Suggests that the poems are characterized by shifting
         point-of-view, and that this is a significant struc-
         tural principle. Observes that all use a frame, and
         all involve confrontation between human and super-
         human perspectives.
      Cf. items 1012, etc.

255. Mathew, Gervase. *The Court of Richard II.* London: Mur-
      ray, 1968.

      Includes speculation about the poems' composition (p.
      116), and comments on the MS (p. 117) and on G's cour-
      tesy (pp. 123-25). Cf. item 1001.

256. Matsui, Noriko. "Allegory of Courtesy in *Pe* and *SGGK.*"
      SELit, 47 (1971), 123-40. English sum. in English num-
      ber, 1971, pp. 165-67.

      Argues that the concept of courtesy is specifically
      Christian, and that it makes a significant contribution
      to the meaning of both poems. (Cf. items 138, etc.).

*   Matsunami, Tamotsu. See item 1298.

257. Mazzelli, Giorgio. "Allegoria e poesia in *Pat* e *Cl.*"
      Diss., Milano, 1972.

258. Medary, Margaret P. "Stanza-Linking in ME Verse." *RR,*
      7 (1916), 243-70.

      Deals with concatenation in *Pe,* and the link between
      first and last lines in *G, Pe,* and *Pat* (pp. 267-68).
      Cf. item 141.

259.   Medcalf, Stephen. "*Piers Plowman* and the Ricardian Age
       in Literature." *Daiches/Thorlby*, pp. 643-96.

       Includes endorsement of the identification of Strode as
       poet, discussion of language and theme in *G*, and a sum-
       mary of *Pe* (pp. 672-74, 655-63, 664). Also various
       passing comments on all four poems.

260.   Menner, Robert J. "Four Notes on the West Midland Dia-
       lect." *MLN*, 41 (1926), 454-58.

       Includes discussion of the spelling -é for final *i* or
       y. Cf. item 243.

  *   Mennicken, Franz. See item 175.

261.   Mills, A.D. "A Comparative Study of the Vocabulary,
       Versification and Style of *Pe*, *Pat*, *Pur* and *SGGK*."
       Ph.D. thesis, Manchester, 1963.

262.   Moorman, Charles. "Some Notes on *Pat* and *Pe*." *SoQ*, 4
       (1965), 67-73.

       Notes on *Pat* 1, 39, 41-45, 54-58, and *Pe* 39, 139-40,
       977-81, 1027-30.

263.   ————. *The "Pe"-Poet*. Twayne's English Authors Ser.,
       64. New York: Twayne, 1968.

       A general introduction.

       1. Summarizes the historical and cultural context; sup-
          ports the theory of common authorship.
       2. *Pe*: Considers the use of conventions (dream vision,
          first-person narrator); reviews critical approaches.
          Emphasizes the Dreamer's progress (based on item
          493).
       3. *Pat*: Discusses the modification of source material
          and the role of the narrator (the latter based on
          item 663).
       4. *Cl*: An account of the relation between theme and
          structure, and the use of source material.
       5. *G*: Discusses form and structure, sources, mythic ele-
          ments, and the moral theme, emphasizing the poet's
          skill and subtlety.
       6. A general summary.

       Includes a selective, annotated bibliography. The poems
       are quoted in translation throughout.

       Review: G.C. Britton and W.A. Davenport, *YWES*, 50 (1969),
             90.

264. Moorman, Frederic W. "The *Gawayne*-Poet." *The Interpretation of Nature in English Poetry from "Beowulf" to Shakespeare.* QF, 95. Strassburg: Trübner, 1905. Pp. 95-106.

Praises the descriptions of nature in *G*, of the Earthly Paradise in *Pe*, of the Flood in *Cl*, and of the storm in *Pat*, emphasizing connections with OE poetry. Cf. items 166, etc.

265. Morley, Henry. *English Writers: An Attempt towards a History of English Literature.* 2nd, rev., ed. 11 vols. London, Paris, and Melbourne: Cassell, 1887-95.

Contains a summary and brief discussion of *Pe* (IV, 144-49), a summary of *G* (VI, 59-61), and support for the theory of common authorship (VI, 240-42).

266. Morse, Ruth. "A Note on Authorship" in her ed. of *StE*. Cambridge: Brewer; Totowa, N.J.: Rowman and Littlefield, 1975. Pp. 45-48.

Concludes that *StE* is probably not by the *G*-Poet. Cf. items 192, etc.

267. Moseley, C.W.R.D. "Chaucer, Sir John Mandeville, and the Alliterative Revival: A Hypothesis concerning Relationships." *MP*, 72 (1974), 182-84.

Mentions evidence of the poet's familiarity with Mandeville, and of Chaucer's with *G* (cf. items 359, etc.; 756, etc.).

268. Muscatine, Charles. "The *Pe* Poet: Style as Defence." *Poetry and Crisis in the Age of Chaucer.* Univ. of Notre Dame Ward-Phillips Lectures in English Language and Literature, 4. Notre Dame and London: Univ. of Notre Dame Press, 1972. Pp. 37-69.

Observes the poet's detachment from contemporary history, and his concern with personal rather than social crisis. Mainly discusses *Pe* and *G*, emphasizing the fusion of courtly and religious values, the formal perfection, and the interplay between formal unity on the one hand and contrasts and variations on the other. Also brief comments at the end of the preceding chapter (pp. 34-35).

Reviews: E. Talbot Donaldson, *CL*, 25 (1973), 262-63.
Nicolas Jacobs, *EIC*, 24 (1974), 71-77.

269. Mustanoja, Tauno F. "The ME Syntactical Type *His Own hand(s)* 'with his own hands, himself,' with Reference to Other Similar Expressions." *NM*, 60 (1959), 267-86.

Discusses the synthetic instrumental in *G* 10, *cors(e)* in *Cl* 683, etc., and *G* 1237, and *þyn awen seluen* (*G* 2301).

*   Nakao, Toshio. See item 1299.

270. Nance, R. Morton. "Northern Ships of Circa 1340." *MM*, 3 (1913), 33-39.

Includes comment on *Cl* 417-20 (erroneously credited to a Miracle Play) and *hurrok* (*Pat* 185, *Cl* 419). Cf. items 307, etc.

*   Naruse, Masaiku. See items 1300-02.

271. Neilson, George. "Huchown of the Awle Ryale." *TGAS*, 4 (1900), 252-393.

See item 274.

272. ————. "Sir Hew of Eglintoun and Huchown off the Awle Ryale: a Biographical Calendar and Literary Estimate." *PRPSG*, 32 (1900-01), 111-50. Also pub. separately.

Argues that Huchown (referred to in Wyntoun's *Chronicle*, V, 4301) is to be identified with Sir Hew (referred to in Dunbar's "Lament"). This poet is assumed to be the author of a number of alliterative poems, including *G*. Cf. items 274, etc.

273. ————. "Huchown of the Awle Reale." *Chambers*.

Briefly mentions *Pe*, *Pat*, and *Cl* as works ascribed to Huchown, and quotes *Cl* 410-24 (I. 171-75). Cf. items 274, etc.

274. ————. *"Huchown of the Awle Ryale" the Alliterative Poet: A Historical Criticism of Fourteenth Century Poems ascribed to Sir Hew of Eglintoun.* Glasgow: MacLehose, 1902. A revised version of item 271.

Identifies Huchown with Sir Hew (see item 272). Presents evidence of common sources and parallels of phrasing and plot in a group of alliterative poems comprising *Pe*, *Cl*, *Pat*, *G*, and nine others, and concludes that Sir Hew is the author of all thirteen. (See, in particular,

pp. 71-77, 113-16). Suggests that the incomplete super-
scription *Hugo de* in the MS (f. 91^r) refers to Sir Hew.
Cf. items 142, 144, 187, 248, 252, 272-73, 342, 1103.

275. Nolan, Barbara, and David Farley-Hills. "The Authorship
of *Pe*: Two Notes." *RES*, NS 22 (1971), 295-302.

A joint introductory note summarizes the material on
Massey in item 89. Nolan ("A Signature and an Anagram
in *Pe*") provides further evidence, and argues that the
poet's Christian name is John (not Hugh). Farley-Hills
("Maister Massy") draws attention to a reference by
Hoccleve to an author of this name. Cf. items 89, 178,
290-93, 347, 349, 367.

276. Oakden, J[ames] P. *Alliterative Poetry in ME: The Dia-
lectical and Metrical Survey.* Pubs. of the Univ. of
Manchester, 205; English ser., 18. Manchester: UP,
1930.

Contains many passing comments and observations. Provides a summary of opinion on the dialect (pp. 5-9), his
own review of language and dialect (pp. 72-87), and a
summary of metrical characteristics (pp. 190-92, 235-36,
241). Supports the theory of common authorship for *G*,
Pat, and *Cl* (pp. 251-53), and possibly *Erk* (pp. 253-55).
Identifies Clitheroe Castle as the GK's castle, and a
nearby site as the Green Chapel (pp. 259-61). Postu-
lates seven scribes responsible for copying the poems
(pp. 261 63). See item 279.

Reviews: A. Brandl, *Archiv*, 159 (1931), 293-96.
Dorothy Everett, *YWES*, 11 (1930), 92-97.
C.T. Onions, *RES*, 9 (1933), 89-94.
(See also under item 279).

277. ———. "The Scribal Errors of the MS. Cotton Nero
A.x." *Library*, 4th ser., 14 (1933), 353-58.

A response to item 195.

278. ———. "The Survival of a Stylistic Feature of Indo-
European poetry in Germanic, especially in ME." *RES*, 9
(1933), 50-53.

Includes examples in *G* 533 and *Pat* 31 of this feature:
the occurrence in one line of three names, of which the
last is qualified by an epithet.

279.   ————. *Alliterative Poetry in ME: A Survey of the Tra-*
        ditions. Pubs. of the Univ. of Manchester, 236; Eng-
        lish ser., 22. Manchester: UP, 1935.

        Includes many incidental references and observations.
        Provides general critical comments on *G*, *Pat*, and *Cl*
        (pp. 46–47, 67–69), and reviews the debate on the inter-
        pretation of *Pe* (pp. 69–76). Suggests that *Erk* may be
        by the poet (pp. 76–78). Discusses problems of estab-
        lishing common authorship; lists parallels among the
        four poems and *Erk* (pp. 83–93), and with various other
        alliterative poems (pp. 96–100, 103). Comments on the
        poet's descriptive style (pp. 104–11). Reviews his vo-
        cabulary (pp. 179–81, 187–88; see also 166–68, 183–86,
        188–93). The review of alliterative phrases (pp. 263–
        312, 343–50) contains many relevant references. Com-
        ments on stylistic features (pp. 392–401). See item
        276.

        Reviews: Mary S. Serjeantson, *YWES*, 16 (1935), 121–22.
                G.V. Smithers, *RES*, 13 (1937), 217–25.

        Review of items 276 and 279: Edgar C. Knowlton, *JEGP*,
                36 (1937), 120–23.

280.   ————. *The Poetry of the Alliterative Revival: Re-*
        printed from "Alliterative Poetry in ME: A Survey of the
        Traditions" (1935). Manchester: UP, 1935.

        Reprints item 279, pp. 1–111, retaining the pagination
        of the original.

281.   ————. *Alliterative Poetry in ME*. n.p.: Archon, 1968.

        A reprint of items 276 and 279 in one volume. Retains
        the original pagination.

   *   Ogoshi, Kazuzo. See item 1298.

282.   Ohlander, Urban. *Studies on Coordinate Expressions in*
        ME. LundSE, 5. Lund: Gleerup; London: Williams and
        Norgate; Copenhagen: Levin and Munksgaard, 1936.

        The four poems are included in a large corpus of ME
        texts used to provide exemplary illustration.

283.   Ohye, Saburo. "Metrical Influences in the Grammar of
        the Four Poems Preserved in MS. Cotton Nero A.x." *SPR*,
        11 (1962), 75–97.

Summarizes each poem's metrical characteristics, and goes on to review the influence which these exert on grammatical forms. In English.

284. Oiji, Takero. *Fourteenth Century English Literature.* Tokyo: Bunri, 1976.

Contains reprints of items 520, 521, and 1066.

285. Olszewska, E.S. "Norse alliterative tradition in ME." *LeedsSE*, 6 (1937), 50-64.

Includes notes on *Pe* 868, *Pat* 473, and *G* 46, 725.

* Orton, Harold. See item 299.

* Owen, D.D.R. See item 1080.

286. Padolsky, Enoch David. "Narrative Technique and the Instruction of the Reader in *Pat* and *Pur*." Diss., California (Berkeley), 1972. Abst.: *DAI*, 33 (1972), 731A.

287. Patch, Howard Rollin. *The Other World, According to Descriptions in Medieval Literature.* Smith College Studies in Mod. Langs., NS, 1. Cambridge, Mass.: Harvard UP, 1950.

Offers brief comments on the Terrestrial Paradise in *Pe* and the Green Chapel in *G* (pp. 190; 292, 318).

288. Pearsall, Derek. *OE and ME Poetry. The Routledge History of English Poetry*, I. London, Henley, and Boston: Routledge, 1977.

Provides a general account of the poet's work; emphasizes dramatic qualities, technical skill, and imaginative subtlety (pp. 169-76).

289. ————, and Elizabeth Salter. *Landscapes and Seasons of the Medieval World.* London: Elek; Toronto: Univ. of Toronto Press, 1973.

On *Pe*, discuss the transformation of the garden into the vision of Paradise (pp. 58-59, 102-08, 147). On *G*, compare seasonal descriptions to the art of the calendars (pp. 147-54). Cf. items 166, etc.

290. Peterson C[lifford] J. "*Pe* and *StE*: Some Evidence for Authorship." *RES*, NS 25 (1974), 49-53.

Endorses the arguments presented in item 275. Suggests
that *StE* contains a similar anagram, and concludes that
it is by the *Pe*-Poet. Cf. items 275, etc.

291.   ———, Clifford J. "The *Pe*-Poet and John Massey of
        Cotton, Cheshire." *RES*, NS 25 (1974), 257-66.

Following on from items 275 and 290, argues for the
identification of Hoccleve's "maistir Massy" (and thus
the poet) with John Massey of Cotton, a Lancastrian re-
tainer. Cf. items 275, etc.

292.   ———, Clifford [J.]. "Introduction to his ed. of *StE*.
        Haney Foundation ser., 22. Philadelphia: Univ. of Penn-
        sylvania Press, 1977.

Reviews the debates on the authorship of the four poems
and of *StE* (cf. items 192, etc.); summarizes the Massey
theory (pp. 15-23; cf. items 275, etc.). Includes passing comments on quatrains in *Pat* and *Cl* (pp. 27-28; cf.
items 161, etc.).

293.   ———, and Edward Wilson. "Hoccleve, the Old Hall Man-
        uscript, Cotton Nero A.x., and the *Pe*-Poet." *RES*, NS 28
        (1977), 49-56.

In response to item 347, Peterson (pp. 49-55) accepts,
with reservations, Wilson's criticisms; rejects Turville-
Petre's argument, providing further evidence about Hoccleve addressees. Wilson replies briefly (pp. 55-56).

294.   Pollard, Alfred W. "ME Literature: from the Eleventh
        Century to the second half of the Sixteenth." *Chambers*.

Includes summaries and brief discussion of *G* and *Pe* (I.
52-54).

295.   Pons, Emile. "Note sur *Gauvain et le Chevalier Vert*."
        *Mélanges de philologie romane et de la littérature mé-
        diévale offerts à Ernest Hoepffner*. Publications de la
        Faculté des lettres de l'université de Strasbourg, 113.
        Paris: Les Belles Lettres, 1949. Pp. 71-75.

A note on *enbaned* (*G* 790, *Cl* 1459), and *bantel* (*Pe* 992,
etc., *Cl* 1459).

296.   Praz, Mario. *Storia della Letteratura Inglesa*. Firenze:
        Sansoni, 1937.

Offers general comments on all four poems, and a summary
of *Pe* (pp. 12-17).

297. Quennell, Peter, and Hamish Johnson. *A History of English Literature*. London: Weidenfeld, 1973.

Provide a brief discussion of *G* and *Pe*; question common authorship (pp. 17-21).

298. Reinhold, Heinz. *Humoristische Tendenzen in der Englischen Dichtung der Mittelalters*. Buchreihe der Anglia Zeitschrift für Englische Philologie, 4. Tübingen: Niemeyer, 1953.

Many passing comments on *Pat*, *Cl*, and *G*. Particular discussion of: mocking humor and the character of *G* (pp. 42-43); courtly humor and laughter in the third fitt of *G* (pp. 117-31); anti-heroic and homely humor in *Pat* (pp. 152-57).

299. Renwick, W.L., and Harold Orton. *The Beginnings of English Literature to Skelton 1509*. Introductions to English Literature, I. Gen. ed. Bonamy Dobrée. London: Cresset Press; New York: McBride, 1940; 2nd, rev., ed., London: Cresset Press, 1952; 3rd ed., rev. Martyn F. Wakelin, 1966.

General comments on all four poems (pp. 62-63, 85, 88); bibliographical guide (pp. 324-27, 400-02).

300. Rynell, Alarik. *The Rivalry of Scandinavian and Native Synonyms in ME, Especially "Taken" and "Nimen", with an Excursus on "Nema" and "Taka" in Old Scandinavian*. LundSE, 13. Lund: Gleerup; London: Williams and Norgate; Copenhagen: Munksgaard, 1948. Diss., Lund, 1948.

Lists the occurrence in all four poems of the Scandinavian and native synonyms *taken* and *nimen* (pp. 175-93). Provides an alphabetical word-list, recording regional variants: this includes references to the poems (pp. 294-348). Also summarizes their usage of *taken/nimen* (p. 351) and *betaken/betechen* (p. 356).

301. Saintsbury, George. *A Short History of English Literature*. London and New York: Macmillan, 1898; corr. ed., 1913.

General comments on *Pe*, *Cl*, and *Pat* (pp. 78-81), and on *G* (pp. 102-04).

302. ————. *From the Origins to Spenser. A History of English Prosody from the Twelfth Century to the Present Day*, I. London and New York: Macmillan, 1906; 2nd ed., London: Macmillan, 1923; rpt., New York: Russell, 1923.

Reviews the versification of all four poems (pp. 102-09).

303.   Saito, Isamu. "The *G*-Poet's Use of the Bible in *Pat* and
       Cl." *Poetica*, 6 (1976), 48-63.

       Considers the poet's treatment of biblical sources, em-
       phasizing the development of descriptive passages, the
       introduction of contemporary details, and the concern
       for human frailty. In English.

*   Sakai, Tsuneo. See item 1303.

304.   Salter, Elizabeth. "The Alliterative Revival." *MP*, 64
       (1966-7), 146-50, 233-37.

       A discussion of the milieu in which the poems were writ-
       ten; makes specific references to *G* and *Pe*.

*   ———. See also item 289.

305.   Sampson, George. *The Concise Cambridge History of Eng-
       lish Literature*. Cambridge: UP, 1941; rev. eds., 1961,
       1970.

       Brief general comments on all four poems (pp. 36-37).

306.   Samson, A.R. "A Reassessment of the Evidence for Common
       Authorship of the poems in MS. Cotton Nero A.x." M.A.
       thesis, Swansea, 1969-70.

307.   Sandahl, Bertil. *The Ship's Hull*. *ME Sea Terms*, I.
       UpsalaE&S, 8. Upsala: Lundequistska Bokhandeln; Copen-
       hagen: Munksgaard; Cambridge, Mass.: Harvard UP, 1951.

       Notes on: *hande-helm* (*Cl* 419: p. 122); *hurrok* (*Cl* 419,
       Pat 185: p. 126). Cf. items 270, 308, 629, 661, 667.

308.   ———. *Masts, Spars, and Sails*. *ME Sea Terms*, II.
       UpsalaE&S, 20. Upsala: Lundequistska Bokhandeln; Copen-
       hagen: Munksgaard; Cambridge, Mass.: Harvard UP, 1958.

       Notes on: *crossayl* (*Pat* 102: p. 32); *lofe* (*Pat* 106: pp.
       54ff.); *sprete* (*Pat* 104: p. 103); *tres* (*Pat* 101: p. 115).
       Cf. items 307, etc.

309.   Sapora, Robert William, Jr. *A Theory of ME Alliterative
       Meter with Critical Applications*. Speculum Anniv. Mono-
       graphs, 1. Cambridge, Mass.: Mediaeval Academy of Amer-
       ica, 1977. Diss., Connecticut, 1976. Abst.: *DAI*, 36
       (1976), 7395A.

Presents a theory of ME alliterative metre. In chap.
4, applies this theory to the complete texts of a number of poems, including *G*, *Cl*, and *Pat*. Appendixes provide a list of the metrical forms found in each of the
poems covered (pp. 81-114) and an annotated list of
problematic lines (pp. 115-17).

310. Savage, Henry L[yttleton]. "Introduction" to his ed.
of *StE: A ME Poem*. YSE, 72. New Haven: Yale UP; London: Milford, Oxford UP, 1926.

Reviews the relationship between *StE* and the four poems,
and endorses the theory of common authorship for all
five. This view is supported with evidence of language,
vocabulary, alliteration, parallels in phraseology,
style, theological views, and thematic concerns (pp.
xxxi-lxxix). Cf. items 192, etc.

311. Schipper, J[akob]. *Grundriss der Englischen Metrik*.
WBEP, 2. Wien und Leipzig: Braumüller, 1895. Enl. Eng-
lish tr., *A History of English Versification*. Oxford:
Clarendon, 1910.

Discusses alliterative rhythm in *Cl*, *Pat*, and *G*, and the
stanza in *Pe* (sects. 56, 272 in the English ed.).

312. Schirmer, Walter F. *Geschichte der Englischen Literatur
von den Anfängen bis zur Gegenwart*. Halle a.S.: Niemeyer, 1937; rev. ed. (... *Englischen und Amerikanischen*
...), Tübingen: Niemeyer, 1954.

Brief comments on all four poems, with a bibliographical note (pp. 142-44, 605 in 1st ed.).

313. Schlauch, Margaret. *English Medieval Literature and Its
Social Foundations*. Warszawa: Panstwowe Wydawnictwo
Naukowe, 1956; rpt., Warszawa: Panstwowe Wydawnictwo
Naukowe; London: Oxford UP, 1967.

A general discussion of the four poems and *Erk* (pp. 218-
21).

* ————. See also item 147.

314. Schofield, William Henry. *English Literature from the
Norman Conquest to Chaucer*. *History of English Literature*, II. London and New York: Macmillan, 1906.

Provides a summary of *G*, and general comments on *G* and
Pe (pp. 215-17, 402).

315. Schubel, Fr[iedrich]. *Die alt- und mittelenglische Pe-*
      riode. Englische Literaturgeschichte, I. Sammlung
      Göschen, 1114. Berlin: De Gruyter, 1954.

      Brief general comments on all four poems (pp. 134-36).

316. Schumacher, Karl. *Studien über den Stabreim in der mit-*
      telenglischen Alliterationsdichtung. BSEP, 11. Bonn:
      Hanstein, 1914. Diss., Bonn, 1913.

      A study of alliteration in ME alliterative poetry. Uses
      29 texts, including *G*, *Cl*, and *Pat*.
      1. The distribution of alliteration in the long line.
         Includes brief sections on each of the three poems
         (pp. 26-28).
      2. The quality of alliteration. Reviews which vowels,
         consonants, and composite sounds alliterate, and dis-
         tinguishes between pure and incomplete or question-
         able alliteration. Includes many passing references
         to all three poems. (Findings tabulated on pp. 212-
         13).
      3. Textual notes on each poem. Makes specific sugges-
         tions on the following lines: *G* 25, 130, 236, 343;
         Cl 28, 228, 327, 380, 745, 778, 1483, 1485, 1518,
         1655 (the last three suggestions by Bülbring); *Pat*
         78.

317. Schwahn, Fr[iedrich]. *Die Conjugation in "Sir Gawayn*
      and the Green Knight" und den sogenannten "Early English
      Alliterative Poems": Ein Beitrag zur mittelenglischen
      Grammatik. Strassburg: Heitz, 1884.

      Supports the theory of common authorship without express-
      ing any strong personal conviction on the subject.
      Reviews and tabulates verb-forms: 1. endings; 2. con-
      struction of preterites and participles in (a) strong
      verbs, (b) weak verbs, (c) preterite-present verbs, (d)
      irregular verbs; 3. composite verb-forms.

318. Serjeantson, Mary S. "The Dialects of the West Midlands
      in ME." *RES*, 3 (1927), 54-67, 186-203, 319-31.

      Assigns the dialect of the MS to Derbyshire (pp. 327-
      28). See also comments on pp. 58, 60. Cf. items 215,
      etc.

*   ————. See also item 88.

*   Shibata, Shozo. See item 1304.

319. Shields, Ellis Gale. "The *G*-Poet and the Latin Rhetorical Tradition." Diss., Southern California, 1956. Abst.: *Univ. of Southern California Abstracts of Dissertations*, 6 (1956), 35-37 (in which it is listed as "Rhetoric and the *G*-Poet").

320. Sisam, K[enneth]. "Epenthesis in the consonant groups *sl, sn.*" *Archiv*, 131 (1913), 305-10.

     Gives examples from *Pe* 1148 and *Cl* 56.

321. Skeat, [Walter W.]. "Notes on English Etymology." *TPS*, 1888-90, art. x, pp. 150-71. Material rpt. in item 324.

     Definition of *noumbles, G* 1347.

322. ———. "Notes on English Etymology." *TPS*, 1891-4, art. iii, pp. 132-48. Material rpt. in item 324.

     Comments on *pentangel* (*G* 620, etc.), *vewters* (*G* 1146).

323. ———. "Rare Words in ME." *TPS*, 1891-4, art. xii, pp. 359-74. Material rpt. in item 324.

     Notes on: *bos* (*Cl* 1075), *bredes* (*Cl* 1405), *ker(re)* (*G* 1421, etc.), *palays* (*G* 769), *pyked* (*G* 769), *stele* (*Pat* 513), *in talle ne in tuch* (*Cl* 48), *tayt* (*Cl* 889), *teuelyng* (*G* 1514), *thulged* (*G* 1859), *type* (*Pat* 506), *totez* (*Cl* 41), *traschez* (*Cl* 40), *treleted* (*G* 960), *troched* (*Cl* 1101, *G* 795).

324. ———, Walter W. *Notes on English Etymology*. Oxford: Clarendon, 1901.

     Includes material reprinted from items 321-23.

325. ———, [Walter W.]. "A Group of Ghost-Words." *TPS*, 1903-6, art. vi, pp. 180-201.

     Note on *aker* (*G* 1421).

326. ———. "English Etymologies." *TPS*, 1903-6, art. viii, pp. 247-60.

     Comments on *angardez* (*G* 681).

327. ———. "Notes on English Etymology." *TPS*, 1903-6, art. xi, pp. 359-72.

     Notes on *bantel* (*Cl* 1459, *Pe* 992, etc.), *scholes* (*G* 160).

328. ————, Walter W. *English Dialects from the Eighth Cen-*
      tury to the Present Day. The Cambridge Manuals of Sci-
      ence and Literature. Cambridge: UP, 1911.

      States that the dialect of *Pe* and *G* is West Midland (pp.
      80-81). Cf. items 215, etc.

329. Snell, F.J. *The Age of Chaucer (1346-1400).* Handbooks
      of English Literature. London: Bell, 1901.

      Includes general comments on the four poems, and sum-
      maries of *Pe* and *G* (pp. 20-28).

 *   Soeda, Hiroshi. See item 1305.

330. Spearing, A.C. *The "G"-Poet: A Critical Study.* Cam-
      bridge and New York: Cambridge UP, 1970.

      1. A general account of the poet and the four poems;
         considers the cultural milieu, the poet's reading,
         and the alliterative revival. Observes the recurring
         pattern of confrontation between man and a super-
         human power. Supports common authorship.
      2. *Cl*: Provides a detailed exposition of structure and
         its relation to theme. Analyzes the poet's treatment
         of biblical sources and his descriptive technique in
         the scenes of divine vengeance.
      3. *Pat*: Discusses structure and purpose, the modifica-
         tion of biblical sources, and the nature of the come-
         dy (partly based on item 675).
      4. *Pe*: Compared to *Cl* and *Pat*. Considers the poet's use
         of traditional concepts and the terminology of reli-
         gious visions and secular dream poetry. After re-
         viewing the critical debate, and rejecting the alle-
         gorical interpretation, goes on to analyze the devel-
         opment of the pearl symbol and the process of the
         Dreamer's enlightenment (partly based on item 560).
      5. *G*: Argues that the linking of the three plots (be-
         heading, temptation, exchange of winnings) conveys
         the meaning of the poem. Discusses the nature of the
         ideals symbolized by the pentangle, and analyzes the
         testing of these values in the temptation scenes;
         comments on parallels between temptations and hunts.
         Adjudicates between the various judgments of G.

      Reviews: Larry D. Benson, *MLQ*, 33 (1972), 183-86.
               W.A. Davenport, *YWES*, 52 (1971), 85-86.
               F.N.M. Diekstra, *DQR*, 2 (1972), 86-88.
               Donald R. Howard, *Speculum*, 47 (1972), 548-51.
               S.S. Hussey, *N&Q*, 217 (1972), 273-75.

David E. Lampe, *Cithara*, 11 (1971), 118-21.
Dieter Mehl, *Archiv*, 210 (1973), 183-85.
D.D.R. Owen, *FMLS*, 8 (1972), 79-84 (item 1080).
Edmund Reiss, *ELN*, 11 (1974), 213-15.
Felicity Riddy, *MAE*, 42 (1973), 96-98.
A.V.C. Schmidt, *RES*, NS 23 (1972), 192-93.

331. Speirs, John. "A Survey of Medieval Verse." *Ford*.

Makes reference to *Pe* and *G* in a brief account of alliterative verse (pp. 30-34).

332. Spendal, Ralph James, Jr. "Narrative Structure in Five ME Poems." Diss., Oregon, 1970. Abst.: *DAI*, 31 (1971), 5376A.

The five poems are *Pe*, *Cl*, *Pat*, *G*, and *Erk*.

333. Stidston, Russell Osborne. *The Use of "Ye" in the Function of "Thou" in ME Literature from MS. Auchinleck to MS. Vernon: A Study of Grammar and Social Intercourse in Fourteenth-Century England*. Prepared for pub. by Arthur G. Kennedy. Leland Stanford Junior Univ. Pubs.: Univ. ser., 28. Stanford: UP, 1917.

Comments on usage in *Pe* (pp. 44, 47, 64, 76), *Cl* and *Pat* (pp. 47, 64), and *G* (pp. 28, 35, 37, 55, 57, 59, 73, 81); summarizes usage in the four poems (pp. 93-94).

334. Sundén, K.F. "The Etymology of ME. *trayþ(e)ly* and *runisch, renisch*." *SN*, 2 (1929), 41-55.

Discusses the etymology and meaning of *trayþ(e)ly* (*Cl* 907, etc.), and of *runisch(ly)* (*Cl* 1545, *Pat* 191, *G* 303, etc.), and *renisch(ly)* (*Cl* 96, etc.). Cf. item 205.

335. ———. "The Etymology of the ME. Verbs *Roþe*, *Roþele*, and *Ruþe*." *A Grammatical Miscellany Offered to Otto Jesperson on his Seventieth Birthday*. Ed. N. Bøgholm, Aage Brusendorff, and C.A. Bodelsen. Copenhagen: Levin and Munksgaard; London: Allen and Unwin, 1930. Pp. 109-22.

Considers the etymology and meaning of *roþeled* (*Cl* 59, etc.) and *ruþen*, *-ed* (*Cl* 895, *G* 1208).

336. Suzuki, Eiichi. "Poetic Synonyms for 'Man' in ME Alliterative Poems." *ESELL*, 49-50 (1966), 209-27.

Investigates the proportion of alliterative to non-alliterative uses of synonyms for "man" in 25 alliterative poems, including *Pe*, *Cl*, *Pat*, and *G*. (Cf. items 731, etc.).

337. ————. "ME *Molde*." *SELit*, English no. (1969), 75-87.

Considers the use of *molde* in a range of ME alliterative verse, including the four poems. (Cf. item 719).

338. Tajima, Matsuji. "The *G*-Poet's Use of *Con* as a Periphrastic Auxiliary." *NM*, 76 (1975), 429-38.

Reviews the occurrence of this linguistic feature in the four poems; concludes that it is used mainly to place the infinitive in the rhyming position.

*   ————. See also items 1306-09.

*   ten Brink, Bernhard. See Brink.

339. Thomas, Julius. *Die alliterierende Langzeile des "Gawayn"-Dichters.* Coburg: Rossteutscher, 1908. Diss., Jena, 1908.

Considers the alliterative long line in *G*, *Cl*, and *Pat* under the following headings: 1. division of long lines and half verses; 2. the end of the verse; 3. stress; 4. measuring of syllables and treatment of unstressed *-e*; 5. tone and intonation; 6. verse forms; 7. alliteration; appendix on short lines in *G*.

*   Thomas, Martha Cary. See item 1229.

340. Thomas, P.G. *English Literature Before Chaucer*. London: Arnold, 1924.

Noncommittal observations on the poet, and brief critical comments on all four poems (pp. 133-41).

*   Traill, H.D. See item 198.

341. Trautmann, Moritz. "*Cl*, *Pat* und *Sir Gawayn*." *Ueber Verfasser und Entstehungszeit einiger Alliterirender Gedichte des Altenglischen.* Halle a.S.: Niemeyer, 1876. Pp. 25-33.

Compares the vocabulary, verse form, and dialect of *G*, *Cl*, and *Pat*, and concludes that they are by the same poet.

342. ————. "Der Dichter Huchown und seine Werke." *Anglia*, 1 (1878), 109-49.

Analyzes the language and metre of the poems sometimes attributed to Huchown. Concludes that *Pe*, *Cl*, *Pat*, and

G are by the same poet, but not by Huchown.   Cf. items
274, etc.

343.   ————.   Review of item 207.   *Anglia*, 5 (1882), anzei-
ger 21-25.

Endorses Horstmann's attribution of *Erk* to the poet.

344.   Treneer, Anne.   *The Sea in English Literature From "Beo-*
wulf" to Donne.   Liverpool: UP; London: Hodder and
Stoughton, 1926.

Discusses the description of the storm in *Pat* and of the
Flood and the Dead Sea in *Cl* (pp. 67-74).   Cf. items
213, etc.

345.   Tristram, Philippa.   *Figures of Life and Death in Medi-*
eval English Literature.   London: Elek, 1976.

G is related to the traditional figure of Youth (pp. 28-
34), Bertilak to Middle Age, and Morgan to Age (pp. 91-
92).   Suggests that New Year in *G* is associated with
both birth and death (pp. 111-13).   *Pe* is seen as a con-
frontation between the Dead and the Living (pp. 205-12).
Various other passing references.

346.   Turville-Petre, Thorlac.   *The Alliterative Revival.*
Cambridge: Brewer; Totowa, N.J.: Rowman and Littlefield,
1977.

Makes many passing references to all four poems (see Index).   Provides brief discussion of the following topics:
dialect (p. 30); contents of the poems (pp. 33-34); major narrative divisions (p. 39); the MS (p. 45); the
storm in *Pat* (p. 48); quatrains in *Pat* and *Cl* and the
stanza in *G* (pp. 61-62).   Also contains separate sections on the following: the form and function of the
metre in *G* (pp. 51-58); the stanzaic and overall form
of *Pe* (pp. 66-68); the narrative structure of *Cl*, and
its relation to the theme (pp. 104-11).

347.   ————, and Edward Wilson.   "Hoccleve, 'Maistir Massy'
and the *Pe* Poet: Two Notes."   *RES*, NS 26 (1975), 129-43.

Turville-Petre ("Maistir Massy," pp. 129-33) rejects
Peterson's identification of John Massey (item 291).

Wilson ("The Anagrams in *Pe* and *StE*," pp. 133-43) argues that the procedures followed by Nolan (item 275)
and Peterson (item 290) are arbitrary, and that their
conclusions are unconvincing.

348. Vantuono, William. "*Pat*, *Cl*, *Pe*, and *G*: the Case for
      Common Authorship." *AnM*, 12 (1971), 37-69.

      Presents evidence of similarity between the four poems
      under the following heads: thematic unity; imagery;
      diction; analogous phrases (with a table of parallels);
      paraphrases for God; methods of introducing a story;
      stating that something is difficult to describe; endings
      which echo beginnings. Cf. item 165.

349. ————. "A Name in the Cotton MS. Nero A.x. Article 3."
      MS, 37 (1975), 537-42.

      Discusses the significance of the inscription *J. Macy* on
      ff. 62^v and 144. Cf. items 275, etc.

350. Vasta, Edward, ed. *ME Survey: Critical Essays*. Notre
      Dame and London: Notre Dame UP, 1965.

      Includes items 443, 462, 810, 846.

351. Von Ende, Frederick Albert Chaffey. "The Prosody of the
      Pe-Poet: A Technical Analysis of the Poems in MS Cotton
      Nero A.x." Diss., Texas Christian Univ., 1972. Abst.:
      DAI, 33 (1973), 3605A-06A.

   * Wakelin, Martyn F. See item 299.

352. Waldron, Ronald A. "Oral-Formulaic Technique and ME Al-
      literative Poetry." *Speculum*, 32 (1957), 792-804.

      Applies the methods of Parry and Magoun to 16 ME alli-
      terative poems, including *G*, *Cl*, and *Pat*. (Cf. item
      1242).

353. Wasserman, Julian Noa. "The Edifice Complex: The Meta-
      phor of the City in *Pur* and *Pat*." Diss., Rice Univ.,
      1975. Abst.: *DAI*, 36 (1975), 2185A.

354. Weichardt, Carl. *Die Entwicklung des Naturgefühls in
      der mittelenglischen Dichtung vor Chaucer (einschlies-
      slich des "G"-Dichters)*. Kiel: Peters, 1900. Diss.,
      Kiel, 1900.

      Praises the creative and subtle use of nature descrip-
      tions in all four poems. Argues that (in *G*) the poet
      was the first in English to appreciate fully the beauty
      of winter (pp. 77-92). Cf. items 166, etc.

   * Whaley, Helen R. See item 1253.

355. Williams, David J. "A Literary Study of the ME Poems
      Pur and *Pat*." B.Litt. thesis, Oxford, 1965.

356. ————, D[avid] J. "Alliterative Poetry in the Four-
      teenth and Fifteenth Centuries." *The Middle Ages*, ed.
      W.F. Bolton. *History of Literature in the English Lan-*
      guage, I. London: Barrie and Jenkins, 1970; p.b.,
      Sphere Books.

      The section on "The *G* Group" (pp. 143-56) provides a
      general account of the theme and structure of each of
      the four poems.

357. Williams, Sr. Margaret, R.S.C.J. "Oriental Backgrounds
      and The *Pe*-Poet." *TkR*, 1, i (1970), 93-107.

      Reviews the Eastern influence on the European Middle
      Ages. Discusses the pentangle in *G*, the description of
      the Earthly Paradise in *Pe*, and the use of Mandeville
      in *Cl*.

358. Wilson, Edward. *The "G"-Poet*. Medieval and Renaissance
      Authors ser. Leiden: Brill, 1976.

      1. *Pe*: Discusses the handling of the relationship be-
         tween the Dreamer and the Maiden, and similarities
         with the story of Abraham and Isaac. Includes mate-
         rial, based on items 576 and 578, on literal inter-
         pretation, the spiritual vision, and verbal echoes.
      2. *Pat*: Deals with the treatment of patience and power
         ty in the Prologue, and the amplification and rear-
         rangement of OT sources in the narrative.
      3. *Cl*: Suggests connections with the Cycle Plays. Dis-
         cusses the mingling of the Matthew and Luke versions
         of the parable of the wedding feast, and the use of
         exegetical and popular traditions in the three major
         exempla.
      4. *G*: Considers the mixture of realism and romance, and
         the function and significance of games.

      Includes a brief bibliography.

      Reviews: Malcolm Andrew, *ES*, 59 (1978), 72-74.
                 J.A. Burrow, *TLS*, 29 July 1978, p. 937.

*   ————. See also items 293 and 347.

359. Wimsatt, James I. *Allegory and Mirror: Tradition and*
      Structure in ME Literature. Pegasus Backgrounds in Eng-
      lish Literature. New York: Pegasus, 1970.

Chap. 5 (pp. 117-36) includes discussion of *Pe* in relation to the Boethian tradition, and comparison of the Maiden to Dante's Beatrice. Chap. 8 (pp. 190-214) includes consideration of *G* in relation to some English and European romances, and analysis of the temptation scenes.

360. Wülcker, Richard. *Geschichte der Englischen Literatur von den altesten Zeiten bis zur Gegenwart*, I. Leipzig und Wien: Bibliographischen Instituts, 1896; 2nd, rev., ed., 1906.

Brief general comments; summaries of all four poems (pp. 116, 120-21).

361. Wyld, Henry Cecil. "The Treatment of OE.y̆ in the Dialects of the Midland, and SE. Counties, in ME." *EStn*, 47 (1913), 1-58.

Reviews relevant spelling forms in *Pe*, *Cl*, and *Pat* (pp. 37-39, 48-49). Assigns the poems to Derbyshire (p. 47). Cf. items 215, etc.

    *   Yamanouchi, Kazuyoshi. See item 1310.

362. Yonekura, Hiroshi. "A Study of the Infinitive in the *G*-Poet's Works." *Ivy*, 8 (1969), 101-23.

Considers the use of the infinitive in the four poems in terms of form, function, tense, and voice. In Japanese. Cf. item 1308.

363. Yoshida, Shingo. "The *G*-Poet's Ethics." *Studies in Chaucer*. Kyoto: Apollon-sha, 1966. Pp. 204-17.

Maintains that the poet shows a concern with the ethics of purity and patience in all four poems. In Japanese.

364. Zavadil, Joseph Benedict. "A Study of Meaning in *Pat* and *Cl*." Diss., Stanford Univ., 1962. Abst.: *DA*, 22 (1962), 4346-47.

365. Zesmer, David M. "The Alliterative Revival: *SG*, *Pe*, and *Piers Plowman*." *Zesmer*, pp. 154-72.

Includes a section on the four poems and *Erk*. Provides brief general comments, and plot summaries of *G* and *Pe*.

B. Critical Writings on *Pearl*

366. Ackerman, Robert W. "The Pearl-Maiden and the Penny."
     RPh, 17 (1964), 614-23. Rpt. in item 397.

     Compares the Maiden with Dame Grace Dieu in Deguile-
     ville's *Pèlerinage*. Argues that a traditional associa-
     tion of the penny with daily bread lies behind the men-
     tion of the Mass in lines 1201-12.

367. Adam, Katherine L. *The Anomalous Stanza of "Pe"*: *Does
     it disclose a six-hundred-year-old secret?* Medieval
     ser., 1. Fayetteville, Ark.: Monograph Pub., 1976.

     A brief monograph. Argues that stanza 76 (lines 901-12)
     should not be considered otiose. Reports the discovery
     of the signature *John Massi* in an acrostic in lines 901-
     05. Briefly mentions another acrostic in *G* 1746-49.
     Includes tables and reproductions from the MS. Cf.
     items 275, etc.

368. Amoils, E.R. "The *endeleʒ rounde*: Poetic Diction and
     Theme in *Pe*." *Middeleeuse Studies/Medieval Studies,
     1974.* Johannesburg: Randse Afrikaanse Universiteit,
     1975. Pp. 3-34.

     Sees the structure of *Pe* as a circle intersected by
     axes -- symbolizing respectively eternity and history.
     Argues for retaining stanza 76.

369. Baird, Joseph L. "*Maskeleʒ, Makeleʒ*: Poet and Dreamer
     in the *Pe*." *AN&Q*, 12 (1973), 27-28.

     Supports the retention of MS *makeleʒ* in 733 and 757.

370. Barron, W.R.J. "*Luf-daungere*." *Medieval Miscellany
     presented to Eugène Vinaver by pupils, colleagues and
     friends*. Ed. F. Whitehead, A.H. Diverres, and F.E. Sut-
     cliffe. Manchester: UP; New York: Barnes and Noble,
     1965. Pp. 1-18.

     Discusses the derivation and usage of OF *dangier* and ME
     da(u)nger. Reviews editorial glosses of *daunger* and *luf-
     daunger* (*Pe* 250, 11), and suggests "frustration" and
     "love-frustration."

371. Billour, Elena. *La XIV Ecloga del Boccaccio "Olimpia"
     e "La Perla," Poemetto inglese del secolo XIV*. Estratto

dall'Annuario del R. Ginnario Liceo "Piazzi" di Sondrio. Sondrio: Washington, 1933.

Maintains that the poet had read Boccaccio's *Olimpia*. Summarizes both poems and specifies parallels. Particularly emphasizes that each daughter acts as a guide and is represented as a Bride of the Lamb. Cf. items 43, 549.

372. Bishop, I[an]. "The Structure of *Pe*: the Interaction of its Liturgical and Poetic Elements." B.Litt. thesis, Oxford, 1951/52.

373. ————, Ian. "The Significance of the *Garlande Gay* in the Allegory of *Pe*." *RES*, NS 8 (1957), 12-21.

Identifies the *garlande gay* (1186) with the ecclesiastical *corona*, which was commonly used to symbolize the New Jerusalem. Discusses the recapitulation of the lapidary formulae of lines 1-2 in lines 1186 and 1188.

374. ————. *"Pe" in its Setting: A Critical Study of the Structure and Meaning of the ME Poem.* Oxford: Blackwell; New York: Barnes and Noble, 1968.

Sets out to study *Pe* in the "setting" of medieval intellectual traditions.

I.   1. Argues that the poem is generically a consolation. (Cf. items 396, etc.).
     2. Discusses the relationship between structure and meaning, and the numerical symbolism. (Cf. items 544, etc.).
     3. Comments on the treatment of salvation in the debate.

II. 4. Considers "the allegory of the theologians" and its application to lines 793-960.
     5-6. Defines "the allegory of the poets," and discusses its application to the poem, commenting on personifications, metaphorical strands, "dark conceits," the treatment of the vision, and the pearl image.

III. Presents liturgical evidence to elucidate the characterization of the Maiden. (Cf. items 432, 513).
     7. Considers her as an Innocent, using material associated with Childermas. (Cf. item 447).
     8. Argues that her dress is that of an adult catechumen.

9. Discusses the interpretation of the parable of
the vineyard. (Cf. items 581, etc.).

Appendix: on the punctuation of lines 821-28 and 803-04.

Reviews: Charles R. Blyth, *Speculum*, 46 (1971), 126-29.
G.C. Britton, *YWES*, 49 (1968), 87.
F. Diekstra, *Neophil*, 56 (1972), 111-12.
S.S. Hussey, *N&Q*, 214 (1969), 436-37.
John MacQueen, *RES*, NS 22 (1971), 180-82.
T. Oiji, *SELit*, 46 (1970), 166-72.
R.M. Wilson, *MLR*, 65 (1970), 394-96.
Rosemary Woull, *SN*, 42 (1970), 259-61.

375. Blanch, Robert J[ames]. "Precious Metal and Gem Symbolism in *Pe*." *LHR*, no. 7 (1965), 1-12. Rpt. in item 132.

Uses contemporary writings, mainly lapidaries, to elucidate the symbolism of gems and precious metals. Apart
from comments on lines 1-2, does not deal with pearl
symbolism. Cf. item 424.

376. ———, Robert James. "An Investigation of Medieval
Color Symbolism and Its Application to *Pe*." Diss., New
York (Buffalo), 1967. Abst.: *DA*, 28 (1967), 1780A-81A.

377. ———, Robert J[ames]. "Color Symbolism and Mystical
Contemplation in *Pe*." *NMS*, 17 (1973), 58-77.

Discusses the use of color symbolism derived from lapidary and exegetical traditions. Argues that the virtues
symbolized are those that the Dreamer needs in order to
attain spiritual enlightenment.

378. Blenkner, Charles Louis. "*Pe* as Spiritual Itinerary."
Diss., Chapel Hill, 1964. Abst.: *DA*, 25 (1965), 6615-
16. Cf. item 379.

379. ———, Louis, O.S.B. "The Theological Structure of
Pe." *Traditio*, 24 (1968), 43-75. Rpt. in item 397.

Sees *Pe* as a poetic account of a spiritual itinerary,
culminating in mystical contemplation. Equates the three
settings with the traditional threefold division of man's
sources of knowledge (sense, intellect, inspiration) and
the stages of the soul's assent to God (without, within,
above).

380. ———. "The Pattern of Traditional Images in *Pe*." *SP*,
68 (1971), 26-49.

Argues that the hierarchical relationship between the
erber, the Terrestrial Paradise, and the New Jerusalem
is reflected in the growing intensity of the imagery of
light, jewels, and vegetation, while the apparently
shifting pearl symbol constantly represents perfection.

*   Bloomfield, Norton W. See item 133.

381.   Bogdanos, Theodore. "*Pe*: A Study in Medieval Poetic
       Symbolism." Diss., California (Berkeley), 1975.

382.   Bone, Gavin. "A Note on *Pe* and *The Buke of Howlat*."
       MAE, 6 (1937), 169-70.

       Comments on the parallel drawn in item 437.

383.   Bradley, Henry. "An Obscure Passage in *The Pe*." *Acad-
       emy*, 38 (1890), 201-02, 249.

       Discusses *Pe* 689-92; cf. item 433.

384.   Brook, Stella. "*Pe*." *JLDS*, 16 (1967), 11-17.

       A general account of dialect, content, and symbolism.

385.   Brown, Carleton F. "Note on the Question of Strode's
       Authorship of *The Pe*." *PMLA*, 19 (1904), 146-48.

       Questions Gollancz's attribution of *Pe* to Ralph Strode,
       distinguishing between three different contemporaries
       with this name. (Cf. items 185, etc.). (Printed as a
       continuation of item 142).

386.   Buchholz, Erich. *Das Verbum substantivum im Mitteleng-
       lischen.* Bottrop i.W.: Postberg, 1936. Diss., Berlin,
       1936.

       Includes a brief section on *Pe* (pp. 67-68).

387.   Campbell, J.M. "Patristic Studies and the Literature of
       Medieval England." *Speculum*, 8 (1933), 465-78.

       Approves of the readings of Schofield and Madeleva
       (items 482, 549, 550).

*   Cargill, Oscar, and Margaret Schlauch. See item 147.

388.   Carrière, Jeanne Louise. "Boethian Narrative Structure
       in Fourteenth-Century English Literature." Diss., Cali-

fornia (Los Angeles), 1975. Abst.: *DAI*, 36 (1976),
5273A.

Includes material on *Pe*.

389. Carroll, Christopher Franklin. "The People in *Pe*:
Audience, Poet, Narrator, Dreamer, and Maiden." Diss.,
Yale, 1970. Abst.: *DAI*, 31 (1970), 2336A.

390. Carson, Mother Angela, O.S.U. "Aspects of Elegy in the
ME *Pe*." *SP*, 62 (1965), 17-27.

Reads *Pe* as an elegy for a woman with whom the poet had
a romantic relationship.

391. Carson, Sr. M. Angela, O.S.U. "A Study of the Technical
Language in the Fourteenth Century *Pe*." Diss., Fordham
Univ., 1968. Abst.: *DA*, 29 (1969), 2668A.

392. Casieri, Sabino. "*Pe* e la critica." *Acme*, 23 (1970),
283-315.

A thorough review of editions, translations, and critical writings from Morris (1864) to 1970. Summarizes
the major scholarly and critical debates (e.g., theories
of authorship, elegiac or allegorical interpretation)
and discusses Gordon's comments (item 44) on the first-
person narrator. Cf. items 574, etc.

393. Casling, Dennis, and V.J. Scattergood. "One Aspect of
Stanza-Linking." *NM*, 75 (1974), 79-91.

Contend that the break in stanza-linking at line 721 is
deliberate (pp. 87-89). Cf. item 544.

394. Chapman, Coolidge Otis. "Numerical Symbolism in Dante
and the *Pe*." *MLN*, 54 (1939), 256-59.

Compares the use of numerological patterning in *Pe* and
the *Divina Commedia*. Cf. items 544, etc.

*   ———. See also item 149.

395. Cohen, Sandy. "The Dynamics and Allegory of Music in
the Concatenations of *Pe*, a Poem in Two Movements."
LangQ, 14, iii-iv (1976), 47-52.

Argues that the structure of *Pe* is based on the modal
system in music (cf. item 148).

396.   Conley, John.   "*Pe* and a Lost Tradition."   *JEGP*, 54
       (1955), 332-47. Rpt. in item 397.

       Provides a mainly negative review of previous criticism.
       Argues that *Pe* is a Christian *consolatio*, "analogous in
       theme, situation, roles, and treatment" to Boethius's
       Consolation. (Cf. items 374, 489, 565, 568, 573).

397.   ————, ed.   *The ME "Pe": Critical Essays*.   Notre Dame
       and London: Univ. of Notre Dame Press, 1970.   ·

       Contains an extract from item 19 (preface); and items
       366, 379, 396, 405, 457, 459, 462, 469, 478, 481, 493,
       532, 539, 540, 560, 563, 568, 571, 572.

       Review: S.S. Hussey, *N&Q*, 216 (1971), 266-67.

398.   Cook, Albert S.   "*Pe* 212 ff."   *MP*, 6 (1908), 197-200.

       Argues for reading *color* "collar" in 215.

399.   Coulton, G.G.   "In Defence of *Pe*."   *MLR*, 2 (1906), 39-
       43.

       An attack on the views expressed in item 549.

400.   ————.   *Medieval Panorama: The English Scene from Con-
       quest to Reformation*.   Cambridge: UP, 1938.

       Makes some general comments, and quotes lines 481-92,
       529-64, and 577-88 from his own translation (item 36)
       (pp. 200-02).

401.   Courthope, W.J.   *A History of English Poetry*, I.   New
       York and London: Macmillan, 1895.

       Unenthusiastic general comments on *Pe* (pp. 349-51).

402.   Coyne, Sr. Therese, R.S.M.   "A Study of the Vision Tra-
       dition in Medieval Literature with Specific Application
       to *The Pe*."   Diss., Michigan State, 1975. Abst.: *DAI*,
       36 (1975), 1491A.

403.   Crawford, John Franklin.   "The Narrative Structure of
       Pe in the Light of the Augustinian Doctrine of Reforma-
       tion."   Diss., Columbia, 1970. Abst.: *DAI*, 33 (1973),
       3578A.

404.   Davenport, W.A.   "Desolation, not Consolation: *Pe* 19-22."
       ES, 55 (1974), 421-23.

       A new interpretation of these lines.

405. Davis, Norman. "A Note on *Pe.*" *RES*, NS 17 (1966), 403-05; 18 (1967), 294. Rpt., with additional material, in item 397.

Suggests that line 1208 embodies a formula of greeting, normally used from parent to child.

406. Day, Mabel. "Two Notes on *Pe.*" *MAE*, 3 (1934), 241-42.

Notes on lines 140 and 210.

407. deFord, Sara "The Miracle of the *Pe.*" *Mount Holyoke Alumnae Quarterly*, Spring 1966, pp. 13-15. (Rpt. from *Goucher Alumnae Quarterly*, Spring 1965).

Describes the preparation of item 39.

408. Donaldson, E. Talbot. "Oysters, Forsooth: Two Readings in *Pe.*" *NM*, 73 (1972), 75-82.

Reads *ostriys* "oysters" in 755, and suggests emending *For soþe* (21) to *forþoȝtes*.

409. Dumbleton, Susanne M. "*Pe*: A Dream-Vision Uniting *Consolatio* and Elegiac Traditions." Diss., New York State (Albany), 1973. Abst.: *DAI*, 34 (1974), 5906A-07A.

410. Earl, James W. "Saint Margaret and the Pearl Maiden." *MP*, 70 (1972), 1-8.

Argues that the Maiden is modelled on the virgin martyr St. Margaret of Antioch. Cf. item 550.

411. Einarsson, Stefan. "Old and ME Notes." *JEGP*, 36 (1937), 183-87.

Includes a reference to *al and sum* (584).

412. Eldredge, Laurence. "The State of *Pe* Studies since 1933." *Viator*, 6 (1975), 171-94.

A review of scholarship since Wellek's survey (item 574). Arranged under thematic headings -- "elegy or allegory," "theology: heresy or orthodoxy," "symbolism," "historicism," "authorship," "miscellaneous." Excludes editions, translations, and notes. Cf. items 574, etc.

413. Elliott, R.W.V. "*Pe* and the Medieval Garden: Convention or Originality?" *LanM*, 45 (1951), 85-98.

Considers the mix of convention and originality in the poet's use of the two settings -- the actual garden and the dream garden. Cf. item 478.

414. Emerson, Oliver Farrar. "Some Notes on the *Pe*." *PMLA*,
      37 (1922), 52-93.

      Reviews scribal errors in the texts of all four poems.
      Notes on the following lines: 8, 10, 24, 29, 53, 66,
      72, 95, 107, 134, 158, 165, 170, 183, 185, 189, 197,
      198, 200, 205, 208, 209, 229, 235, 249, 262, 270, 283,
      303, 307, 309, 311, 313-19, 321, 349, 369, 381, 383,
      388, 415, 431, 441, 442, 457-67, 470, 473, 513, 541, 542-
      51, 560, 563, 567, 572, 584, 585, 591, 601-07, 609, 611,
      616, 617, 634, 647, 648, 692, 697, 698, 709, 711, 721,
      730, 752, 778, 791, 792, 795-97, 800, 802, 803, 813,
      826, 829-30, 838, 841, 845, 850-52, 865, 892, 898, 905,
      908, 910, 911, 914-21, 922, 934, 938, 947, 962-71, 981,
      1000, 1004, 1013, 1041, 1064, 1066, 1074, 1075, 1083,
      1097, 1141, 1142, 1156, 1161, 1177, 1180, 1190, 1196,
      1201.

415. ————. "More Notes on *Pe*." *PMLA*, 42 (1927), 807-31.

      Discusses new readings in the text of item 43. Notes
      on the following lines: 14-16, 32, 54, 56, 57, 66, 81,
      109, 110, 111, 125, 127, 134, 136, 139-40, 154, 155,
      167, 177, 188, 190, 205, 210, 215, 229, 236, 243, 249,
      250, 254, 261-64, 267, 272, 273, 290, 311, 313, 316,
      323, 326, 331-32, 358, 378, 396, 402, 431, 439, 477, 482,
      488, 505, 510, 518, 544, 546, 558, 565, 567, 575, 581,
      595, 604, 613, 626, 645, 660, 672, 674-76, 692, 721,
      733, 767, 780, 799, 820, 822, 824, 860, 872, 873-74,
      884, 919, 922, 930, 936, 944, 947-48, 998, 1001, 1031,
      1050, 1064, 1069, 1086, 1108, 1109, 1117, 1123, 1125-28,
      1183, 1193.

*   ————. See also items 167, 598.

416. Emert, Joyce Rogers. "*Pe* and the Incarnate Word: A
      Study in the Sacramental Nature of Symbolism." Diss.,
      New Mexico, 1969. Abst.: *DAI*, 30 (1970), 4940A-41A.

417. Everett, Dorothy, and Naomi D. Hurnard. "Legal Phrase-
      ology in a Passage in *Pe*." *MAE*, 16 (1947), 9-15.

      Argue that the poet is using a well-known legal expres-
      sion in 703; reconsider 697-708. Cf. items 468, 535.

418. Fairchild, Hoxie Neale. "Of Vyrgyn Flour." *TLS*, 5 Mar.
      1931, p. 178.

      In response to item 575, glosses "flower of the Virgin"
      (line 426).

419. Faris, David Earl. "Symbolic Geography in ME Literature: *Pe, Piers Plowman, Ywain and Gawain*." Diss., Yale, 1973. Abst.: *DAI*, 34 (1974), 7228A.

* Farley-Hills, David. See item 275.

420. Farnham, Anthony Edward. "The Principles of Allegory and Symbolism Illustrated by the ME Poem *Pe*." Diss., Harvard, 1964.

421. Farragher, Bernard Patrick. "*Pe* and Scriptural Tradition." Diss., Boston, 1956.

422. Fehr, Bernhard. "Zu *The Pe*, Z. 51-56." *Archiv*, 131 (1913), 154-55.

    Characterizes the view in these lines as mystic.

423. Fick, Wilhelm. *Zum mittelenglischen Gedicht von der "Perle." Eine Lautuntersuchung*. Kiel: Lipsius und Tischer, 1885. Diss., Kiel, 1885.

    An investigation into the sounds of the language of *Pe*.

    1. Discusses existing emendations and/or suggests new ones for the following lines: 8, 10, 23, 24, 124, 203, 229, 290, 323, 557, 588, 591, 609, 610, 759, 802, 829, 849, 1086, 1097.
    2. Argues that the poet's dialect was West Midland, and the scribe's Southern.
    3. Analyzes the sound system of the poet's language under the following headings: (a) short vowels; (b) long vowels; (c) consonants.

    Review: Fr[iedrich] Knigge, *LfGRP*, 6 (1885), 495.

424. Finkelstein, Dorothee Metlitzki. "The *Pe*-poet as Bezalel." *MS*, 35 (1973), 413-32.

    Suggests that the poet identifies himself with Bezalel, the jeweller who shaped, for Aaron's breastplate (Exod. 28:6-21), the stones which become the foundations of the New Jerusalem in Revelation. Argues that the structure of section XV shows the influence of Hebrew numerology. Cf. items 375, 467.

425. Finlayson, John. "*Pe*: Landscape and Vision." *SP*, 71 (1974), 314-43.

    Emphasizes that the three *loci* are created through the eyes of the Dreamer. Investigates the relationship be-

tween the Dreamer and the *loci*, arguing that they represent the stages of his understanding, and that his developing perceptions of them mark his progress from ignorance to enlightenment.

426.   Fletcher, Jefferson B. "The Allegory of the *Pe*." *JEGP*,
       20 (1921), 1-21.

       Suggests that "Paradise Regained" would be an apt sub-
       title (cf. items 443, 479). Maintains that *Pe* is essen-
       tially an allegorical interpretation of the parable of
       the pearl of price (the pearl standing for innocence),
       but does not reject the elegiac reading. Cf. items 482,
       etc.

427.   Fowler, David C. "*Pe* 1. 558: *Waning* ." *MLN*, 74 (1959),
       581-84.

       Argues for glossing "lamentation."

428.   ———. "On the Meaning of *Pe*, 139-40." *MLQ*, 21 (1960),
       27-29.

       Offers a new interpretation of these lines, glossing
       deuyse "deception."

429.   Fritz, Donald Wayne. "The Arbor of Wisdom: An Essay on
       the *Pe*." Diss., Stanford, 1969. Abst.: *DA*, 30 (1969),
       1523A-24A.

430.   Gardner, Lloyd Alan. "*Pe* and the Medieval Vision of
       Peace." Diss., Vanderbilt Univ., 1972. Abst.: *DAI*, 33
       (1973), 4344A.

431.   Garrett, Robert Max. "*The Pe*: An Interpretation." *UWPE*,
       4 (1918), 1-45. Also pub. separately: Seattle, Wash.:
       The Univ., 1918.

       Argues that eucharistic doctrine is central to the mean-
       ing of *Pe*. Reviews traditions of the pearl symbolizing
       the eucharist and the pearl of price symbolizing Christ.
       Summarizes the poem. Suggests line 39 refers to the
       Feast of the Holy Name of Jesus (August 7). Provides a
       translated text of a letter from Hilary of St. Poitiers
       to his daughter (*c*. 358), in which she is compared to a
       pearl. Includes a bibliography. Cf. items 482, etc.

       Reviews: Carleton Brown, *MLN*, 34 (1919), 42-45.
                 Clark S. Northup, *JEGP*, 20 (1921), 288-89.

432. Gatta, John, Jr. "Transformation Symbolism and the Lit-
      urgy of the Mass in Pe." MP, 71 (1974), 243-56.

      Considers the significance of liturgical allusions; sug-
      gests that the development of the Dreamer's state of
      mind conforms to the pattern of transformation in the
      liturgy of the Mass. Cf. items 374, 513.

433. Gollancz, I[srael]. "An Obscure Passage in The Pe."
      Academy, 38 (1890), 223-24.

      Discusses Pe 689-92 in reply to item 383.

434. ————. "Notes on the Review of Pe." Academy, 40
      (1891), 36-37.

      Comments on lines 115, 140, 349, 415, 513, 607-12, 678-
      82, 687, 826, in response to item 496.

435. ————. "Pe." Academy, 40 (1891), 116-17.

      Comments on lines 140, 415, 513, 607-12, 826, in reply
      to item 497.

436. G[ollancz], I[srael]. "The Pe." Enc. Brit., XXI, 27-
      28.

      A brief summary of the poem.

437. Gordon, E.V., and C.T. Onions. "Notes on the text and
      interpretation of Pe." MAE, 1 (1932), 126-36; 2 (1933),
      165-88.

      Discusses the question of the preterite and past par-
      ticiple of weak verbs without -d in all four poems (cf.
      item 160). Notes on the following lines: 8, 10, 51, 56,
      61-62, 115, 139-40, 142, 197, 210-12, 359, 364-66, 375,
      431, 432, 457-62, 492, 565, 568, 572, 599-600, 604, 607-
      08, 609-11, 630, 672, 733, 755, 762, 802, 815, 817, 855-
      56, 884, 992, 1013, 1041, 1086, 1193.

438. Gosse, Edmund. "Pe." More Books on the Table. London:
      Heinemann; New York: Scribner's, 1923. Pp. 179-86.

      Provides a summary with general critical comments; en-
      dorses Gollancz's theory about Strode (cf. items 185,
      etc.).

439. Greene, Walter Kirkland. "The Pe -- A New Interpreta-
      tion." PMLA, 40 (1925), 814-27.

An allegorical reading, in which the Maiden is taken as
a literary device used to express the lesson of divine
grace. Comments on item 549. Cf. items 482, etc.

*   Grelle, L. Le. See under Le Grelle.

440. Haber, Richard. "The English Renaissance Novella and
      Hawthorne's *The Scarlet Letter*: Toward a Theory of Fic-
      tion." Diss., Massachusetts, 1976. Abst.: *DAI*, 37
      (1977), 5850A-51A.

      Includes material on *Pe*.

441. Hackel, Ruth. "Meditations on the Mediaeval Allegory
      Pe." *UES*, 4 (1968), 35-41.

      Suggests that *Pe* reflects the poet's struggle to accept
      Christian doctrine.

442. Hamilton, Marie P[adgett]. "The Orthodoxy of *Pe* 603-4."
      MLN, 58 (1943), 370-72.

      Discusses these lines, glossing *payed inlyche* (603)
      "completely satisfied, profoundly at peace." Cf. items
      539, etc.

443. ———, Marie Padgett. "The Meaning of the ME *Pe*."
      PMLA, 70 (1955), 805-24. Rpt. in items 132 and 350.

      Describes the poem as "a Catholic Paradise Lost and Re-
      gained," epitomized in one man's loss and recovery of
      immortal life (cf. items 426, 479). Provides extensive
      elucidation of the relevant Christian traditions, e.g.,
      on the symbolic significance of gardens, hills, spices,
      etc. Cf. items 482, etc.

444. ———, Marie P[adgett]. "Notes on *Pe*." *JEGP*, 57
      (1958), 177-91.

      Argues against the elegiac approach in Gordon's edition
      (item 44), commenting specifically on the following
      lines: 10, 13-14, 19-20, 49, 53, 233, 269-72, 364-65,
      375, 381-84, 393-96, 411, 429-32, 546, 572, 603-04, 697-
      704, 740, 749-52. Cf. items 482, etc.

445. Hammerle, Karl. "*The Castle of Perseverance* und *Pe*."
      Anglia, 60 (1936), 401-02.

      Draws attention to similarities in phraseology.

446. Hansen, Niels Bugge. *That Pleasant Place: The Represen-
tation of Ideal Landscape in English Literature from the
14th to the 17th Century.* Copenhagen: Akademisk Forlag,
1973.

Includes discussion of the Earthly Paradise in *Pe* (pp.
33-35). Cf. items 166, etc.

447. Hart, Elizabeth. "The Heaven of Virgins." *MLN*, 42
(1927), 113-16.

Cites the Prioress's Tale to demonstrate that a fourteenth-century writer could have considered a child a
fitting member of the 144,000 (in answer to item 482;
cf. also item 526).

448. Harvey, Patricia A. "ME *Point* (*Troilus and Criseyde*
III. 695)." *N&Q*, 213 (1968), 243-44.

Mentions the usage in *Pe* 891.

449. Heiserman, A.R. "The Plot of *Pe*." *PMLA*, 80 (1965),
164-71.

Demonstrates how the major ideas derive their significance from their context in the developing structure of
the poem.

450. Hieatt, Constance B. "Dream Allegory in ME Poetry: the
Use of Dream Effects in Fourteenth Century Dream Visions." Diss., Yale, 1959.

451. ———, Constance [B]. "*Pe* and the Dream-Vision Tradition." *SN*, 37 (1965), 139-45. Rpt., in modified form,
in her *The Realism of Dream Visions: The Poetic Exploi-
tation of the Dream Experience in Chaucer and his Contemporaries.* De Proprietatibus Litterarum, Series Prac-
tica, 2. The Hague and Paris: Mouton, 1967.

Discusses dream psychology in *Pe*, and relates this to
the shifting quality of images and word-senses. Cf.
items 554, 561.

452. Higgs, Elton Dale. "The Dream as a Literary Framework
in the Works of Chaucer, Langland, and the *Pe* Poet."
Diss., Pittsburgh, 1965. Abst.: *DA*, 27 (1966), 1030A.

453. ———, Elton D[ale]. "The Progress of the Dreamer in
Pe." *SMC*, 4 (1974), 388-400.

Argues that the movement of the poem is supplied by the development of the Dreamer's understanding.

454. Hillmann, Mary V[incent]. "*Pe: Inlyche* and *Rewarde*." *MLN*, 56 (1941), 457-58.

Offers evidence from Hilton in support of the interpretation of lines 603-04 in item 557.

455. ————, Sr. Mary Vincent. "*The Pe: west ernays* (307); *Fasor* (432)." *MLN*, 58 (1943), 42-44.

Glosses *west ernays* (307) "empty pledge," and *Fasor* (431, misnumbered 432) "Maker, Creator."

456. ————. "*Pe: Lere Leke*, 210." *MLN*, 59 (1944), 417-18.

Argues for retaining MS *lere leke*, suggesting three possible glosses.

457. ————. "Some Debatable Words in *Pe* and Its Theme." *MLN*, 60 (1945), 241-48. Rpt. in item 397.

Discusses the theme of renouncing attachment to worldly goods; translates and comments on lines 49-60, 483, 1177-88, and 1201-12.

458. [————], Sr. Mary Vincent. "*Pe*, 382: *mare reʒ mysse?*" *MLN*, 68 (1953), 528-31.

Rejects the interpretation of item 460. Advocates reading *mare reʒ mysse* "lack great power [of speech]."

459. Hoffman, Stanton de Voren. "The *Pe*: Notes for an Interpretation." *MP*, 58 (1960), 73-80. Rpt. in item 397.

Suggests basing interpretation on four points: the pearl symbol, innocence, physical death, and flower-fruit-jewel metaphors. Raises objections to various allegorical readings; sees *Pe* essentially as an elegy.

460. Holman, C. Hugh. "*Mareeʒ Mysse* in *The Pe*." *MLN*, 66 (1951), 33-36.

Argues for glossing "a botcher's mistake" (cf. item 458).

461. Holthausen, F. "Zur Textkritik me. Dichtungen." *Archiv*, 90 (1893), 143-48.

Comments on the following lines: 11, 51, 53, 54, 81, 134, 209, 231, 323, 359, 369, 382, 451, 462, 513, 528, 572, 581, 599, 630, 681, 687, 721, 752, 763, 802, 874, 893, 944, 1004.

*   Hurnard, Naomi D. See item 417.

*   Hyprath, Heide. See item 532.

462.   Johnson, Wendell Stacy. "The Imagery and Diction of *The Pe*: Toward an Interpretation." *ELH*, 20 (1953), 161-80. Rpt. in items 350 and 397.

Investigates how diction and imagery contribute to the poem's central purpose: the revelation of the contrast between the nature of heaven and that of earth.

463.   Johnston, G.K.W. "Northern Idiom in *Pe*." *N&Q*, 204 (1959), 347-48.

Argues that *mysse* (382) is a noun.

464.   Jugaku, Bunsho. "A Reading of *Pe*." *The Climate of English Literature*. Tokyo: Taishukan, 1961. Pp. 52-81.

Emphasizes the importance of seeing the poem from the medieval point of view and argues that it should be interpreted as an allegory. In Japanese. Cf. items 482, etc.

465.   Kaske, R.E. "Two Cruxes in *Pe*: 596 and 609-10." *Traditio*, 15 (1959), 418-28.

Glosses *pertermynable* (596) "speaking enduringly," and provides a new interpretation of lines 609-10.

466.   Kawasaki, Masatoshi. "Notes on *Pe*." *JFFL*, no. 5 (1976), 79-99.

Discusses the meaning of the pearl symbol in relation to gold, the garden, and the *garlande*; also considers the significance of light in the poem. In Japanese.

467.   Kean, P.M. "Numerical Composition in *Pe*." *N&Q*, 210 (1965), 49-51.

A numerological defence of the "extra" stanza in section XV. Cf. items 367, 394, 424, 510, 544.

468.   ————. *"The Pe"*: *An Interpretation*. London: Routledge; New York: Barnes and Noble, 1967.

     I.   1. Analyzes the proem (lines 1-60), demonstrating how it establishes the subject of *Pe*. Specifies rhetorical devices, traditions drawn on, and biblical allusions. Cf. items 443, 527.
          2. Discusses the description of the garden, relat-

ing relevant *topoi,* and emphasizing the significance of associations of death and rebirth. Cf.
items 413, 478.
3. Specifies central images--gardens, treasure,
   growth and decay, spices, seed, etc.--to be
   transformed in the settings of the Earthly Paradise and the New Jerusalem.

II. 1. Emphasizes that the Earthly Paradise is a land-
        scape rather than a garden, relating the *Iter
        ad Paradisum* tradition and other paradisal de-
        scriptions.
     2. Compares the Maiden to various female guides and
        instructors, especially Dante's Beatrice; sees
        the Dreamer as a quasi-personification of Will.
     3. Discusses symbols of perfection--crown, gold,
        rose, and (particularly) pearl--drawing illus-
        trative material from a variety of sources, in-
        cluding alchemical writings.

III. 1. Considers the theme of "less and more" in the
        debate, and the use of legal terms in the dis-
        cussion of salvation. Cf. items 417, 535.
     2. Specifies connections between the Earthly Para-
        dise and the New Jerusalem; provides a reading
        of the account of the heavenly city.

IV.   Comments on the last sixty lines; suggests that
        the poet resumes his own voice towards the end.

        (Includes various passing comments on the other
        three poems: see Index).

Reviews: Charles R. Blyth, *Speculum,* 43 (1968), 348-51.
           G.C. Britton, *YWES,* 48 (1967), 74.
           R.T. Davies, *RES,* NS 19 (1968), 63-65.
           Stanley B. Greenfield, *CL,* 21 (1969), 164-66.
           S.S. Hussey, *N&Q,* 212 (1967), 438-39.
           R.E. Kaske, *ELN,* 6 (1968), 48-52.
           Charles Moorman, *MLQ,* 29 (1968), 91-93.
           T. Oiji, *SELit,* 46 (1970), 166-72.
           R.M. Wilson, *MLR,* 63 (1968), 672-73.

469. Kellogg, Alfred L. "Note on Line 274 of the *Pe.*" *Tra-
     ditio,* 12 (1956), 406-07. Rpt., as "*Pe* and the August-
     inian Doctrine of Creation," in item 397.

     Suggests that this line makes reference to the August-
     inian concept of *creatio ex nihilo.*

470. Knightley, William J., Jr. "Symbolic Imagery in *Pe.*"
     Diss., Princeton Univ., 1956. Abst.: *DA,* 17 (1957),
     1339-40.

471. ———, William J. [Jr.]. "*Pe*: The *hyȝ seysoun*." *MLN*,
      76 (1961), 97-102.

      Reviews the various identifications; argues in favor of
      the Feast of the Transfiguration.

472. Kölbing, E. Review of item 41. *EStn*, 16 (1892), 268-
      73.

      Significant notes on the following lines: 10, 11, 21,
      23, 37-38, 89, 115, 165, 203, 229, 335, 349, 362, 378,
      462, 470, 505, 565 66, 609 10, 630, 687, 709, 721, 758-
      60, 786, 802, 849, 859, 874, 892, 893, 921, 969, 1006,
      1115, 1159.

473. Kuranaga, Makoto. "*Pe*: A Medieval Religious Poem."
      Kuranaga, pp. 80-107.

      An introductory account of the poem. In Japanese.

474. Kuriyagawa, Fumio. "On *The Pe*." *SELit*, 12 (1932), 557-
      91.

      Provides a review of scholarship on the poem, giving
      particular emphasis to the problem of authorship, the
      rhyme-scheme, sources, and the dream-vision tradition.
      Includes a lengthy plot-summary. In Japanese. Cf.
      items 574, etc.

475. Le Grelle, L. "La *Perle*: Essai d'Interprétation Nou-
      velle." *EA*, 6 (1953), 315-31.

      After summarizing previous critical approaches, empha-
      sizes the poem's religious lyricism, discusses the use
      of convention (dream, debate, etc.) and concatenation,
      and praises the poem's unity in diversity.

476. Lucas, Peter J. "Pearl's Free-Flowing Hair." *ELN*, 15
      (1977), 94-95.

      Considers the significance of the Maiden's unbound hair.

477. Luttrell, C.A. "The Mediaeval Tradition of the Pearl
      Virginity." *MAE*, 31 (1962), 194-200.

      Discusses evidence, in the liturgy and in homiletic and
      moral writings, of the symbolic identification of the
      pearl with virginity.

478. ———. "*Pe*: Symbolism in a Garden Setting." *Neophil*,
      49 (1965), 160-76. Rpt. in items 132 and 397.

A response to item 413. Discusses the meaning of key
words (*erber*, *huyle*, etc.) in the garden description,
and suggests--drawing parallels from contemporary French
poets--that entry into the garden symbolizes the onset
of deep thought. Cf. also item 468.

479. McAndrew, Bruno. "*The Pe*, a Catholic Paradise Lost."
     ABR, 8 (1957), 243-51.

     Summarizes the contrasting literal and allegorical ap-
     proaches; endorses the latter. Interprets the pearl as
     a symbol of Paradise. (Cf. items 426, 443).

480. McGalliard, John C. "Links, Language, and Style in
     The Pe." *Willard*, pp. 279-99.

     Provides a detailed discussion of the use of link-words.
     Defends the poet against the accusation of artificiality
     and praises the fluidity of his diction. Makes specific
     points about lines 267, 274, 417, 630. (Cf. item 481).

481. Macrae-Gibson, O.D. "*Pe*: The Link-Words and the Thematic
     Structure." *Neophil*, 52 (1968), 54-64. Rpt. in item 397.

     Discusses the function of the link-words in each stanza-
     group; concludes that they form a key to the structure
     of *Pe*. (Cf. item 480).

482. Madeleva, Sr. M. "*Pe*": *A Study in Spiritual Dryness*.
     New York and London: Appleton, 1925. Rpt., New York:
     Phaeton Press, 1968.

     1. Reviews interpretations of *Pe*; argues that it is a
        spiritual autobiography and a study in dryness.
     2. Defines spiritual dryness, illustrating the concept
        from the writings of the mystics.
     3. Discusses medieval mysticism as a context for *Pe*,
        drawing some parallels with Rolle and Dame Julian.
     4. Offers a reinterpretation of *Pe*: (a) the five intro-
        ductory and the five concluding stanzas are inter-
        preted respectively as accounts of spiritual desola-
        tion and spiritual initiation, the argument being
        supported by quotations from the mystics; (b) the
        Maiden is taken to stand for the Dreamer's soul, and
        the debate interpreted accordingly (483 is taken to
        refer to the age of a religious in a community--i.e.,
        the length of time since he joined); (c) concludes
        that *Pe* is about the state of soul of a religious;
        (d) draws parallels with thirteenth- and fourteenth-

century spiritual autobiography.
5. Summarizes the argument. Cf. items 387, 426, 431,
439, 443, 444, 462, 479, 483, 549, 550, 580.

Reviews: Anon., *TLS*, 21 Jan. 1926, p. 46.
Dorothy Everett, *YWES*, 6 (1925), 94-96.
J.M., *Month*, 147 (1926), 544-46.
Robert J. Menner, *MLN*, 41 (1926), 411-14.
Howard R. Patch, *Speculum*, 3 (1928), 411-14.

483. Mahl, Mary R. "The Pearl on the Church." *EngR*, 17, i
(1966), 27-29.

Suggests that the pearl and the Maiden symbolize the
Church.

484. Manzalaoui, Mahmoud. "English Analogues to the *Liber
Scalae*." *MAE*, 34 (1965), 21-35.

Includes discussion of parallels between *Pe* and the *Liber Scalae* and some other works of Moslem eschatology.
Cf. item 233.

485. Martin, Elizabeth Petroff. "Psychological Landscape in
Fourteenth Century Poetry and Painting." Diss., California (Berkeley), 1973. Abst.: *DAI*, 33 (1973), 6877A.

Includes material on *Pe*.

486. Matsui, Noriko. "The *Pe*-Poet's Psychological Insight."
RIKK, no. 37 (1977), 43-62.

Concludes that interpretation of *Pe* as an elegy does not
necessarily preclude interpreting it as an allegory. In
Japanese. Cf. item 426.

487. Mead, W.E. [Title unknown]. *Quest*, Jan. 1913.

Article on *Pe*. Not seen.

488. Means, Michael Hugh. "The *Consolatio* Genre in ME Literature." Diss., Florida, 1963. Abst.: *DA*, 29 (1968),
875A.

Includes material on *Pe*.

489. ————, Michael H[ugh]. *The "Consolatio" Genre in Medieval Literature*. Univ. of Florida Humanities Monographs,
36. Gainesville: Univ. of Florida Press, 1972.

Sees *Pe* as a poem in the Boethian tradition, in which
the narrator is educated by an authoritative instructor
(pp. 49-59). Cf. items 396, etc.

490. Mendillo, Louise Dunlap. "Word Play in *Pe*: Figures of
      Sound and Figures of Sense." Diss., California (Berke-
      ley), 1976. Abst.: *DAI*, 37 (1977), 5811A.

491. Milroy, James. "*Pe*: The Verbal Texture and the Linguis-
      tic Theme." *Neophil*, 55 (1971), 195-208.

      Discusses the way in which the handling of language and
      point-of-view are used to define central concepts and
      themes.

492. Mitchell, Bruce. "*Pe*, lines 609-610." *N&Q*, 209 (1964),
      47.

      Supports Gordon's interpretation (item 44).

493. Moorman, Charles. "The Role of the Narrator in *Pe*."
      MP, 53 (1955), 73-81. Rpt. in item 397.

      Emphasizes the importance of the narrator as the poem's
      "central intelligence," and gives a critical account of
      his progress. Concludes that *Pe* is an elegy. (Cf.
      items 263, 663).

494. Moran, Dennis [William]. "*Pe* and Its Moral Poet."
      NDEJ, 6, i (1968), 51-57.

      Treats *Pe* as a poem of practical moral instruction writ-
      ten in an age of controversy.

495. ———, Dennis William. "Style and Theology in the ME
      Pe: Patterns of Change and Reconciliation." Diss.,
      Notre Dame, 1976. Abst.: *DAI*, 37 (1976), 1539A.

496. Morris, R[ichard]. Review of item 41. *Academy*, 39
      (1891), 602-03.

      Specific notes on lines 115, 140, 307, 349, 513, 607-12,
      676, 681, 814, 826. Cf. item 434.

497. ———. "*Pe*." *Academy*, 40 (1891), 76.

      Comments on lines 115, 140, 349, 415, 513, 607-12, 826,
      in response to item 434. Cf. item 435.

498. Murtaugh, Daniel M. "*Pe* 462: *þe Mayster of Myste*."
      Neophil, 55 (1971), 191-94.

Provides evidence for glossing "the Master of mini-
stries."

499. Nakajima, Yoshio. "Allegory and Symbolism in English
      Religious Poems in the Middle Ages." *Essays and Studies
      in English Language and Literature in Celebration of
      the Sixtieth Birthday of Prof. Tamihei Iwasaki.* Tokyo:
      Kenkyusha, 1954. Pp. 295-314.

      Suggests that allegory and elegy are combined in *Pe.*
      In Japanese.

500. Naruse, M[asaiku]. "On the ME Poem *Pe.*" *EigoS*, 117
      (1971), 489-91, 564-67.

      Analyzes the debate between the Dreamer and the Maiden.
      Emphasizes the importance of the debate to the poem's
      meaning. In Japanese.

501. ————. "On the Figure of the Pearl-Maiden in the ME
      Pe." *JCulS*, 8 (1972-3), 183-250, 289-382.

      Provides a detailed survey of previous interpretations.
      Goes on to argue that *Pe* is an elegy and that the Maiden
      stands for the poet's daughter. In Japanese.

502. ————. "A Study of the ME Poem *Pe.* Part II: The Mean-
      ing of *Pe.*" *JCulS*, 10 (1974-5), 1-58, 111-60, 181-225;
      11 (1975), 66-112.

      Considers the history of the MS, and suggests dates and
      order of composition (*Cl-Pat-Pe-G*). Maintains that of
      the four poems, only *Pe* was not intended primarily for
      recitation. Discusses the region and the historical
      setting in which the poet was working. Emphasizes the
      influence of the *Legenda Aurea*. In Japanese. See item
      1293.

503. ————. "On the So-Called 'Otiose' Stanza in the ME
      Pe." *JCulS*, 12 (1976), 81-127.

      Argues that stanza 76 (lines 901-12) was added after the
      completion of the poem, and functions as an apology to
      the Maiden. Suggests that the 101 stanzas of both *Pe*
      and *G* signify completeness (100) made imperfect by the
      addition of one (cf. item 202). In Japanese.

504. Neilson, George. "Crosslinks between *Pe* and *The Awn-
      tyrs of Arthure.*" *ScA*, 16 (1902), 67-78.

Discusses connections between the *Trentalle Sancti Gre-gorii* and both *The Awntyrs* and *Pe*. Suggests that Hu-chown is the author of *The Awntyrs*, *Pe*, and *Erk*. Cf. items 197, 1009.

*   ————. See also items 271-74.

505. Nelson, Cary Robert. "The Incarnate Word: Studies in Verbal Space." Diss., Rochester, 1970. Abst.: *DAI*, 31 (1971), 6623A.

Includes material on *Pe*: cf. item 506.

506. ————, Cary [Robert]. "*Pe*: the circle as figural space." *The Incarnate Word: Literature as verbal space.* Urbana, Chicago, and London: Univ. of Illinois Press, 1973. Pp. 25-49.

Considers the function of circular form in *Pe*, empha-sizing the close relationship between form and meaning. Suggests that the omission of line 472 may have been in-tentional: the purpose being to symbolize, in this struc-tural defect, man's flawed perception.

507. Niemann, Thomas Charles. "*Pe* and the Medieval Christian Doctrine of Salvation." Diss., Duke Univ., 1971. Abst.: *DAI*, 33 (1973), 5133A-34A.

508. ————, Thomas C[harles]. "*Pe* and the Christian Other World." *Genre*, 7 (1974), 213-32.

Suggests that *Pe* may be identified generically as vision of the other world; summarizes the development of this genre. Draws parallels with the *Vision of Tundale* and Dante's *Commedia*.

509. Nolan, Barbara Frances. "An Approach to a Reading of the *Pe*." Diss., Wisconsin (Madison), 1967. Abst.: *DA*, 28 (1968), 3153A-54A.

510. ————, Barbara [Frances]. "*Pe*: A Fourteenth-Century Vision in August." *The Gothic Visionary Experience.* Princeton: UP, 1977. Pp. 156-204.

Provides a reading of *Pe* as a visionary quest. Discus-ses the Dreamer's initial self-absorption, his instruc-tion by the Maiden, and the poem's culmination in escha-tological vision. Also emphasizes the importance of the Earthly Paradise as a setting, and considers symbolism of herbs and numbers.

*   ————, and David Farley-Hills. See item 275.

511. Northup, Clark S. "A study of the metrical structure
      of the ME poem *Pe*." *PMLA*, 12 (1897), 326-40.

      Discusses some factors relevant to metrical structure:
      the treatment of *-e*, *-o*, *-y*, etc.; the occurrence of an
      extra syllable before the caesura and of seven-syllable
      lines; and alliteration.

512. ————. "Recent Studies of The *Pe*." *MLN*, 22 (1907),
      21 22.

      A review article on items 36, 52, 142, and 549.

513. Oakden, James P. "The Liturgical Influence in *Pe*."
      Chaucer und seine Zeit: Symposion für Walter F. Schir-
      mer. Buchreihe der *Anglia*: Zeitschrift für englische
      Philologie, 14. Tübingen: Niemeyer, 1968. Pp. 337-53.

      Mainly concerned with the influence of liturgical rites
      for the burial of children, and of the cycle of reading
      for Septuagesima and Sexagesima. Suggests that the
      Feast mentioned in 39 is Lammas. Cf. items 374, 432.

514. Oiji, Takero. "An Interpretation of the ME Poem *Pe*."
      EALit, no. 3 (1955), 60-71.

      An abbreviated version of item 515. In Japanese.

515. ————. "On the ME *Pe*." *BYU*, 3 (1956), 227-63.

      Examines the psychological process of the conversion of
      the Dreamer. Considers the central issues in the poem's
      alleged heresy. Sees the poet among contemporary pre-
      cursors of the Renaissance and Reformation. In Japanese.
      Cf. items 539, etc.

516. ————. "An Interpretation of the ME *Pe*." *LAR*, 4
      (1959), 172-60.

      Argues that the poem should be regarded primarily as an
      elegy on the death of an infant girl. In Japanese.

517. ————. "The ME *Pe* and its Theology." *SELit*, English
      Number, 1961, 39-57.

      Reviews the critical debates on elegiac or allegorical
      interpretation and on the orthodoxy or unorthodoxy of
      the poet's theology. In English. Cf. items 539, etc.

518. ————. "Recent Studies on *Pe*." *Shiron*, no. 6 (1964), 115-25.

A survey of studies published since 1950. In Japanese. Cf. items 574, etc.

519. ————. "A Reconsideration of the ME Poem *Pe*." *EigoS*, 112 (1966), 668-70.

Reaffirms the author's view that *Pe* is primarily an elegy (cf. item 516). In Japanese.

520. ————. "The Genre of the Alliterative *Pe*." *Oiji*, pp. 119-49. Rpt. in item 284.

After surveying discussions of genre, denies the possibility of the poem's being primarily an allegory. In Japanese.

521. ————. "Heresy in the *Pe*." *Oiji*, pp. 150-60. Rpt. in item 284.

Argues that the poet's views on salvation are not unorthodox, but do anticipate Protestant evangelicism. In Japanese. Cf. items 539, etc.

522. Olmsted, Mary Macniel. "A Reading of *Pe*: Faith, Art, and Reconciliation." Diss., Denver, 1971. Abst.: *DAI*, 32 (1971), 2065A.

  *   Onions, C.T. See item 437.

523. Otten, Charlotte. "A Note on the *Gyltes Felle* in *Pe*." *ES*, 52 (1971), 209-11.

Translates "the bitterness of sin" (line 655).

  *   Oyama, Toshiko. See item 1311.

524. Palgrave, Francis T. *Landscape in Poetry from Homer to Tennyson, with many illustrative examples.* London and New York: Macmillan, 1897.

Discusses the description of the Earthly Paradise (pp. 115-17). Cf. items 289, 446.

525. Palmer, Barbara. "The Guide Convention in *Piers Plowman*." *LeedsSE*, NS 5 (1971), 13-27.

Includes comment on the use of this convention in *Pe* (pp. 14-15).

526. Pardy, Averil. "The Theological Background to *Pe*."
      BSC, no. 9 (1962), 8-13.

      Maintains that the poet's views concerning the position
      of innocents in heaven is orthodox. Cf. items 447, 482;
      539, etc.

527. Parr, Roger P. "Rhetoric and Symbol in *The Pe*." *SMC*,
      3 (1970), 177-87.

      Examines the poet's use of conventional rhetorical de-
      vices; concludes that he handles them with considerable
      freedom and individuality. Cf. item 468.

528. Patten, Clara Lucille. "A Consideration of *Pe* as a Me-
      dieval Romance." Diss., Denver, 1967. Abst.: *DA*, 28
      (1968), 4139A-40A.

529. Paul, James Allen. "Aporia and *Pe*: Medieval Narrative
      Irony." Diss., Michigan, 1977. Abst.: *DAI*, 38 (1977),
      3476A.

  *   Peterson, Clifford J. See items 290, 291, and 293.

530. Piehler, Paul H.T. "Landscape and Dialogue. A Study
      of Allegorical Tradition in Medieval Literature." Diss.,
      Columbia, 1962.

      Includes material on *Pe*. Cf. item 531.

531. ————, Paul [H.T.]. "*Pe*." *The Visionary Landscape: A
      Study in Medieval Allegory*. London: Arnold, 1971. Pp.
      144-62.

      Discusses patterns of transformation; argues that the
      Maiden has both human and allegorical dimensions, and
      relates her to the Jungian archetype of the child (cf.
      item 561).

532. Pilch, Herbert. "Das mittelenglische *Perlengedicht*:
      Sein Verhältnis zum *Rosenroman*." *NM*, 65 (1964), 427-46.
      Rpt. in item 397, tr. Heide Hyprath, as "The ME *Pe*: Its
      Relation to the *Roman de la Rose*."

      Argues that connections between *Pe* and the *Roman* have
      been exaggerated, maintaining that the poet's intentions
      are so distinct that *Pe* is virtually an "anti-*Roman*."

533. Rathborne, Isabel E. "New Light on *Pe* 690." *Traditio*,
      19 (1963), 467-69.

Provides evidence of liturgical usage in support of
Gollancz's emendation of *Pe* 690.

534. Reisner, Thomas A[ndrew]. "*Pe*, 44." *Expl*, 31 (1973),
      item 55.

      Suggests that *powdered* (44) alludes to the coat of arms
      of the Prat family. Cf. item 147.

535. ————, Thomas Andrew. "The *Cortaysye* Sequence in *Pe*:
      A Legal Interpretation." *MP*, 72 (1975), 400-03.

      Discusses the poet's use of legal terms associated with
      marriage and tenure in 409-80 (cf. items 417, 468).

536. Revard, Carter. "A Note on *stonden*[,] *Pe* 113." *N&Q*,
      207 (1962), 9-10.

      Argues for glossing "shone."

537. ————. "A Note on *at þe fyrst fyne* (*Pe* 635)." *ELN*, 1
      (1964), 164-66.

      Translates "according to the original contract."

538. Richardson, F.E. "*The Pe*": A Poem and Its Audience."
      Neophil, 46 (1962), 308-16.

      Reviews interpretations; argues that the central theme
      is salvation and that the poet was writing for a lay
      audience.

539. Robertson, D.W., Jr. "The 'Heresy' of *The Pe*." *MLN*,
      65 (1950), 152-55. Rpt. in item 397.

      Refutes the view that the poet's interpretation of the
      parable of the vineyard is heretical. Cf. items 142,
      442, 515, 517, 521, 526, 546; 581, etc.

540. ————. "The Pearl as a Symbol." *MLN*, 65 (1950), 155-
      61. Rpt. in item 397.

      Provides evidence of the meaning of the pearl symbol in
      scriptural and exegetical tradition; offers a fourfold
      interpretation. Cf. item 563.

541. Robinson, Ian. "*Pe* and Ontology." *In Geardagum II: Es-
      says on Old and ME Language and Literature*. Ed. Loren
      C. Gruber and Dean Loganbill. Denver: Soc. for New Lang.
      Study, 1977; corr. rpt., 1978. Pp. 1-8.

Suggests that the Dreamer's achievement of love is de-
pendent on his achievement of faith.

542. Robson, J.A. *Wyclif and the Oxford Schools: the Relation of the "Summa de Ente" to Scholastic Debates at Oxford in the Later Fourteenth Century.* Cambridge: UP,
1961.

Considers that *Pe* provides evidence of the interest of
the laity in theological matters (p. 33).

543. Rønborg, Cort. " A Note on *Endorde* in *Pe* (368)." *ES*,
57 (1976), 198-99.

Glosses "gilt" or "gold-adorned" (OF *endorer*).

544. Røstvig, Maren-Sofie. "Numerical Composition in *Pe*: a
Theory." *ES*, 48 (1967), 326-32.

Specifies the symbolic appropriateness of the significant numbers (5, 6, 8, 12, 60, 101). Argues that the
lack of concatenation between 720 and 721 is part of the
numerological scheme. Cf. items 394, 424, 467, 510.

545. Rupp, Henry R. "Word-Play in *Pe*, 277-278." *MLN*, 70
(1955), 558-59.

Suggests double meanings for *geste* and *iuelez*.

546. Saito, Isamu. "An Interpretation of the ME *Pe*." *SHumD*,
no. 55 (1961), 103-43.

Provides a close exegetical reading of the parable of
the vineyard, stressing the poet's orthodoxy. Discusses
the idea of salvation as reward for the purification of
the soul with special reference to the pearl symbol and
the medieval concept of "like attracts like." In Japanese. Cf. items 539, etc.; 581, etc.

547. Salter, Elizabeth. "Medieval Poetry and the Figural
View of Reality." Sir Israel Gollancz Memorial Lecture,
1968. *PBA*, 54 (1968), 73-92. Also pub. separately, London: Oxford UP, 1969.

Applies the figural approach to *Pe* (pp. 81-83; see also
pp. 75, 79-80).

*   Scattergood, V.J. See item 393.

548.   Schipper, J. *Altenglische Metrik. Englische Metrik in Historischer und Systematischer Entwicklung Dargestellt,* I. Bonn: Strauss, 1881.

Brief comments on the form of the stanza (pp. 223-24, 317-18, 421-22).

*   Schlauch, Margaret. See item 147.

549.   Schofield, William Henry. "The Nature and Fabric of *The Pe.*" *PMLA*, 19 (1904), 154-215. Also pub. separately, Baltimore: MLA, 1904.

Takes issue with the usual elegiac reading of *Pe*. Suggests that the Maiden is an allegorical figure representing "clean maidenhood," and provides illustrations of this concept in medieval religious literature. Draws parallels with other female allegorical figures, particularly those in Boethius and the *Roman de la Rose*. Discusses similarities between *Pe* and contemporary vision and debate poems. In an appendix, argues that Boccaccio's *Olympia* is the main source of *Pe*, and specifies parallels between the two poems. Cf. items 371, etc.; 482, etc.

Review: Clark S. Northup, *MLN*, 22 (1907), 21-22 (item 512).

550.   ————. "Symbolism, Allegory, and Autobiography in *The Pe.*" *PMLA*, 24 (1909), 585-675. Also pub. separately, Baltimore: MLA, 1909.

Recommends literal interpretation of the first stanza, which is related to the lapidaries. Analyzes the development of the pearl symbol, and draws attention to possible connections with legends of St. Margaret. Recognizes many allegorical suggestions, but concludes that the poem is probably not a systematic allegory of clean maidenhood (contrast item 549). Argues that there is no evidence that *Pe* is an elegy written by a father on his daughter's death, or that the poet was a layman. Cf. items 375; 410; 482, etc.

551.   Schroeder, Sr. Margaret Ann, O.S.F. "*Pe*: A Study of Style in the Light of Literary Traditions and the Poet's own Genius." Diss., Cincinnati, 1960. Abst.: *DA*, 21 (1960), 903.

552.   Seib, Kenneth. "A Note on Hawthorne's Pearl." *ESQ*, 39 (1965), 20-21.

Considers that the influence of *Pe* is reflected in Hawthorne's *The Scarlet Letter*, chap. 29. (Cf. item 440).

553. Shibata, Yoshitaka. "The Meaning and Function of *lyttel* (1. 1147) in *Pe*." *Tohoku*, no. 7 (1972), 32-47.

Argues that, in addition to the literal meaning, *lyttel* implies endearment and tender feeling. In Japanese.

554. ————. "The Dream Vision Form in ME Literature." *ESELL*, no. 62 (1974), 1-32.

Includes consideration of the dream vision form in *Pe*. In Japanese. Cf. items 451, 561.

555. Singh, Catherine. "The Alliterative Ancestry of Dunbar's 'The Tretis of the Tua Mariit Wemen and the Wedo.'" *LeedsSE*, NS 7 (1974), 22-54.

Suggests that the "Tretis" is indirectly influenced by *Pe*, probably *via* "Tayis Banke."

556. Sklute, Larry M. "Expectation and Fulfillment in *Pe*." *PQ*, 52 (1973), 663-79.

Discusses how *Pe* instructs its readers by exploring the frustrations which occur between their expectation for the Dreamer and their failure with him to comprehend divine truth rationally.

557. Sledd, James. "Three Textual Notes on Fourteenth-Century Poetry." *MLN*, 55 (1940), 379-82.

Argues for glossing *rewarde* (604) "reward" (p. 381).

558. Smith, Thomas Norris. "The Garden Image in Medieval Literature." Diss., Connecticut, 1968. Abst.: *DA*, 29 (1969), 2685A.

Includes material on *Pe*.

559. Smithers, G.V. "Four Cruces in ME Texts." *EGS* (1948-49), 59-67.

Translates *marere₃ mysse* (382) as "dung-raker's muck" (pp. 60-62).

560. Spearing, A.C. "Symbolic and Dramatic Development in *Pe*." *MP*, 60 (1962), 1-12. Rpt. in items 132 and 397.

Suggests that the poem has no hidden allegorical meaning. Demonstrates the development of the pearl symbol

through the dramatic encounter between the Dreamer and
the Maiden.

561. ————. *Medieval Dream-Poetry*. Cambridge, etc.: Cambridge UP, 1976.

Relates the dream-vision in *Pe* to the traditions of religious and secular visions, and the Maiden to the Jungian archetype of the child (cf. item 531). Discusses
the debate between the Dreamer and the Maiden. (Pp.
111-29). Cf. items 451, 554.

562. Speedie, D.C. "*Pe*: a Semantic Study of the Vocabulary."
B.Phil. thesis, St. Andrews, 1973/5.

563. Stern, Milton R. "An Approach to *The Pearl*." *JEGP*, 54
(1955), 684-92. Rpt. in item 397 and in *Studies in Memory of John Jay Parry, by members of the English Depart-
ment, Univ. of Illinois*, Urbana: Univ. of Illinois Press,
1955.

Recommends applying the fourfold method of scriptural
exegesis and the gemological interpretations of the lapidary tradition to *Pe*. Cf. items 375, 540, 550.

564. Stiller, Nikki. "The Consolation of Poetry: A Study of
the ME *Pe*." Diss., New York (City Univ.), 1972. Abst.:
DAI, 33 (1973), 4366A.

565. Sutton, Robert F. "Characterization and Structure as
Adjuncts to Theme in *Pe*." *MSE*, 3 (1970), 88-94.

Argues that the poet's skillful handling of characterization and structure reinforce his theme--the attainment
of consolation through grace.

566. Takenaka, Keiko. "On the ME Poem *Pe*." *KenK*, no. 2
(1967), 26-43.

Supports interpretation of the poem as an elegy. In
Japanese.

567. Thomas, P.G. "Notes on *The Pe*." *LMS*, 1 (1938), 221-24.

Comments on the following lines: 18, 79, 107, 115, 117,
119, 179, 185, 249, 254, 260, 269, 277, 283, 321, 351,
356, 359, 572, 584, 609, 703, 857, 921, 931, 1050, 1066,
1086, 1177.

568. Tristman, Richard. "Some Consolatory Strategies in *Pe*."
Item 397, pp. 272-87.

Argues that *Pe* reflects the dual purpose of Christian
consolation: to comfort human bereavement and to awaken
the spirituality of the afflicted. Cf. items 396, etc.

* Turville-Petre, Thorlac, and Edward Wilson. See item
  347.

569. Tuttle, Edwin H. "Notes on *The Pe.*" *MLR*, 15 (1920),
     298-300.

     Discusses the variation of word-forms for the purposes
     of rhyme. Cf. item 167.

570. Ueno, Naozo. "On the ME Poem *Pe.*" *SELit*, 13 (1933),
     147-53.

     Gives an outline of the poem, and interprets it as an
     elegy rather than an allegory. In Japanese.

571. Vasta, Edward. "*Pe*: Immortal Flowers and the Pearl's
     Decay." *JEGP*, 66 (1967), 519-31. Rpt. in item 397.

     Discusses the third stanza; argues for understanding
     fede (29) as "fed" (instead of "faded, decayed"), and
     discusses the ramifications of this new interpretation.

* Vincent, Sr. Mary. See Hillmann.

572. Visser, F.Th. "*Pe* 609-611." *ES*, 39 (1958), 20-23.
     Rpt. in item 397.

     Reviews previous interpretations and suggests a new one.

573. Watts, V.E. "*Pe* as a *Consolatio.*" *MAE*, 32 (1963), 34-
     36.

     Argues that *Pe* is a Christian *consolatio*. Cf. items
     396, etc.

574. Wellek, René. "The *Pe*: An Interpretation of the ME Po-
     em." *Studies in English by Members of the English Sem-
     inar of the Charles Univ., Prague*, 4. Praze: Rivnáče,
     1933. Rpt., with some rev., in item 132.

     A thorough chronological review of editions, transla-
     tions, and critical writings on *Pe*. Goes on to express
     some personal views: that the poem is a response to the
     death of a child, and that exclusively elegiac and al-
     legorical interpretations are both inadequate. Cf.
     items 392, 412, 474, 518.

575. Whiteley, M. "Of Vyrgyn Flour." TLS, 15 Jan. 1931, p.
      44.

      Asks the meaning of this phrase (Pe 426). Answer in
      item 418.

576. Wilson, Edward. "The Gostly Drem in Pe." NmQ, 69
      (1968), 90-101.

      Suggests that the treatment of the Dreamer's vision re-
      flects both the classification of visions and the ter-
      minology used by fourteenth-century mystics.

577. ———. "Gromylyoun (Gromwell) in Pe." N&Q, 216
      (1971), 42-44.

      Provides evidence that gromwell was called margarita
      rusticorum in some herbals (cf. items 374, 579).

578. ———. "Word Play and the Interpretation of Pe." MAE,
      40 (1971), 116-34.

      Argues that the text should be interpreted literally ex-
      cept where there is a clear indication to the contrary.
      Demonstrates that the moral growth of the Dreamer is
      given emphasis by a pattern of verbal echoes.

*   ———. See also items 293 and 347.

579. Wintermute, Edwin. "The Pe's Author as Herbalist."
      MLN, 64 (1949), 83-84.

      Specifies the association of gromwell with pearls; sug-
      gests that the poet was a monastic apothecary. (Cf.
      items 374, 577).

580. Wolff, Mary Madeleva. "Pe—A Study in Spiritual Dry-
      ness." Diss., California (Berkeley), 1925.

      Cf. item 482.

581. Wood, Ann Douglas. "The Pe-Dreamer and the Hyne in the
      Vineyard Parable." PQ, 52 (1973), 9-19.

      Considers the role and character of the Dreamer in the
      light of traditional interpretations of the parable. Cf.
      items 374, 539, 546, 581.

582. Wrenn, C.L. "On re-reading Spenser's Shepheardes Calen-
      der." E&S, 29 (1943), 30-49.

Includes discussion of the symbolism of the garden in
Pe (pp. 31-32).

583. Wright, Elizabeth M. "Additional Notes on *SGGK*."
JEGP, 38 (1939), 1-22.

The title is misleading: this article consists of notes
on *Pe*. Lines discussed are as follows: 2, 22, 49, 51,
66, 95, 162, 173, 199, 215-16, 217, 226, 238, 313, 333,
358, 359, 375, 390, 462, 476, 512, 560, 604, 609-12, 617,
618, 630, 631, 635, 674, 683, 812, 824, 860, 865, 903,
905, 911, 933, 940, 947, 1064, 1069, 1094, 1141, 1193.

584. ———. "Additional Notes on *The Pe*." *JEGP*, 39 (1940),
315-18.

Comments on the following lines: 17, 19, 56, 80, 132,
174, 276, 434.

585. Wright, M.J. "Comic Perspective in Two ME Poems." *Parergon*, no. 18 (Aug. 1977), 3-15.

Includes discussion of the comedy generated in *Pe* by the
gap between earthly and heavenly perception.

C. Critical Writings on *Cleanness*

* Ackerman, Robert W. See item 119.

586. Anhorn, Judy Schaaf. "*Sermo Poematis*: Homiletic Traditions of *Pur* and *Piers Plowman*." Diss., Yale, 1976.
Abst.: *DAI*, 37 (1976), 3605A.

587. Armstrong, Elizabeth. "*Pur*." *Expl*, 36 (1977), 29-31.

Discusses the mingling of Christian and courtly senses
of "purity."

588. Bateson, Hartley. "The Text of *Cl*." *MLR*, 13 (1918),
377-86.

Comments on the following lines: 3, 30, 48, 54, 69, 106,
148, 201, 208, 214, 215, 216, 222, 224-25, 230, 257-61,
313, 341, 353, 379, 411, 431-34, 449, 456, 550, 553,
599, 629, 630, 765, 795, 820, 846, 848, 935, 956, 958,
1038, 1048, 1075, 1124, 1153, 1234, 1261, 1358, 1381,

1385, 1393, 1410, 1414, 1463, 1469, 1470, 1472, 1483,
1514, 1516, 1520, 1525, 1527, 1543, 1566, 1584, 1634,
1686, 1697, 1735, 1747, 1776.

589.   ———. "Looking over the Left Shoulder." *F-L*, 34
        (1923), 241-42.

        An interpretative note on *Cl* 981-82.

590.   ———. "Three Notes on the ME *Cl*." *MLR*, 19 (1924),
        95-101.

        Discusses the problem of word-division and provides
        notes on lines 599 and 982-83.

591.   Bennett, Josephine Waters. *The Rediscovery of Sir John
        Mandeville*. MLA Monograph ser., 19. New York: MLA,
        1954.

        Alludes to borrowing from the French Mandeville in *Cl*
        (p. 221). Cf. items 593, etc.

592.   Bödtker, A. Trampe. "*Covacle*, not *conacle*." *MLN*, 26
        (1911), 127.

        The word occurs in lines 1461 and 1515.

 *   Brett, Cyril. See item 136.

593.   Brown, Carleton F. "Note on the Dependence of *Cl* on the
        Book of Maundeville." *PMLA*, 19 (1904), 149-53.

        Argues that the poet is drawing on the French *Mande-
        ville* in lines 1015-51. (This note is printed as a con-
        tinuation of item 142). Cf. items 267, 357, 591.

 *   ———. See also item 142.

 *   Bülbring, K.D. See item 316.

 *   Clark, John W. See item 152.

594.   Doob, Penelope B.R. *Nebuchadnezzar's Children: Conven-
        tions of Madness in ME Literature*. New Haven and Lon-
        don: Yale UP, 1974.

        Discusses the poet's modification of biblical sources in
        the story of Nebuchadnezzar (pp. 81-87).

595.   Emerson, Oliver F[arrar]. "Legends of Cain, Especially
        in Old and ME." *PMLA*, 21 (1906), 831-929.

        Considers the description of the giants in lines 269-92
        (pp. 901-02).

596. ————, Oliver Farrar. "A Note on the ME *Cl*." *MLR*, 10
      (1915), 373-75.

      Suggests that lines 817-28 and 994-1000 reflect the in-
      fluence of Hebrew commentaries.

597. ————. "ME *Clannesse*." *PMLA*, 34 (1919), 494-522.

      Comments (mainly in response to items 19 and 588) on the
      following lines: 17-22, 39, 63-70, 72, 106-07, 110, 117,
      119, 127, 168, 201, 204-08, 211, 215, 222, 224, 225, 226,
      230, 243, 257-62, 265-68, 269, 271, 313, 322, 341, 399,
      408, 421, 433-34, 455, 456, 459, 469, 491, 514, 522,
      550, 577, 578, 590, 599, 629, 636-37, 654, 655, 695-96,
      721, 731, 752, 771, 791, 795, 799, 819-21, 827, 846,
      848, 855, 912, 915, 945, 956, 958, 961-62, 979, 981,
      984, 985, 1000, 1002, 1035, 1037, 1040, 1057, 1076,
      1092, 1099, 1111, 1123, 1124, 1127, 1141, 1165, 1226,
      1234, 1267, 1291, 1303, 1336, 1358, 1381, 1384, 1391,
      1393, 1394, 1396, 1397, 1398, 1402, 1403, 1406, 1410,
      1414, 1423, 1458-60, 1463, 1473, 1474, 1476, 1477,
      1484, 1491, 1507, 1512, 1518, 1525, 1532, 1540, 1543,
      1551, 1559, 1595, 1629, 1646-48, 1661, 1681, 1684, 1687,
      1690, 1692, 1695, 1697, 1698, 1703, 1717, 1747, 1761,
      1764, 1776, 1777, 1808.

598. ————. Review of item 62. *JEGP*, 20 (1921), 229-41.

      Includes specific notes on the following lines: 16, 41,
      49-50, 64, 71, 72, 104, 110, 117, 143, 167, 180, 210,
      211, 231, 304, 341, 408, 447, 463, 473, 476, 529, 543,
      590, 620, 655, 681, 747, 757, 765, 889, 915, 926, 966,
      1010, 1044, 1093, 1189, 1211, 1231, 1253, 1256, 1315,
      1385, 1389, 1391, 1395-96, 1491-92, 1507, 1542, 1543,
      1577, 1687, 1692, 1716. Also on: *Pe* 115, 532, 784; *Pat*
      474; *G* 813, 1825, 2377.

*   ————. See also item 414.

599. Fowler, David C. "Cruxes in *Cl*." *MP*, 70 (1973), 331-
      36.

      Discusses lines 216, 596, 655, 686, 1155, 1231, 1584,
      1687-90, 1761, 1764.

600. Gollancz, I[srael]. "The Text of *Cl*." *MLR*, 14 (1919),
      152-62.

      A response to item 588. Comments on all Bateson's notes
      except those on the following lines: 69, 216, 353, 449,
      958, 1048, 1153, 1261, 1381, 1516, 1525, 1527, 1566, 1735.

601. Holthausen, F. "Zu dem mittelenglischen Gedicht *Cl*."
      Archiv, 106 (1901), 349.

      Suggests that lines 265-68, 459-64, 695-96, and 1015-48
      are reminiscent of the *Historia Scholastica* of Petrus
      Comestor.

*   Irwin, John T. See item 602.

602. Kelly, T.D., and John T. Irwin. "The Meaning of *Cl*:
      Parable as Effective Sign." *MS*, 35 (1973), 232-60.

      Argues that the four sections of *Cl* (introduction and
      three main narratives) are linked by the theme of the
      authority of God, and by the motifs of the body as ves-
      sel (cf. items 613, 614) and of purification by water.
      The organization is based on the use of parabolic sto-
      ries in both hortatory and eschatological traditions.
      Cf. item 657.

*   Ker, W.P. See item 621.

603. Kittendorf, Doris Ethel Krueger. "*Cl*: The Unity of
      Structure and Theme." Diss., Michigan, 1975. Abst.:
      DAI, 36 (1975), 3678A-79A.

604. Kock, Ernst A. "Interpretations and Emendations of
      Early English Texts, II." *Anglia*, 26 (1903), 364-76.

      Includes discussion of lines 257-62 and 348.

605. Kolve, V.A. *The Play Called Corpus Christi*. Stanford:
      UP, 1966.

      Considers the attribution of human motivation to God in
      Cl (pp. 254-55).

606. Luttrell, C.A. "Baiting of Bulls and Boars in the ME
      Cl." *N&Q*, 197 (1952), 23-24.

      Provides evidence for glossing *bayted* (55) "worried by
      dogs" (cf. items 607, 612).

607. ———. "The Baiting of Bulls and Boars." *N&Q*, 201
      (1956), 398-401.

      Further evidence in support of the interpretation in
      item 606 (cf. item 612).

608. ———. "*Cl* and the Knight of La Tour Landry." *MAE*, 29
      (1960), 187-89.

Argues that *Cl* was not directly influenced by the *Book of the Knight* (cf. items 59, 60, 610).

609. McGowan, Thomas Andrew. "A Textual Study of *Cl*." Diss., Virginia, 1975. Abst.: *DAI*, 36 (1976), 4472A.

610. Menner, Robert J. Review of item 59. *MLN*, 37 (1922), 355-62.

Includes comments on the influence of the *Book of the Knight of La Tour Landry* and the quatrain arrangement. Specific notes and suggestions on the following lines: 229, 385, 458, 491, 553, 1267, 1838-84, 1396, 1423, 1618, 1635, 1717. (Cf. items 161, etc.; 608, etc.).

611. ————. Review of item 60. *MLN*, 50 (1935), 336-38.

Specific suggestions on the following lines: 65, 364, 599, 668, 914, 951, 1179, 1564, 1584, 1674.

612. Morgan, F.C. "Bull Baiting and Bear Baiting." *N&Q*, 197 (1952), 107.

Support for item 606 (cf. also item 607).

613. Morse, Charlotte C. "The Image of the Vessel in *Cl*." *UTQ*, 40 (1971), 202-16.

Suggests that each story in *Cl* is a type of the Last Judgment. Argues that Belshazzar's sacrilege is comparable to sexual uncleanness because man has traditionally been represented by the image of the vessel. Cf. item 614.

614. ————. "*Cl*." *The Pattern of Judgment in the "Queste" and "Cl*." Columbia and London: Univ. of Missouri Press, 1978. Pp. 129-99.

A reading of *Cl* based on the propositions that the paradigm of the vessel as an image of man is of central significance (see item 613), and that the three major narratives adhere to the model established in the parable of the wedding feast, and demonstrate God's judgment in history. These ideas are introduced and summarized in other chapters, which also contain many passing comments on *Cl*.

615. Naruse, Masaiku. "A Study of *Cl*, an Alliterative Poem in the Fourteenth Century--on the *G*-Poet's Attitude towards Earthly Love." *ShoR*, no. 62 (1964), 200-26.

Comments on lines 1052-68. Argues that the poet contrasts earthly and heavenly love, exhorting his audience
to seek the latter. In Japanese.

616. Nevanlinna, Saara. "Background and History of the Par-
      enthetic *As Who Say/Saith* in Old and ME." *NM* (1974),
      568-601.

      Comments on *As so saytz* (29) on p. 584.

617. Ohlander, Urban. "A Passage in *Cl*: A note on ME Con-
      struction-Change." *GHÅ*, 56 (1950), 311-23.

      Discusses the change of construction between the indica-
      tive *wysses* (1564), and *make* (1566), which can be inter-
      preted as a subjunctive or an infinitive. Specifies
      parallels in other ME texts.

618. Olszewska, E.S. "Some English and Norse Alliterative
      Phrases." *Saga-Book*, 12 (1942), 238-45.

      Discusses *raynande ryg* (382) on pp. 244-45.

619. Spendal, R.J. "The Manuscript Capitals in *Cl*." *N&Q*,
      221 (1976), 340-41.

      Argues that the placing of capitals in the MS is not
      haphazard.

620. Thomas, P.G. "Notes on *Cl*." *MLR*, 17 (1922), 64-66.

      Comments, in response to item 62, on the following lines:
      16, 72, 76, 145, 226, 230, 433-34, 470, 473, 527, 553,
      577, 655, 751, 1141, 1155, 1231-32, 1502, 1566, 1683,
      1687.

621. ————. "Notes on *Cl*." *MLR*, 24 (1929), 323-24.

      Records the views of W.P. Ker on lines 145, 375, 655,
      1687, 1701.

622. Yanko, Nadina Robin. "*Pur* and the Social Order." Diss.,
      California (Berkeley), 1977. Abst.: *DAI*, 38 (1978),
      4813A.

                  D. Critical Writings on *Patience*

623. Anderson, J.J. "The Prologue of *Pat*." *MP*, 63 (1966),
      283-87.

Argues, in reply to item 663, that *pouerte* (35, etc.) is physical; also that the prologue provides immediate contemporary relevance for the Jonah story. Cf. also item 657.

624. Andrew, Malcolm. "Jonah and Christ in *Pat*." *MP*, 70 (1973), 230-33.

Suggests that Jonah functions as both a type and a sub-fulfillment of Christ. Cf. items 635, etc.

625. ————. "Pat' the minnnng lol," *DEN*, 14 (1977), 164-67.

Considers the effect of the simile in line 268, and the traditions it embodies.

626. Berlin, Normand. "*Pat*: A Study in Poetic Elaboration." *SN*, 33 (1961), 80-85.

Discusses the relationship between the Jonah story in *Pat* and the OT Book of Jonah. Cf. items 159, 303, 358, 628, 675.

627. Bloomfield, Morton W. "*Pat* and the *Mashal*." *Hornstein*, pp. 41-49.

Maintains that *Pat* is not a homily, but a *mashal* ("a narrative with a small amount of moralizing"). Cf. items 159, 680.

628. Bowers, R.H. *The Legend of Jonah*. The Hague: Nijhoff, 1971.

Includes consideration of the poet's treatment of biblical sources and exegetical tradition (pp. 61-67). Cf. items 626, etc.; 677.

629. Callender, Geoffrey. "*Pat*." *MM*, 4 (1914), 97-105.

Translates lines 101-08, 137-68, and 181-86; provides notes on lines 101-08 and on *hurrok* (185). Cf. items 307, etc.

630. Camiciotti, Gabriella Del Lungo. "Sulla struttura e sul significato del poemetto medio-inglese *Pazienza*." *StG*, 13 (1975), 15-31.

Not seen. Cf. item 634.

631. Cazamian, Louis. *From the Early Times to the Renaissance. The Development of English Humor*, I. New York: Macmillan, 1930. Rpt. Durham, N.C.: Duke UP, 1951.

Discusses the description of Jonah in the whale; translates lines 268-81 and 289-302 (pp. 55-56).

632. Day, Mabel. "Introduction" to *"The Siege of Jerusalem"*:
*edited from MS. Laud. Misc. 656 with variants from all
other extant MSS.* Ed. E. Kölbing and Mabel Day. EETS,
OS 188. London: Milford, Oxford UP, 1932. Rpt. New
York: Kraus, 1971.

Considers the influence of *Pat* (particularly lines 137-
52) on *The Siege of Jerusalem* (pp. xxix-xxx).

633. ───. "A Note on *Pat*, 1. 54." *MLR*, 33 (1938), 564.

Supports suggested emendations with a parallel from the
alliterative *Wars of Alexander*.

634. Del Lungo, Gabriella. "Esame critico e traduzione del
poemetto medio-inglese *Pazienza*." Diss., Firenze, 1973.

Cf. item 630.

635. Diekstra, F.N.M. "Jonah and *Pat*: The Psychology of a
Prophet." *ES*, 55 (1974), 205-17.

Discusses the meaning of "patience" in Christian tradition, and argues that the poet's treatment of the Jonah
story is not at odds with that of the commentators. Cf.
items 624, 628, 648, 677.

636. Eberhard, Oscar. *Der Bauernaufstand vom Jahre 1381 in
der englischen Poesie.* AF, 51. Heidelberg: Winter,
1917.

Detects a reference to the Peasants' Revolt in the open-
ing of *Pat* (pp. 33-35).

637. Ekwall, Eilert. "Kleinigkeiten zur englischen Wortfor-
schung, II.[2]" *Archiv*, 119 (1907), 442-43.

Discusses *caraldes* (159).

638. ───. "Some notes on the Text of the alliterative
Poem *Pat*." *EStn*, 44 (1911), 165-73.

Notes on the following lines: 77, 101-05, 143, 148, 150,
157, 173, 185, 186, 188, 189, 226, 275, 279, 299-302,
316, 354, 355, 372, 427-28, 448, 460.

639. ───. "Another Note on the Poem *Pat*." *EStn*, 47
(1913), 313-16.

Comments on lines 77, 101-08, 185, 299-302, 316, in response to item 644.

640. ———. Review of item 67. *AnglB*, 24 (1913), 133-36.

Includes specific comments on lines 51, 187, 188, 428, 509.

641. ———. Review of item 68. *EStn*, 49 (1915), 144-46.

Comments on Gollancz's treatment of various lines; suggests that *rome* (52) should be read *Rome*.

642. ———. "Zu *Pat* 143." *EStn*, 49 (1916), 483-84.

Discusses *breed fysches* (143), *swey* (429), and *flee3* (*Cl* 956).

643. Emerson, Oliver Farrar. "A Parallel between the ME Poem *Pat* and an Early Latin Poem attributed to Tertullian." *PMLA*, 10 (1895), 242-48.

Suggests that the poet knew the pseudo-Tertullian poem *De Jona* (and Tertullian's treatises *De Patientia* and *De Modestia*). Cf. items 653, 662, 679.

644. ———. "A Note on the Poem *Pat*." *EStn*, 47 (1913), 125-31.

Offers suggestions on lines 299-302, in response to item 638. Also comments on the following lines: 77, 101-08, 121-22, 159 (misnumbered 139), 185, 269, 279, 316.

645. ———. Review of item 67. *MLN*, 28 (1913), 171-80, 232.

Includes comments and suggestions on the following lines: 1, 6, 11, 36, 37, 47, 53, 54-56, 58, 62, 67, 69, 71, 78, 84, 86, 88, 92, 93, 106, 108, 122, 126, 136, 154, 157, 160, 163, 167-68, 173, 188, 189, 195, 219, 220, 228, 230, 235, 238, 250, 253, 255, 267, 270, 272, 275, 289, 298, 300, 306, 317, 319, 325, 338, 344, 350, 353, 362, 383, 401, 402, 419, 423, 425, 428, 435, 439, 451, 452, 454, 458, 460, 463, 474, 492, 502, 504, 509, 511.

646. ———. "Two Notes on *Pat*." *MLN*, 29 (1914), 85-86.

Suggests reading *apoynt* (1) and understanding *ne* (231) as an adverb "nigh."

647. ———. "More Notes on *Pat*." *MLN*, 31 (1916), 1-10.

Expresses opposition to the quatrain arrangement and reservations about various glosses in the *OED*. Comments on the following lines: 77, 101, 104, 106, 185, 188, 269, 279, 316, 338; and on *Cl* 417 and 1520. Cf. items 161, etc.

*   ———. See also items 414, 598.

648.   Fàj, Attila. "Marbodean and Patristic Reminiscences in *Pat*." *RLC*, 49 (1975), 284-90.

Argues that *Pat* reflects the influence of a poem by Marbodus of Rennes, and of various patristic writings. Cf. items 635, etc.; 679.

649.   Grant, W. Michael. "Comedy, Irony, and Compassion in *Pat*." *WVUPP*, 20 (1973), 8-16.

Suggests that the conflict of wills between Jonah and God generates comedy and irony, tempered by the poet's compassion. Draws some parallels with *Cl*. Cf. item 675.

650.   Grattan, J.H.G. Review of item 68. *MLR*, 9 (1914), 403-05.

Specific comments on the following lines: 54-56, 104, 116, 117, 122, 143, 216, 219, 230, 256, 259, 289, 292, 320, 350, 354, 375, 380, 449, 451, 454, 530.

651.   Greg, W.W. "Sottez for Madde." *MLR*, 20 (1925), 185-86.

A comment on these words in 509.

652.   Heather, P.J. "The Seven Planets." *F-L*, 54 (1943), 338-61.

Mentions the reference to the worship of the sun and the moon in *Pat* 167 (p. 353).

653.   Hill, Ordelle G. "The Late-Latin *De Jona* as a Source for *Pat*." *JEGP*, 66 (1967), 21-25.

Reviews the controversy between Emerson and Liljegren (items 643, 662); concludes that the poet did know the *De Jona*.

654.   ———. "The Audience of *Pat*." *MP*, 66 (1968), 103-09.

Suggests that *Pat* was intended for an audience concerned with the problems of preaching, possibly clergy.

*   ————. See also item 204.

655. Hill, Thomas D. "Raguel and Ragnel: Notes on the Liter-
      ary Genealogy of a Devil." *Names*, 22 (1974), 145-49.

      Suggests that *Ragnel/Raguel* (*Pat* 188) is derived from
      the Book of Enoch.

656. Hiraoka, Teruaki. "Studies in ME: West-Midland Dialect
      Analysis of the language of *Pat*." *SETG*, 7 (1972), 25-
      39.

      Classifies prepositions, conjunctions, adverbs, adjec
      tives, nouns, and verbs according to their origin.   In
      Japanese.

657. Irwin, John T., and T.D. Kelly. "The Way and the End
      are One: *Pat* as a Parable of the Contemplative Life."
      ABR, 25 (1974), 33-55.

      Contend that the *pouerte* of the prologue is spiritual
      (cf. items 623, 663). Suggest that structurally *Pat* is
      parabolic rather than homiletic, and provide a detailed
      interpretation of it as a parable of the contemplative
      life. Cf. item 602.

658. Johnson, Lynn Staley. "*Pat* and the Poet's Use of Psalm
      93." *MP*, 74 (1976), 67-71.

      Observing that Ps. 93:8-9 is paraphrased in lines 119-
      24, relates exegetical discussion of the psalm to the
      theme of the poem. Cf. item 679.

659. Kelly, Ellin M. "Parallels between the ME *Pat* and *Hym-
      nus Ieiunantium* of Prudentius." *ELN*, 4 (1967), 244-47.

      Suggests that *Pat* reflects the influence of this poem.
      Cf. item 679.

*   Kelly, T.D. See item 657.

660. Kuranaga, Makoto. "*Pat*: An Alliterative Poem." *Kura-
      naga*, pp. 12-29.

      A part of the author's consideration of the Book of Jo-
      nah in English literature. In Japanese.

661. Laughton, L.G. Carr. "*Pat*." *MM*, 4 (1914), 186-95.

      Contains notes on lines 101-08, 184, 185 (in reply to
      item 629. Cf. items 307, etc.).

662. Liljegren, S.B. "Has the Poet of *Pat* read *De Jona?*" *EStn*, 48 (1914), 337-41.

    A destructive reply to item 643, arguing that the poet did not know the *De Jona*. Cf. also item 653.

*   Lungo, Gabriella Del. See Del Lungo.

663. Moorman, Charles. "The Role of the Narrator in *Pat*." *MP*, 61 (1963), 90-95.

    Emphasizes the importance of the "preacher-narrator," suggesting that the Jonah story is structurally an *exemplum* in a sermon. Interprets *pouerte* (35, etc.) as spiritual. (Cf. items 263, 623, 657).

664. Munson, Miriam Grove. "The Sign of Jonah: Rhetorical Strategy in *Pat*." Diss., Washington, 1974. *DAI*, 36 (1975), 280A-81A.

665. Naruse, Masaiku. "On the Possible Omission in the Text of *Pat*." *EigoS*, 111 (1965), 90-93.

    Suggests that a line is missing between lines 512 and 513. In Japanese.

666. ———. "On *Pat*, 11. 509-15." *JCulS*, 4 (1968), 83-95.

    Offers interpretations of various words in these lines. In Japanese.

667. O., D. "'Boat' for 'Ship.'" *MM*, 4 (1914), 156.

    Comments on the usage in line 184. Cf. items 307, etc.

668. Onions, C.T. "Professor Emerson's Note on *Pat*." *EStn*, 47 (1913), 316-17; 48 (1914), 172.

    Deals with lines 101, 185, 269, 279, 316, in response to item 644. The second note modifies comments on line 185.

669. Park, James Mellon. "*Pat*: The Story of Jonah in a ME Poem." Diss., Yale, 1972. Abst.: *DAI*, 33 (1973), 3599A.

670. Ritter, Otto. "Englische Etymologien." *Archiv*, 119 (1907), 436-42.

    Glosses *breedfisches* (143) "turbot, brill."

671. Sanderlin, George. "The Role of Jonah in *Pat*." *LangQ*, 16, i-ii (1977), 39-40.

Emphasizes the centrality of Jonah.

672. Schless, Howard H. "Dante: Comedy and Conversion." *Genre*, 19 (1976-7), 413-27.

Discusses the comedy generated by the contrast between God's grandeur and Jonah's inadequacy (pp. 422-23). Cf. item 675.

673. Schleusener, Jay. "*Pat*, Lines 35-40." *MP*, 67 (1969), 64-66.

Relates these lines to patristic interpretation of the Beatitudes.

674. ———. "History and Action in *Pat*." *PMLA*, 86 (1971), 959-65.

Sees the action of *Pat* in terms of providential history, Jonah's failings serving to reveal God's power, justice, and mercy.

675. Spearing, A.C. "*Pat* and the *G*-Poet." *Anglia*, 84 (1966), 305-29. Extract rpt. in item 827.

Suggests that all four poems reflect a tragi-comic view of man. Discusses the poet's modification of the OT narrative; emphasizes the comedy which results when human impotence is confronted by divine power and mercy. Comments briefly on similarities in *Cl*, *Pe*, and *G*.

676. Spendal, R.J. "The Narrative Structure of *Pat*." *MichA*, 5 (1972), 107-14.

Argues that the structure of the *exemplum* is five-fold, and repeats a pattern of prayer followed by manifestation of divine power and mercy. Cf. item 679.

677. Szarmach, Paul E. "Two Notes on *Pat*." *N&Q*, 216 (1971), 125-27.

Discusses possible sources for Jonah's snoring (186), and suggests patristic precedent for using the Jonah story to illustrate patience (cf. item 628).

678. Vantuono, William. "The Question of Quatrains in *Pat*." *Manuscripta*, 16 (1972), 24-30.

Reviews opinion on the matter, and argues that Pat was
not written in quatrains. Cf. items 161, etc.

679.   ————. "The Structure and Sources of Pat." MS, 34
        (1972), 401-21.

Argues that the structure of Pat follows the traditional
fivefold division of the sermon. Reviews the poet's use
of sources: the Book of Jonah; Psalms 6 and 93; three
Latin poems (De Jona, Marbod's Naufragium, and Pruden-
tius's "Hymnus Ieiunantium"); Jerome's commentary on the
Book of Jonah; and Tertullian's De Patientia. Cf. items
643, etc.; 648, 659, 676.

680.   Williams, David [J.]. "The Point of Pat." MP, 68
        (1970), 127-36.

Expresses reservations about treating Pat as a sermon;
suggests a universalizing intention in the handling of
both prologue and narrative. Cf. item 627.

E. Critical Writings on Sir Gawain and the Green Knight

681.   Ackerman, Robert W. "G's Shield: Penitential Doctrine
        in GGK." Anglia, 76 (1958), 254-65.

Quotes from vernacular penitential writings to demonstrate that the figure of the fyue wytte₃ (640) is to be
associated with confession. Cf. items 1066, etc.

682.   ————. "SGGK and Its Interpreters." On Stage and Off:
        Eight Essays in English Literature. Ed. John W. Ehr-
        stine, John R. Elwood, and Robert C. McLean. [Seattle]:
        Washington State UP, 1968. Pp. 66-73.

Reviews trends in critical writing on G during the 1960s.
Cf. items 716, 889.

683.   ————. "Castle Hautdesert in SGGK." Frappier, I, 1-7.

Relates lines 753-72 to castle descriptions in romance,
and to a visionary tradition based on Revelation (and
reflected in Pe 977-82).

684.   ————. "Madden's G Anthology." Hornstein, pp. 5-18.

Includes some comments on Madden's edition of SGGK (item
97).

*   ————.   See also items 119, 1276.

685.   Akkartal, T.   "A Point of Syntax in *SGGK*."   *N&Q*, 198
       (1953), 322.

       Discusses the meanings of *þeroute* and *þerwyth*.

686.   Aljubouri, A.H.   "The Treatment of Chivalric Ideals in
       SGGK."   *BBCA*, 9· (1966), 37-49.

       Argues that the ideals of chivalry are central to the
       poem, and that G is portrayed as an epitome of Christian
       knighthood.   Cf. items 842, 960, 1001.

687.   Amours, F.J.   "*Capados*."   *N&Q*, 9th ser., 4 (1899), 308.

       Argues that the *capados* (186, etc.) is a gambison of
       Cappadocian leather.

688.   Anderson, Heather Jerrim.   "The Terrestrial Paradise: A
       Study in the 'Intermediacy' and Multi-Levelled Nature of
       the Medieval Garden of Eden."   Diss., New York (Buffalo),
       1973.   Abst.: *DAI*, 34 (1974), 5830A.

       Includes material on *G*.

689.   Andrew, S.O.   "The Text of *Sir Gawayn and the Grene
       Knyʒt*."   *RES*, 6 (1930), 175-82.

       Suggests emendations on grounds of alliteration in the
       following lines: 60, 93, 157, 335, 377, 541, 649, 835,
       939, 971, 1169, 1187, 1223, 1293, 1372, 1390, 1422, 1501,
       1526-27, 1833, 1909, 1912, 1962, 2149, 2212, 2439; and
       on grounds of sense in the following lines: 814, 1265,
       1304, 1351, 1447, 1569, 1606, 1724, 1729, 1969, 2123,
       2179, 2320.   Also suggests various alterations to the
       punctuation of Tolkien and Gordon's edition (item 111).

690.   Anttila, Raimo.   "Sound Preference in Alliteration."
       SML, 5 (1969), 44-48.

       Analyzes the occurrence in *G* of particular initial
       sounds in relation to a predicted norm.

691.   Baker, Sr. Imogen, O.S.B.   *The King's Household in the
       Arthurian Court from Geoffrey of Monmouth to Malory*.
       Washington, D.C.: Catholic Univ. of America, 1937.
       Diss., Washington, 1937.

       Argues that G is pre-eminent among the knights in *G* (pp.
       116-18).

692. Barber, R[ichard] W. *Arthur of Albion: An Introduction to the Arthurian Literature and Legends of England.* London: Barrie and Rockliff, Pall Mall Press; New York: Barnes and Noble, 1961; corr. rpt., London: Boydell Press, 1971.

Includes a plot summary, an account of sources, and comments on descriptions and the moral theme (pp. 95-107).

693. Barnet, Sylvan. "A Note on the Structure of *SGGK*." *MLN*, 71 (1956), 319.

Discusses the poet's use of tripartite patterning. Cf. items 1098, etc.

694. Barron, W.R.J. "French romance and the structure of *SGGK*." *Studies in medieval literature and languages in memory of Frederick Whitehead.* Ed. W. Rothwell, W.R.J. Barron, David Blamires, and Lewis Thorpe. Manchester: UP; New York: Barnes and Noble, 1973. Pp. 7-25.

Demonstrates that the meaning of *G* is revealed through its structural patterning. Argues that, since source study suggests that the structure is original, the thematic conception should be considered original too.

695. Barton, Robert Joyce. "A Figural Reading of *SGGK*." Diss., Stanford, 1969. Abst.: *DAI*, 30 (1970), 3423A.

696. Baughan, Denver Ewing. "The Role of Morgan Le Fay in *SGGK*." *ELH*, 17 (1950), 241-51.

Contends that Morgan's role has been underestimated and that she sends Bertilak to Camelot to purge it of moral corruption. Cf. items 748, 801, 829, 854, 1019, 1032, 1211. 967

697. Bayley, A.R. "The Five Wounds." *N&Q*, 171 (1936), 266.

A reply to item 1097; cf. also items 818, 1203.

698. Bayley, John. Letter. *Scrutiny*, 17 (1950), 128-30.

Expresses reservations about item 1192.

699. Bazire, Joyce. "ME ę̄ and ẹ̄ in the Rhymes of *SGGK*." *JEGP*, 51 (1952), 234-35.

Argues that most of these rhymes are perfect and specifies a few that are suspect.

700. Becker, Ph[ilipp] Aug[ust]. "Der grüne Ritter." *Archiv*, 159 (1931), 275-76.

On the "Green Count" (Amadeus VI). Cf. items 776, 893.

701. Benham, Allen Rogers. *English Literature from "Widsith" to the Death 'of Chaucer: A Source Book.* New Haven: Yale UP; London: Milford, Oxford UP, 1916.

Mentions *G* as illustrative of chivalry; prints W.F. Parish's translation of lines 500-669 (with revisions by Benham). (Pp. 368-73).

702. Bennett, H.S. "Medieval Literature and the Modern Reader." *E&S*, 31 (1945), 7-18.

Comments on the poet's use of detail in descriptions (pp. 14-15).

703. Bennett, J.A.W. *Supplementary Notes on "SGGK."* 4 fascs. Cambridge: privately pr., 1972-76.

The fascicles are each between 20 and 30 pages in length, and provide explanatory and interpretative notes of the kind found in critical editions.

* Bensel, Elise ... Ven-Ten. See Ven-Ten Bensel.

704. Benson, Larry D. "The Art and Meaning of *SGGK*." Diss., California (Berkeley), 1959.

Cf. item 706.

705. ————. "The Sources of the Beheading Episode in *SGGK*." *MP*, 59 (1961), 1-12.

Demonstrates, by comparing passages, that *Le Livre de Caradoc* is the main source for the beheading episode in *G*.

706. ————. *Art and Tradition in "SGGK."* New Brunswick, N.J.: Rutgers UP, 1965. Extracts rpt. in items 827, 891.

Investigates the relevant literary traditions in order to provide a context for the evaluation of the art of *G*.

1. After a general discussion of the function of sources in romance, reviews the origins of the beheading and temptation episodes in turn, emphasizing the Caradoc version of the former and the poet's use of the latter as a test of courtesy. (Cf. items 934, etc.).

2. Considers the description of the Green Knight, relating it to the literary conventions of the green
man and the wild man, and to the various symbolic
associations of green. Goes on to relate the poet's
characterization of the hero to the traditionally imperfect G. (Cf. items 802, etc.; 1209, etc.).

3. Provides an account of the development of the ME alliterative style. Considers the poet's use of this
style, discussing synonyms and their aesthetic function, syntactical variation, the analytic function of
syntax, and variation in the narrative structure.
(Cf. items 731, etc.).

4. Reviews narrative and descriptive techniques. Discusses the ordering of the narrative, the concrete-
ness of alliterative description, the use of alter-
nating viewpoints, the contribution of narrative
technique to characterization, and the function of
the narrator's voice. (Cf. items 1012, etc.).

5. A critical reading. Stresses the themes of reputation in the challenge and of identity in the testing.
Analyzes the major episodes of the fourth fitt. Concludes that *G* is at once an affirmation and a comic
rejection of romance values. (Cf. items 707, etc.).

Appendix: Text of the prose redaction of the Caradoc
beheading tale.

Reviews: G.C. Britton and Betty Hill, *YWES*, 46 (1965),
70-71.
J.A. Burrow, *N&Q*, 211 (1966), 191-93.
Cecily Clark, *MAE*, 36 (1967), 89-92.
D.L. Farley-Hills, *RES*, N.S. 18 (1967), 187-88.
J. Finlayson, *MP*, 65 (1967), 152-54.
John Gardner, *JEGP*, 65 (1966), 705-08 (rpt. in
item 891).
Kemp Malone, *Speculum*, 41 (1966), 726-29.
Dieter Mehl, *Anglia*, 85 (1967), 82-90.
Helaine Newstead, *RPh*, 20 (1967), 583-85.
Rossell Hope Robbins, *RBPH*, 46 (1968), 545-48.
P.J. Verhoeff, *Neophil*, 51 (1967), 100-01.
R.M. Wilson, *MLR*, 62 (1967), 108-09.
See also item 870.

✗ 707. Bercovitch, Sacvan. "Romance and Anti-Romance in *SGGK*."
PQ, 44 (1965), 30-37. Rpt. in item 891.

Argues that through the tempering of romance convention
with comedy and realism, *G* becomes a profound celebra-

tion of courtly values. Cf. items 706, 732, 741, 846, 1126.

708. Berry, Francis. "The Sublime Ballet: An Essay on *SGGK*." *W&R*, 6 (1949-50), 165-74.

Relates the metre to OE antecedents; praises nature descriptions and emphasizes the significance of seasonal ritual. Cf. items 1192, etc.

/09. ——— —. "*Sir Gawayne and the Grene Knight*." *Ford*, pp. 146-56.

Provides comments on language and metre, a plot-summary, and critical analysis which emphasizes ritualistic and mythic elements. Cf. items 1192, etc.

710. Billings, Anna Hunt. *A Guide to the ME Metrical Romances dealing with English and Germanic Legends, and with the Cycles of Charlemagne and of Arthur.* YSE, 9. New Haven: Yale UP, 1901. Rpt., New York: Russell, 1967.

Provides basic information on *G*, under the following headings: 1. subject; 2. specimen (lines 2374-8/); 3. story; 4. origin (i.e., sources); 5. metre; 6. dialect; 7. date; 8. author; 9. bibliography (pp. 160-68).

711. Björkman, Erik. *Scandinavian Loan Words in ME.* 2 pts. SEP, 7, 11. Halle a.S.: Niemeyer, 1900-02.

Numerous passing references to the occurrence of various words in *G*.

712. Black, Nancy BreMiller. "The Hero's Fight with a Dragon or Giant Adversary in Medieval Narrative." Diss., Columbia, 1971. Abst.: *DAI*, 32 (1971), 3243A.

713. Blake, Norman. *The English Language in Medieval Literature.* London, Melbourne, and Toronto: Dent; Totowa, N.J.: Rowman and Littlefield, 1977.

Considers the use of traditional themes in *G* (pp. 130-32); also makes various passing references.

714. Blanch, Robert J. "Games poets play: the ambiguous use of Color Symbolism in *SGGK*." *NMS*, 20 (1976), 64-85.

Reviews "mythic" criticism of *G* (cf. items 1192, etc.). Discusses the poet's use of color symbolism, and con-

cludes that its ambiguity reinforces the significant
element of play and game in the poem. Cf. items 769,
etc.; 802, etc.

715. Blenkner, Louis, O.S.B. "Sin, Psychology, and the
Structure of *SGGK*." *SP*, 74 (1977), 354-87.

Emphasizes the structural significance of all nine MS
divisions. Proposes a complex pattern of structural
and thematic triads (e.g., G undergoes three tests--be-
heading, exchange of winnings, temptation--testing respectively *fortitudo*, *sapientia*, and chastity; his responses reveal the wounds of mortality, concupiscence,
and ignorance, while his acceptance of the girdle follows the three psychological steps of *suggestio*, *delec-
tatio*, and *consensus*)--etc. (Cf. items 1098, etc.).

716. Bloomfield, Morton W. "*SGGK*: An Appraisal." *PMLA*, 76
(1961), 7-19. Rpt. in item 891 and in Morton W. Bloomfield, *Essays and Explorations: Studies in Ideas, Language, and Literature*, Cambridge, Mass.: Harvard UP;
London: Oxford UP, 1970.

A detailed review of critical writing on *G*. Considers
the theory of common authorship not conclusively proven;
predicts growing interest in the poem's religious aspects. Cf. items 682, 889.

*   ————. See also item 133.

717. Bonjour, Adrien. "*werre and wrake and wonder* (*SG*, 1.
16)." *ES*, 32 (1951), 70-72.

An interpretative note on this phrase.

718. Borroff, Marie Edith. "The Style of *GGK*." Diss., Yale,
1955.

Cf. item 719.

719. ————, Marie [Edith]. "*SGGK*": *A Stylistic and Metrical
Study*. YSE, 152. New Haven and London: Yale UP, 1962.
Rpt., Hamden, Conn.: Archon, 1973. Extracts rpt. in
items 827 and 891.

I.   Style.
      1. Discusses the relationship between style and
         meaning as they affect the expressive value of
         words.

   2. Reviews the historical study of style, the aim
      of which is to recover lost expressive values in
      the language of literary texts.
   3. Using the discoveries of Brink (item 731) as a
      starting-point, discusses the relation between
      alliterative status and expressive value in the
      vocabulary of *G*. Concentrates on words for
      "man, warrior" and "earth, field." Also offers
      some discussion of adjectives.
   4. After general observations on the criticism of
      style, offers detailed analysis of lines 37-59
      and 136-50. Discusses the effect of the narra-
      tor and his viewpoint, especially in the chal-
      lenge episode.

   II. Metre.
   5. Considers phonological evidence for the accen-
      tuation of romance words and the pronunciation
      of final -*e*.
   6. Establishes a metrical pattern for the "wheels,"
      specifying chief and intermediate syllables;
      considers the treatment of -*e* and romance words.
   7. Presents evidence of the accentuation of romance
      words in the long line. Reviews four- and
      seven-stress theories, favoring the latter.
   8. Suggests that in "extended" half-lines, one of
      the heavy syllables should be subordinated.

   Reviews: Larry D. Benson, *MLQ*, 24 (1963), 307-08.
            J.A. Burrow, *EIC*, 13 (1963), 172-77.
            Basil Cottle, *JEGP*, 62 (1963), 364-65.
            Norman Davis, *RES*, NS 15 (1964), 194-96.
            G.N. Garmonsway, *UTQ*, 36 (1967), 295-301.
            A. Macdonald and Betty Hill, *YWES*, 43 (1962),
              67.
            Dieter Mehl, *Archiv*, 201 (1964), 64-66.
            James P. Oakden, *MAE*, 33 (1964), 145-47.
            Alain Renoir, *Speculum*, 39 (1964), 494-96.
            Ewald Standop, *Anglia*, 81 (1963), 477-81.
            Yoshio Terasawa, *SELit*, 40 (1964), 248-51.
            R.M. Wilson, *MLR*, 58 (1963), 234-35.

720. Bowen, E.G., and Gwyn Jones. Review of item 88. *MAE*,
      13 (1944), 58-65.

      Consider the significance of *G*'s origin in the "Highland
      zone" on Britain, and offer specific suggestions on the
      following lines: 171, 184, 574, 608, 654, 802, 932, 1141,
      1172, 2223, 2316, 2329, 2343.

721. Bowers, R.H. "*GGK* as Entertainment." *MLQ*, 24 (1963),
      333-41. Rpt. in item 891.

      Discusses the interpretations in items 739, 997, and
      1033. Argues that the warm humor of *G* has not been
      acknowledged.

722. Braddy, Haldeen. "SG and Ralph Holmes the Green Knight."
      MLN, 67 (1952), 240-42.

      Suggests that the GK was modelled on Sir Ralph Holmes
      (d. 1369).

723. Branford, William. "Bercilak de Hautdesert: An Inter-
      rogation of the GK." *ESA*, 7 (1964), 54-64.

      Discusses the role of the GK/Bercilak, and the possible
      meanings of *Bercilak* and *Hautdesert*.

724. Brett, Cyril. "Notes on *Sir Gawayne and the Green
      Knight*." *MLR*, 8 (1913), 160-64.

      Notes on lines 681, 967, 1440, 1730.

725. ———. "Notes on Passages of Old and ME." *MLR*, 14
      (1919), 1-9.

      Includes notes on lines 477 and 2424 (misnumbered 2423).

726. ———. Review of item 111. *MLR*, 22 (1927), 451-58.

      Specific comments on the following lines: 46, 67-70,
      113, 160, 186, 197-99, 211, 235, 296, 350, 372, 574,
      790, 1053, 1377, 1395-97, 1431, 1457-59, 1570, 1726,
      1755, 1968, 1999, 2012, 2079-80, 2102, 2110, 2173, 2316,
      2399, 2418.

  *   ———. See also item 136.

727. Breuer, Rolf. "Die Funktion der Naturschilderungen in
      den mittelenglischen Versromanzen." Diss., Göttingen,
      1966. Abst.: *EASG*, 1968, pp. 24-26.

      Includes material on *G*.

728. Brewer, D[erek] S. "Gawayn and the Green Chapel." *N&Q*,
      193 (1948), 13.

      Suggests that the Green Chapel is a long barrow. Cf.
      items 764, 781.

729. ————, Derek [S.]. "The Interpretation of Dream, Folk-
      tale and Romance with Special Reference to *SGGK*." *NM*,
      77 (1976), 569–81.

      Interprets *G* as a *rite de passage*, with the GK/Bertilak
      as an ambivalent father-figure, and the Lady and Morgan
      respectively as seductive and hostile aspects of the
      mother figure. Cf. items 795, 993, 1033, 1261.

730. Brewer, Elisabeth, tr. *From Cuchulainn to G: Sources
      and analogues of "SGGK."* Cambridge: Brewer, 1973.

      Consists of a brief introduction, followed by transla-
      tions of sources and analogues, arranged as follows:

      1. The Beheading Game (*Bricriu's Feast*, the first and
         second versions of the Carados story, *Perlesvaus*,
         La Mule sanz Frain, and *Hunbaut*).
      2. The Temptation Theme (*Yder*, the Vulgate *Lancelot*,
         Hunbaut, *Le Chevalier à l'Epée*).
      3. Later Versions (the prose *Caradoc*, The *GK*, *SG* and the
         Carl of Carlisle).

      Review: V.J. Scattergood, *EIC*, 25 (1975), 370–71.

731. Brink, August. *Stab und Wort im "G": eine stilistische
      Untersuchung.* SEP, 59. Halle a.S.: Niemeyer, 1920.
      Diss., Göttingen, 1920.

      An investigation of the relationship between the use of
      nouns and adjectives in the alliterative line and their
      stylistic qualities. Demonstrates that among synonymous
      words, some invariably alliterate while others alliter-
      ate only sometimes; and that those used exclusively in
      alliterating positions are rarely found in Chaucer and
      do not survive in ModE. Concludes that words of "high
      alliterative rank" were archaic and elevated. Cf. items
      336, 719.

      Review: Karl Luick, *EStn*, 56 (1922), 411–14.

732. Broes, Arthur T. "*SGGK*: Romance as Comedy." *XUS*, 4
      (1965), 35–54.

      Argues that *G* is a mixture of jest and earnest, the poet
      delicately satirizing chivalric attitudes which he re-
      gards as outdated. Cf. items 707, etc.

733. Bruce, J[ames] Douglas. "The breaking of the deer in
      Sir Gawayne and the Green Knight." *EStn*, 32 (1903) 23–
      36.

Uses evidence from hunting manuals and *The Parlement of the Thre Ages* (65-91) to clarify the meaning of *G* 1325-61.

734.   ───────, James Douglas. *The Evolution of Arthurian Romance: From the Beginnings Down to the Year 1300,* I. Hesperia: Ergänzungsreihe: Schriften zur englischen Philologie, 8. Göttingen, Vandenhoeck und Ruprecht; Baltimore: Johns Hopkins, 1923; 2nd. ed., with supp. by Alfons Hilka, Baltimore: Johns Hopkins, 1928; rpt., Gloucester, Mass.: Smith, 1958.

Comments on the relationship between *G* and its sources (pp. 88-89, 125-27).

735.   Bruten, Avril. "*G*'s Green Girdle as a 'Sign.'" *N&Q*, 211 (1966), 452-54.

An Augustinian view of Camelot's response to the girdle. Cf. item 858.

736.   Buchanan, Alice. "The Irish Framework of *GGK*." *PMLA*, 47 (1932), 315-38.

Takes issue with Kittredge's view (item 934) that the Beheading Test in *G* is derived from a single episode in the Curoi cycle; discusses and tabulates parallels to *G* in other episodes from this cycle. Cf. items 969, etc.

737.   Burnley, J.D. "The Hunting Scenes in *SGGK*." *YES*, 3 (1973), 1-9.

Suggests that the audience's emotional response to the hunting scenes conditions their emotional and moral response to the temptation scenes. Cf. items 1127, etc.

738.   ───────. "*SGGK*, lines 3-7." *N&Q*, 218 (1973), 83-84.

Argues that the reference is to Aeneas, comparing *Cl* 977-84.

739.   Burrow, John [A.]. "The Two Confession Scenes in *SGGK*." *MP*, 57 (1959), 73-79. Rpt. in item 132.

Emphasizes the penitential theme. Suggests that G's confession is imperfect, and is completed before the GK. Cf. items 741, 820, 821, 825, 857, 858, 896, 911, 1039.

740.   ───────, J[ohn] A. Letter. *RES*, NS 15 (1964), 56. Rpt. in item 891.

Argues, in response to item 820, that *couetyse* (2374) should be taken in its literal sense.

741. ————. *A Reading of "SGGK."* London: Routledge, 1965;
New York: Barnes and Noble, 1966. Extract rpt. in item
827.

  1. Fitt 1: States that, in view of the linear nature of
  G, this reading will follow the order of events in
  the poem. Emphasizes the conflicting expectations
  and the ambivalence in the account of the challenge.

  2. Fitt 2: Discusses the pentangle and the meaning of
  trawþe (626); suggests that the winter journey has
  penitential aspects, and that, on arrival at tho
  castle, G is disarmed metaphorically as well as lit
  erally.

  3. Fitt 3: Emphasizes the fitt's symmetry and its pre-
  cisely synchronized time-scheme. Analyzes the temptation scenes, concluding that G's acceptance of the
  girdle is a breach of *trawþe*, and his confession in-
  valid (cf. item 739).

  4. Fitt 4: Points out parallels with Fitt 2 and eschatological motifs in the journey to the Green Chapel.
  Interprets the meeting with the GK as a scene of recognition, confession, and judgment; considers G's
  reincorporation into the society of Camelot.

  5. Conclusion: Discusses the testing of G; suggests that
  the poem combines romantic (older) and realistic
  (newer) modes; emphasizes its comic nature. (Cf.
  items 707, etc.).

  Appendixes deal with the pentangle (lines 625-29) and
  the geography of G's journey (lines 698-701).

  Reviews: Anon., *TLS*, 23 Dec. 1965, p. 1198.
  J. Boswinkel, *LT*, 242 (1967), 729-30.
  G.C. Britton and Betty Hill, *YWES*, 46 (1965),
  69-70.
  T.P. Dunning, C.M., *RES*, NS 18 (1967), 58-60.
  Arthur Heiserman, *MLQ*, 27 (1966), 449-57 (item
  870).
  Donald R. Howard, *Speculum*, 42 (1967), 518-21.
  P.M. Kean, *MAE*, 36 (1967), 92-93.
  Dieter Mehl, *Anglia*, 85 (1967), 82-90.
  Gordon M. Shedd, *MLR*, 63 (1968), 932-33.
  Rosemary Woolf, *CritQ*, 8 (1966), 383-84.

742. ————. "Two Notes on *SGGK*." *N&Q*, 217 (1972), 43-45.

  On lines 1304 and 2515.

743. ————. "Bards, Minstrels, and Men of Letters."
      Daiches/Thorlby, pp. 347-70.

      Includes an analysis of alliterative technique in *G*
      (pp. 357-59).

744. Butler, Norbert Patrick. "An Analysis of the Metrics
      of *SGGK*." Diss., Wisconsin, 1930.

745. Butturff, Douglas R. "Laughter and Discovered Aggres-
      sion in *SGGK*." *L&P*, 22 (1972), 139-49.

      Argues that the cruelty of the comedy makes the reader's
      laughter uneasy and encourages identification with G.

   * C., O.G.S. See item 764.

746. Campbell, Alphonsus M. "The Character of King Arthur in
      the ME Alliterative Poems." *RUO*, 45 (1975), 26-41.

      Presents a positive view of the character of Arthur in
      G (pp. 26-30). Cf. items 839, 1158, 1159, 1241.

747. Carrière, Jean Louise. "*SGGK* as a Christmas Poem."
      Comitatus, 1 (1970), 25-42.

      Argues that in being obliged to recognize his own im-
      perfection, G learns the true significance of Christmas.
      An appendix, by W[illiam] M[atthews] (pp. 40-42), inter-
      prets one of the MS illustrations (f. 125).

748. Carson, Mother Angela, O.S.U. "Morgain la Fée as the
      Principle of Unity in *GGK*." *MLQ*, 23 (1962), 3-16.

      Suggests that both young and old ladies are Morgain;
      that she is the most significant character in *G*, and
      functions to unify the plot. Cf. items 696, etc.

749. ————. "The Green Chapel: Its Meaning and Its Func-
      tion." *SP*, 60 (1963), 598-605. Rpt. in item 891.

      Argues that there is a sustained ambiguity between the
      two senses of *chapel*, "chapel" and "place of slaughter."

750. ————. "The GK's Name." *ELN*, 1 (1963), 84-90.

      Considers the meaning of *Bercilak de Hautdesert* (2445)
      and its significance for the poem.

751. Cavallo, Simonetta. "*SGGK*." Diss., Milano, 1969.

752. Chambers, E.K. *English Literature at the Close of the Middle Ages. Oxford History of English Literature*, II, 2. Ed. F.P. Wilson and Bonamy Dobrée. Oxford: Clarendon, 1945; 2nd, corr., ed., 1947.

Discusses the meaning of *caroles* (43, etc.) and of *coundutes* (1655) on pp. 75-76.

753. Chambers, R.W. *"Sir Gawayne and the Green Knight*, lines 697-702." *MLR*, 2 (1907), 167.

Comments on the geography of G's journey. Cf. items 792, 875, 1028.

754. Champion, Larry S. "Grace Versus Merit in *SGGK*." *MLQ*, 28 (1967), 413-25.

Argues that *G* reflects the contemporary debate as to whether salvation is achieved through divine grace or human merit; briefly discusses the other three poems.

755. Chapman, Coolidge Otis. "Ticius to Tuskan, *GGK*, line 11." *MLN*, 63 (1948), 59-60.

Contends that *Ticius* is a scribal error for *Turnus*.

756. ————. "Chaucer and the *G*-Poet: A Conjecture." *MLN*, 68 (1953), 521-24.

Suggests that the influence of *G* is reflected in the *Squire's Tale*. Cf. items 267, 991.

757. Chisnell, Robert Emmett. "Unconventionality and Irony: A Reading of *SGGK*." Diss., Auburn Univ., 1971. Abst.: *DAI*, 32 (1971), 910A.

758. Christmas, Peter. "A Reading of *SGGK*." *Neophil*, 58 (1974), 238-47.

Argues that G's failure is not major; considers the effect of laughter in the poem. Cf. items 916, 1201.

759. Christophersen, Paul. "The Englishness of *SGGK*." *On the Novel: A present for Walter Allen on his 60th birthday from his friends and colleagues*. Ed. B.S. Benedikz. London: Dent, 1971. Pp. 46-56.

Considers that despite the foreign origin of romance, G has close links with the native tradition going back to Anglo-Saxon poetry. Cf. item 789.

760.   Clark, Cecily. "The Green Knight Shoeless: A Reconsid-
       eration." *RES*, NS 6 (1955), 174-77.

       Glosses *scholes* (160) "shoeless."

761.   ————. "*SGGK*: Characterisation by Syntax." *EIC*, 16
       (1966), 361-74. Extract rpt. in item 827.

       Following item 1191, discusses the poet's use of syn-
       tactical variation to portray the characters of the GK/
       Bertilak, the Guide, and the Lady.

762.   ————. "*SGGK*: Its Artistry and its Audience." *MAE*, 40
       (1971), 10-20.

       Argues that the subtle use of linguistic nuances and
       parallels implies a sophisticated audience; discusses
       the meaning of line 1237.

  *   Clark, John W. See item 152.

763.   Coffer, Karin Boklund. "Myth, Code, Order: Transforma-
       tions in the Narrative Structure of Courtly Romance."
       Diss., Colorado, 1975. Abst.: *DAI*, 36 (1976), 5273A.

764.   Colgrave, Bertram. "Sir Gawayne's Green Chapel." *An-
       tiquity*, 12 (1938), 351-53.

       Suggests that the Green Chapel is a neolithic round or
       long barrow. Additional brief note by O.G.S. C[rawford].
       Cf. items 728, 781.

765.   Conley, John. "The Meaning of *fare* in *SGGK* 694." *N&Q*,
       202 (1957), 2.

       Glosses "going, way."

766.   Conner, J.E. "Phonemic Discrimination of ME Dialects."
       RKHS, 56, ii (1958), 17-32.

       Reference from item 1281, not verified. Item not seen,
       but believed to include phonemic analysis of *G*.

767.   Cook, Arthur Bernard. "The European Sky God: The Celts
       (cont.)." *F-L*, 17 (1906), 308-48, 427-53.

       Quotes the plot-summary from item 1252; relates the GK
       to the folk figures Viribius and the king of the wood
       (pp. 338-41, 427). Cf. items 1192, etc.

768.   Cook, James Rhodes. "Aesthetic and Religious Symbolism
       in *SGGK*." Diss., Georgia State, 1977. Abst.: *DAI*, 39
       (1978), 277A.

769. Cook, Robert G. "The Play-Element in *SGGK*." *TSE*, 13 (1963), 5-31.

Interprets various events in *G* (e.g., the challenge, the exchange of winnings, the temptations) in the light of the discussion of play in Huizinga's *Homo Ludens*. Cf. items 959, 1196, 1201.

770. Coomaraswamy, Ananda K. "*SGGK*: Indra and Namuci." *Speculum*, 19 (1944), 104-25.

Discusses parallels in Indian mythology and ritual to the motif of the beheading game in *G*.

771. Cottle, Basil. *The Triumph of English 1350-1400*. London: Blandford; New York: Barnes and Noble, 1969.

Some general observations; particular discussion of the use of second-person pronouns (pp. 279-85). Cf. items 816, etc.

772. Crane, John Kenny. "The Four Levels of Time in *SGGK*." *AnM*, 10 (1969), 65-80.

Considers the significance in *G* of the cosmic, historical, psychological, and sacred levels of time.

* C[rawford], O.G.S. See item 764.

773. Curley, Michael J. "A Note on Bertilak's Beard." *MP*, 73 (1975), 69-73.

Argues that traditional associations of the beaver (see *G* 845) may suggest the theme of debt-payment.

774. Curry, Walter Clyde. *The ME Ideal of Personal Beauty; as Found in the Metrical Romances, Chronicles, and Legends of the XIII, XIV, and XV Centuries*. Baltimore: Furst, 1916. Diss., Stanford, 1916.

Refers to various features of the GK (e.g., pp. 28, 37, 50, 66, 108, 114-16) and the Lady (e.g., pp. 66, 73-76, 113).

775. Cutler, John L. "The Versification of the '*G* Epigone' in Humfrey Newton's Poems." *JEGP*, 51 (1952), 562-70.

Includes comments on the stanza-form of *G*. Cf. items 1115, 1116.

776. d'Ardenne, S.R.T.O. "'The Green Count' and *SGGK*." *RES*, NS 10 (1959), 113-26.

Argues that the GK may have been modelled on the "Green
Count," Amadeus VI, Count of Savoy. Cf. items 700, 893.

777. Davenport, W.A. "A Study of the Word Order and Sentence
     Structure of *SGGK* with References to other poems of the
     North-West Midland Alliterative Group." M.A. thesis,
     London, 1957/8.

778. ————. "SG's Courteous 'Whoa!'" *ELN*, 11 (1973), 88–
     89.

     Provides evidence that *hoo* (2330) was a formal word,
     used for stopping combat.

779. ————. "The Word *Norne* and the Temptation of SG." *NM*,
     78 (1977), 256–63.

     Discusses the meaning and derivation of *norne*, and the
     textual and interpretative problems of 1760–72.

780. David, Alfred. "G and Aeneas." *ES*, 49 (1968), 402–09.

     Argues that lines 3–4 refer to Aeneas, and that the mix-
     ture of nobility and treachery is later paralleled in G.

781. Davies, R.T. "Gawayn and the Green Chapel." *N&Q*, 193
     (1948), 194.

     Questions the suggestion in item 728 that the Chapel is
     a barrow. (Cf. also item 764).

782. Davis, Norman. "*SGGK* 611–12." *N&Q*, 211 (1966), 448–51.

     Suggests reading *peruyng* (611) "periwinkle" and glossing
     trulofes (612) "quatrefoils."

783. ————. "*SGGK* 2073." *N&Q*, 215 (1970), 163–64.

     Discusses the syntax and meaning of *G* 2073a.

784. Day, Mabel. "The Word *Abloy* in *Sir Gawayne and the
     Green Knight*." *MLR*, 18 (1923), 337.

     Considers that this is a past participle lacking *-ed*.

  * ————. See also item 88.

785. Dean, Christopher. "*SGGK*, 2231–2232." *Expl*, 22 (1964),
     item 67.

     Suggests that these lines reflect a folk superstition.

786. ————. "The Temptation Scenes in *SGGK*." *LeedsSE*, NS
5 (1971), 1-12.

Argues that the sexual temptation is a stratagem to
throw G off his guard, so that the real temptation (to
accept the girdle) may succeed. Cf. items 1024, etc.

787. Delany, Paul. "The Role of the Guide in *SGGK*." *Neophil*, 49 (1965), 250-55. Rpt. in item 891.

An analysis of the Guide's temptation of G. Cf. item
1059.

788. Dendinger, Lloyd N. "The Dynamic Structural Balance of
SGGK." *Essays in Honor of Esmond Linworth Marilla*. Ed.
Thomas Austin Kirby and William John Olive. Baton Rouge:
Louisiana State UP, 1970. Pp. 367-78.

Argues that seeing the structure of G as tripartite
(with divisions at 841 and 1997) clarifies the definition of the two plots (challenge and temptation).

789. Diamond, Arlyn. "*SGGK*: An Alliterative Romance." *PQ*,
55 (1976), 10-29.

Suggests that G embodies two kinds of romance--the courtly continental tradition and the heroic alliterative
tradition--and that its meaning is generated by tension
between the two. Cf. item 759.

790. Dickins, Bruce. "A Yorkshire Chronicler (William of
Newburgh)." *TYDS*, 5, xxxv (1934), 15-26.

Mentions parallels to the GK in a story by this chronicler (p. 19).

791. ————. "Going at G." *TLS*, 6 Jan. 1966, p. 10.

Comments on Burrow's views (item 741) on fox-hunting in
G.

792. Dodgson, John McNeal. "SG's Arrival in Wirral." *Early
English and Norse Studies Presented to Hugh Smith in
Honour of His Sixtieth Birthday*. Ed. Arthur Brown and
Peter Foote. London: Methuen, 1963. Pp. 19-25.

Suggests that line 799 alludes to a legendary ford at
the mouth of the Dee estuary. Cf. items 753, etc.

793. Donaldson, E. Talbot. Introductory note to the tr. of
G in *Abrams*. Extract rpt. in item 827.

A brief account, which emphasizes the moral theme (pp. 183-84 in 1962 ed.).

794.   Donner, Morton. "Tact as a Criterion of Reality in *SGGK*." *PELL*, 1 (1965), 306-15.

Discusses G's tact in various awkward situations; suggests that these scenes are used to "flesh out" the narrative.

795.   Dossetor, R.F. "*GGK*": *The myth of an intuitive*. Guild of Pastoral Psychology: Guild Lecture, 15. London: Guide of Pastoral Psychology, 1942.

Maintains that *G* describes the progress towards integration and incarnation of a "feeling intuitive" (Jungian classification). Includes a lengthy summary with some loose translation. Cf. item 993.

796.   Dove, Mary. "G and the *Blasme des Femmes* Tradition." *MAE*, 46 (1972), 20-26.

A discussion of lines 2414-28; cites earlier works in which G is associated with anti-feminism. Cf. items 1025, etc.

797.   Dowden, P.J. "*Sir Gawayne and the Green Knight*." *MLR*, 44 (1949), 229.

Mentions two books, of relevance to the pentangle, in the library of John of Erghome (cf. item 149).

798.   Duncan, Patricia Jean. "From Folklore to Archetype: Analyses of Four ME Romances." Diss., New York State (Albany), 1976. Abst.: *DAI*, 37 (1976), 3606A.

Includes material on *G*.

799.   Dunn, Thomas Peckham. "Comic Effect in *SGGK*." Diss., Cincinnati, 1972. Abst.: *DAI*, 33 (1973), 3581A.

800.   Dykstra, Timothy Eugene. "Humor in the ME Metrical Romances." Diss., Ohio State, 1975. Abst.: *DAI*, 36 (1976), 5313A.

Includes material on *G*.

801.   Eadie, J. "Morgan la Fée and the Conclusion of *SGGK*." *Neophil*, 52 (1968), 299-304.

Sees the reference to Morgan as a reminder of the continuing conflict between good and evil. Cf. items 696,
etc.

802. Eagan, Joseph F., S.J. "The Import of Color Symbolism
      in *SGGK*." *SLUS*, ser. A, 1 (Nov. 1949), 12-86.

      Summarizes medieval color symbolism, reviewing the sig-
      nificance of individual colors. Argues that *G* repre-
      sents both a literal test of chivalric virtues and a
      satirical reflection on the false values of contemporary
      romance. Specifies the function of colors in the poem,
      concluding that its meaning is reinforced by the use of
      traditional color symbolism. Cf. items 714, 1118.

803. Edwards, A.S.G. "*SGGK*, 250-255 and 2239-40." *Expl*, 29
      (1971), item 73.

      Discusses the parallel phrasing of lines 252 and 2240.

804. Ekwall, Eilert. "A few notes on English etymology and
      word-history." *AnglB*, 29 (1918), 195-201.

      Includes a note on *strothe* (1710).

805. Elliott, Ralph W.V. "*SG* in Staffordshire: A Detective
      Essay in Literary Geography." *Times*, 21 May 1958, p.
      12. Rpt. in item 827.

      Identifies sites for the castle and the Green Chapel,
      near Dieulacres Abbey, North Staffordshire. Cf. items
      88, 97, 276, 921, 924.

806. ————. "Some Northern Landscape Features in *SGGK*."
      *Iceland and the Mediaeval World: Studies in Honour of Ian
      Maxwell*. Ed. Gabriel Turville-Petre and John Stanley
      Martin. Melbourne: [Univ. of Melbourne Press], 1974.
      Pp. 132-43.

      Observes that topographical vocabulary derived from ON
      is used more extensively in particular and realistic
      passages than in general and romantic ones. Specific
      comments on the following lines: 507, 699-701, 723, 1074,
      1421, 1430, 1431, 1466, 1568-71, 1709, 1710-11, 2077-83,
      2144, 2162, 2167, 2173-74, 2183, 2222; and *Pe* 57, 115,
      860. Cf. items 116, etc.

807. Embler, Weller B. "The Sanity of True Literature."
      CEA, 26, viii (May 1964), 1, 3-4.

Summarizes the story; praises the literary truth of G.

808. Emerson, Oliver Farrar. "Two Notes on SGGK." MLN, 36
      (1921), 212-15.

      Glosses scholes (160) "shoeless"; discusses and trans-
      lates lines 864-74.

809. ————. "Notes on SGGK." JEGP, 21 (1922), 363-410.

      Notes on the following lines: 28, 33, 46, 55, 60, 62,
      63, 67, 68, 72, 74-80, 88, 98, 113, 118, 132-33, 144,
      149, 152-60, 178, 180, 184, 185, 221, 229, 262, 267,
      271, 296, 305, 310, 372, 380, 420, 435, 440, 460, 465,
      472, 478, 488, 504, 508, 513, 518, 531, 537, 563, 568,
      577, 599, 613, 635, 660, 681, 683, 723, 726, 729, 745,
      750, 751, 762, 769, 777, 790, 795, 798, 820, 821, 841,
      849, 863, 884, 890, 932, 941-42, 943, 945, 946, 958,
      965, 985, 992, 1006, 1009, 1012, 1032, 1038, 1060, 1068-
      70, 1072, 1074, 1092, 1096, 1100, 1114, 1116, 1150,
      1153, 1157, 1158, 1161, 1167, 1168, 1169, 1170, 1175,
      1177, 1183, 1199, 1206, 1210, 1215, 1224, 1238, 1250,
      1256, 1265-66, 1283-87, 1293, 1301, 1304, 1315, 1328,
      1329, 1333, 1336, 1345, 1356, 1358, 1360, 1381, 1386,
      1399, 1403, 1407, 1421, 1422, 1423, 1426, 1440, 1444,
      1445, 1452, 1463, 1476, 1480, 1481-84, 1512, 1514, 1515,
      1523, 1561-66, 1570, 1573, 1580, 1590, 1593, 1603, 1604,
      1623, 1627, 1634, 1639, 1648, 1666, 1680, 1699-1700,
      1704, 1706, 1710, 1711, 1713, 1722, 1727, 1729, 1734,
      1736, 1738, 1750, 1755, 1769, 1770, 1780, 1796, 1805,
      1825, 1826, 1830, 1833, 1847, 1859, 1863, 1868, 1875,
      1895, 1902, 1915, 1941, 1946, 1956, 1958, 1964, 1968,
      1970, 1972, 1975, 1999, 2026, 2032, 2035, 2053, 2071,
      2082, 2084, 2103, 2111, 2123, 2140, 2167, 2173, 2177,
      2181, 2189, 2207, 2251, 2263, 2274, 2275, 2294, 2297,
      2305, 2312, 2316, 2326, 2337, 2344, 2346, 2350, 2354,
      2370, 2379-80, 2387, 2396, 2409, 2411, 2422-26, 2431,
      2447, 2448, 2452, 2460, 2461, 2494.

*   ————. See also items 167, 414, 598.

810. Engelhardt, George J. "The Predicament of G." MLQ, 16
      (1955), 218-25. Rpt. in item 350.

      Discusses G's failure to live up to the values of the
      pentangle--symbolized by the substitution of the green
      girdle for the "endless knot." Cf. items 741, 814, 821,
      896, 1039.

811. Enkvist, Nils Erik. *The Seasons of the Year: Chapters*
      on a Motif from "Beowulf" to the "Shepherd's Calendar."
      Societas Scientiarum Fennica: Commentationes Humanorum
      Litterarum, XXII, 4. Helsingfors, 1957.

      Praises the description of the changing seasons in lines
      500-35 (pp. 85-87). Cf. item 1171.

*   Enomoto, Tsuneya. See item 1312.

812. Evans, W.O. "The Five Virtues of Gawayn's Shield and
      their contemporary equivalents." B.Litt. thesis, Oxford,
      1959.

813. ———. "G's New Pentangle." *Trivium*, 3 (1968), 92-94.

      Interprets line 636 to mean that G had newly adopted the
      pentangle.

814. ———. "The Case for SG Re-opened." *MLR*, 68 (1973),
      721-33.

      While acknowledging that G has to recognize his own fal-
      libility, argues that many critics are excessively harsh
      in their judgments of him. Cf. items 810, etc.

815. Evans, William W., Jr. "The Second-Person Pronoun in
      SGGK." Diss., Florida, 1959. Abst.: *DA*, 24 (1964),
      4184.

816. ———, William W. [Jr.]. "Dramatic Use of the Second-Per-
      son Singular Pronoun in *SGGK*." *SN*, 39 (1967), 38-45.

      Emphasizes the subtlety with which the choice of pronoun
      underlines the speaker's attitude to the person ad-
      dressed. Cf. items 771, 915, 1020.

817. Everett, Dorothy. "A Characterization of the English
      Medieval Romances." *E&S*, 15 (1929), 98-121.

      Comments on the use of hunting terms (p. 103) and the
      poet's descriptive power (p. 112).

*   ———. See also item 170.

818. F., J.R. "The Five Wounds." *N&Q*, 171 (1936), 335-36.

      Further comments on line 642. Cf. items 697, etc.

*   F., T.G. See T.G. F[oster], item 826.

819. Farley-Hills, D[avid] L. "Poetic Structure, and its re-
      lation to Meaning, in *SGGK*." B.Litt. thesis, Oxford,
      1961.

820. ———, David [L.]. "G's Fault in *SGGK*." *RES*, NS 14
      (1963), 124-31. Rpt. in item 891.

      Argues that *couetyse* (2374, etc.) should be understood
      not in its literal sense, but as the broad concept of
      Augustinian tradition. Cf. item 740; also items 810,
      etc. (Note: the author's name is printed as David
      Farley Hills, but is here normalized to the form in
      which it appears elsewhere.)

821. Field, P.J.C. "A Rereading of *SGGK*." *SP*, 68 (1971),
      255-69.

      Takes issue with Burrow's estimate of G's sinfulness
      (items 739, 741), emphasizing that the withholding of
      the girdle is venial, not mortal, sin. Cf. items 810,
      etc.

822. Figgins, Robert Harrison. "The Character of G in ME
      Romance." Diss., Washington, 1973. Abst.: *DAI*, 34
      (1973), 2556A.

823. Fletcher, P.C.B. "SG's Anti-Feminism." *Theoria*, 36
      (1971), 53-58.

      Suggests that in lines 2414-28 G is rejecting the fem-
      inine (courtly) aspects of chivalry. Cf. items 1025,
      etc.

824. Förster, Max. "Der Name des GK." *Archiv*, 147 (1924),
      194-96.

      Favors the form *Bercilak*; discusses the meaning and der-
      ivation of *Hautdesert*.

825. Foley, Michael M. "G's Two Confessions Reconsidered."
      ChauR, 9 (1974), 73-79.

      Argues that G is guilty not of mortal sin but of a minor
      contravention of the knightly code. Cf. items 739, etc.

826. F[oster], T.G. "The Revised Text of *Sir Gawayne and the
      Green Knight*." *MLQ* (Lon), 1 (1897), 53-55.

      A review of the 1897 revision of item 100. Makes spe-
      cific points on lines 156-57, 1114, 1497, 1540.

827. Fox, Denton, ed. *Twentieth Century Interpretations of
      "SGGK": A Collection of Critical Essays.* Twentieth Cen-
      tury Interpretations ser. Englewood Cliffs, N.J.:
      Prentice-Hall, Spectrum, 1968.

      Fox's introductory essay provides general comments on
      the poet and the alliterative revival, and a brief cri-
      tical account of *G*. Other contents are as follows:
      items 805, 887, 1001, 1192, 1259; extracts from items
      170, 706, 719, 741; brief extracts from items 675, 761,
      793, 957, 1272.

      Review: S.S. Hussey, *N&Q*, 214 (1969), 225-26.

828. Frankis, P.J. "*SGGK*, line 35: *with lel lettres loken.*"
      N&Q, 206 (1961), 329-30.

      Glosses "enclosed in true letters, embodied in truthful
      words."

829. Friedman, Albert B. "Morgan le Fay in *SGGK*." *Speculum*,
      35 (1960), 260-74. Rpt. in item 132.

      Rejects the views of Baughan (item 696). Regards the
      poet's use of Morgan as a flaw, and suggests that this
      reflects the difficulties he encountered in combining
      the two stories. Cf. items 696, etc.

830. ————, and Richard H. Osberg. "G's Girdle as Tradi-
      tional Symbol." *JAF*, 90 (1977), 301-15.

      Relates the girdle to tradition in both folklore and
      literature, emphasizing its ancient magical associations
      and clear sexual connotations. Cf. item 992.

831. Fry, Nancy Mallet. "A Study of Play and Festivity in
      Literature: Four Essays." Diss., Yale, 1975. Abst.:
      DAI, 36 (1975), 8032A.

      Contains material on *G*.

832. Gaffney, A.C. "An Analysis of Certain Romance Elements
      in *SGGK*." M.A. thesis, Cardiff, 1969/70.

833. Gallagher, Joseph E. "*Trawþe* and *Luf-Talkyng* in *SGGK*."
      NM, 78 (1977), 362-76.

      Analyzes the temptation scenes; argues that G must even-
      tually refuse the Lady unequivocally, since *luf-talkyng*
      is contrary to the *trawþe* defined by the pentangle. Cf.
      items 1024, etc.

834.   Gallant, Gerald. "The Three Beasts: Symbols of Tempta-
        tion in *SGGK*." *AnM*, 11 (1970), 35-50.

        Considering the relationship between hunts and tempta-
        tions, suggests that each animal represents a sinful
        mode of behavior: the deer, youthful passion; the boar,
        lust and malice; the fox, fraudulence. Cf. items 1127,
        etc.

835.   Ganim, John M. "Disorientation, Style, and Conscious-
        ness in *SGGK*." *PMLA*, 91 (1976), 376-84.

        Discusses the poet's technique of undermining his own
        statements, thus disorienting his audience and challeng-
        ing their perceptions. Cf. item 897.

836.   Garrett, Robert Max. "The Lay of *Sir Gawayne and the
        Green Knight*." *JEGP*, 24 (1925), 125-34.

        Considers the features *G* has in common with the Breton
        lais. Cf. item 1184.

837.   Gilbert, A.J. "A New Analogue for *SGGK*." *NM*, 77 (1976),
        365-68.

        Specifies parallels in *Karlamagnus saga ok kappa hans*.
        Cf. items 1155, 1214, 1222.

838.   Gillie, Christopher. *Character in English Literature*.
        London: Chatto; New York: Barnes and Noble, 1965.

        Comments on the GK's character. Sees *G* as about the
        conflict between civilization and nature (cf. items 840,
        etc.).

839.   Göller, Karl Heinz. *König Arthur in der Englischen Lit-
        eratur des Späten Mittelalters*. Palaestra, 238. Gött-
        ingen: Vandenhoeck und Ruprecht, 1963.

        Contrasts the youthful and spirited Arthur in *G* to the
        middle-aged figure of French romance (pp. 99-101). Cf.
        items 758, etc.

840.   Goldhurst, William. "The Green and the Gold: The Major
        Theme of *GGK*." *CE*, 20 (1958), 61-65.

        Suggests that *G* is about the conflict between natural
        forces and courtly civilization—symbolized by green and
        gold respectively. Cf. items 838, 892, 1220.

841. Gollancz, I[srael]. "Gringolet, G's Horse." *Saga-Book*,
      5 (1907), 104-09.

      Mentions the occurrence of the name in *G*.

842. ————, Sir Israel. "Chivalry in Medieval English Po-
      etry." *Chivalry: A Series of Studies to Illustrate Its
      Historical Significance and Civilizing Influence by Mem-
      bers of King's College, London*. Ed. Edgar Prestage.
      London: Kegan Paul; New York: Knopf, 1928. Pp. 167-81.

      Sees *G* as a poem in praise of chivalry (pp. 175-78).
      Cf. items 686, etc.

843. Grattan, J.H.G. Review of item 111. *RES*, 1 (1925),
      484-87.

      Offers suggestions on lines 113, 352, 372, 473, 504,
      783, 1009, 1109, 1161, 1174, 1368, 1440, 1595, 1726.

844. Gray, D. "*SGGK*." *N&Q*, 203 (1958), 487-88.

      Argues for emending *more* to *innore* (649).

845. Green, D.H. "Irony and Medieval Romance." *FMLS*, 6
      (1970), 49-64. Rpt. in *Arthurian Romance: Seven Essays*,
      ed. D.D.R. Owen. London and Edinburgh: Scottish Aca-
      demic Press; New York: Barnes and Noble, 1971.

      Discusses the function of irony in a number of romances
      including *G*. Cf. item 897.

846. Green, Richard Hamilton. "G's Shield and the Quest for
      Perfection." *ELH*, 29 (1962), 121-39. Rpt. in items
      132 and 350.

      Suggests that the comic tone of this serious poem modi-
      fies the hero's stature in accord with the tastes
      of an age of satire. Provides a detailed discussion of
      the symbolic significance of G's shield. Cf. items 707,
      etc.

847. Greg, W.W. "*SGGK*." *TLS*, 8 Feb. 1941, p. 67.

      On the spelling of *Bertilak*.

848. Gross, Laila. "Time in the Towneley Cycle, *King Horn*,
      SGGK, and Chaucer's *Troilus and Criseyde*." Diss., Toron-
      to, 1967. Abst.: *DA*, 29 (1969), 3097A.

849. ———. "Telescoping in Time in *SGGK*." *OL*, 24 (1969), 130-37.

Discusses the technique of "telescoping" time from the general to the particular.

850. ———. "G's Acceptance of the Girdle." *AN&Q*, 12 (1974), 154-55.

Observes that wearing a magic object in single combat contravenes the chivalric code (cf. item 954).

851. Guest, Edwin. *A History of English Rhythms*. 2 vols. London: Pickering, 1838. Rev., in 1 vol., by Walter W. Skeat, London: Bell, 1882.

Prints the text of *G* 1126-77 marked to indicate rhythmic patterns, with parallel translation and a few general comments (1st ed., II, 166-70; rev. ed., pp. 458-63).

852. Gunn, Alan M.F. "The Polylithic Romance: With Pages of Illustrations." *Studies in Medieval [,] Renaissance [and] American Literature: a Festschrift: Honoring Troy C. Crenshaw [,] Lorraine Sherky [and] Ruth Speer Angel*. Ed. Betsy Feagan Colquitt. Fort Worth: Texas Christian Univ. Press, 1971. Pp. 1-18.

Designates *G* a romance of wonder and mystery (pp. 3, 11-16).

853. Habicht, Werner. "*SGGK*: Die individuellen Gebärden." *Die Gebarde in englischen Dichtungen des Mittelalters*. Bayerische Akademie der Wissenschaften: philosophisch-historische klasse: abhandlungen, neue folge, 46. München: Beck, 1959. Pp. 148-56.

Discusses the poet's use of individual gestures to fill out his characters. Elsewhere in the book comments on the GK's gestures (pp. 60-61) and on courtly lifestyle (pp. 105-07); various passing references.

854. Haines, Victor Yelverton. "Morgan and the Missing Day in *SGGK*." *MS*, 33 (1971), 354-59.

Suggests that G (possibly the victim of Morgan's magical powers) slept through the "missing day" of 28 December (cf. item 1247).

855. ———. "Allusions to the *felix culpa* in the Prologue of *SGGK*." *RUO*, 44 (1974), 158-77.

Argues that *G* is figural of the *felix culpa*, and that
this is suggested in the first stanza--of which a detailed explication is provided. Cf. item 1175.

856. ———. "*SGGK*: As *Figura of the Felix Culpa*." Diss.,
     McGill Univ., 1975. Abst.: *DAI*, 36 (1976), 6703A-04A.

857. ———. "When G Sins?" *RUO*, 46 (1976), 242-46.

     Discusses the nature and timing of G's fault in accept-
     ing the girdle. Cf. items 739, etc.

858. Halpern, R[ichard] A[vram]. "The Last Temptation of *G*:
     Hony Soyt Qui Mal Pence." *ABR*, 23 (1972), 353-84.

     Argues that G's final temptation is to accept Bertilak's
     estimate of his conduct. G sees taking the girdle as
     "spiritual fornication": Camelot sees the girdle as sig-
     nifying prowess. The motto restates the poem's theme:
     the contrast between true and false evaluation. Cf.
     item 735.

859. ———, Richard Avram. "Spiritual Vision and the City
     of God in *SGGK*." Diss., Princeton, 1976. Abst.: *DAI*,
     37 (1977), 6471A-72A.

860. Halstead, W.L. "Artifice in *SG*." *A Chaucerian Puzzle
     and other Medieval Essays*. Ed. Natalie Grimes Lawrence
     and Jack A. Reynolds. Univ. of Miami Pubs. in English
     and American Literature, 5. Coral Gables, Fla.: Univ.
     of Miami Press, 1961. Pp. 63-70.

     A general critical reading, with emphasis on the poet's
     artistry.

861. Halverson, John. "Template Criticism: *SGGK*." *MP*, 67
     (1969), 133-39.

     Discusses "template criticism" (i.e., the imposition on
     a work of an existing pattern); concentrates on items
     1033 and 1185.

862. Hamilton, George L. "*Capados* and the Date of *Sir Gawayne
     and the Green Knight*." *MP*, 5 (1908), 365-76.

     Argues that evidence of the use of this word suggests
     that *G* was written between 1348 and 1377.

863. Harada, Haruo. "The Vocabulary of *SGGK*." *HSELL*, 8
     (1961), 92-113.

Specifies and discusses "alliterative words," "poetic words," and ON words. In English.

864. Hare, Kenneth. "*SGGK*." *TLS*, 6 Sept. 1923, p. 588.

Opposes the emendation of MS *sage* (531) to *fage* (cf. items 1070, etc.).

865. Hargest-Gorzelak, Anna. "A Brief Comparison of the *Knight's Tale* and *SGGK*." *RH*, 15, iii (1967), 91-102.

Suggests that symmetry serves a more organic purpose in *G* than in the *Knight's Tale*.

866. Hark, Ina Rae. "G's Passive Quest." *Comitatus*, 5 (1974), 1-13.

Points out that G's quest is passive, in that he goes not to fight but to submit to a blow.

867. Harris, V. "Bertilak the Fox: A reassessment of the character of the GK." *StEng*, no. 3 (Dec. 1972), 1-18.

Argues that the conduct of Bertilak and Morgan is treacherous and unfair. Analyzes the hunting and temptation scenes. Concludes that Bertilak is a human fox--cowardly and treacherous. Cf. items 723, 1206.

868. Haworth, Mary. "*Barlay--SGGK* (line 296)." *N&Q*, 204 (1959), 104.

Glosses "my turn now!"

869. Haworth, Paul. "*Warthe* in *SGGK*." *N&Q*, 212 (1967), 171-72.

Suggests glossing "ford."

870. Heiserman, Arthur. "G's Clean Courtesy, or, The Task of Telling of True Love." *MLQ*, 27 (1966), 449-57.

A review article, which discusses items 706 and 741.

871. Henderson, Hamish. "The Green Man of Knowledge." *ScS*, 2 (1958), 47-85.

Contains a version of folktale no. 313 in the Aarne-Thompson classification. Motifs which the tale has in common with *G* are discussed on pp. 73-80. Cf. item 893.

872. Henry, Avril. "Temptation and Hunt in *SGGK*." *MAE*, 45 (1976), 187-99.

Suggests reading the symbolic relationship between temptations and hunts "vertically" instead of "horizontally":
thus the correspondence is of progressive diminution
and reduction of dignity. Cf. items 1127, etc.

873. Herzog, Michael Bernard. "The Development of G as a
Literary Figure in Medieval German and English Arthurian
Romance." Diss., Washington, 1971. Abst.: *DAI*, 32
(1972), 6377A-78A.

874. Heyworth, P.L. "Notes on Two Uncollected ME Proverbs."
N&Q, 215 (1970), 86-88.

Includes discussion of lines 1531-34.

875. ————. "SG's Crossing of Dee." *MAE*, 41 (1972), 124-
27.

Provides evidence to support the view that lines 698-
701 refer to fording the Dee. Cf. items 753, etc.

876. Hieatt, A. Kent. "*SG*: Pentangle, *Luf-Lace*, Numerical
Structure." *PLL*, 4 (1968), 339-59. Rpt., in somewhat
modified form, in *Silent Poetry: Essays in numerological
analysis*, ed. Alastair Fowler. London: Routledge, 1970.

Argues that the pentangle and the lace form a symbolic
structure of opposites (imperfection being signified by
the lace's need for a knot). Goes on to propose various
patterns--in particular, parallels between Fitts I and
IV, and within Fitt III, and the use of five (or a multiple thereof) plus one to symbolize imperfection. Cf.
items 206, etc.

877. Hieatt, Constance B. "The Rhythm of the Alliterative
Long Line." *Robbins*, pp. 119-30.

Ideas (developed from Pope's analysis of OE verse) are
illustrated mainly with lines from *G*.

878. Highfield, J.R.L. "The Green Squire." *MAE*, 22 (1953),
18-23.

Suggests that the GK may have been modelled on Simon
Newton, the "Green Squire."

879. Hill, Archibald A. "The GK's castle and the translators." *CJL*, 17 (1972), 140-58.

Compares the treatment of lines 794-802 in items 8, 32,
76, 77, 81, 102, 104, 105, 107, 110, 116, and 117, and

in the notes to item 4. Discusses specific problems
and general principles. Cf. item 1238.

880. Hill, Laurita Lyttleton. "Madden's Divisions of *SG* and
the 'Large Initial Capitals' of Cotton Nero A.X." *Speculum*, 21 (1946), 67-71.

Questions the traditional fourfold division of *G*, suggesting that the nine initial capitals may mark stages
in the narrative. Cf. items 715, 1236.

*   Hills, David Farley. See Farley-Hills, David.

881. Hiraoka, Teruaki. "Some Notes on the Language of *Sir
Gawayn and the Grene Knyght.*" *SETG*, 3 (1968), 69-81; 5
(1970), 41-47.

Grammatical description of nouns, pronouns, adjectives,
and verbs. Also comments on syntax, spelling, and
sound. In Japanese.

882. ————. "An Analysis of the Language of *Sir Gawayn and
the Greene Knyght.*" *Mimesis*, 5 (1973), 29-33.

Discusses alliteration and rhyme. In Japanese.

883. ————. "Studies in ME: West-Midland Dialect Analysis
of the Language of *Sir Gawayn and the Greene Knight.*"
SETC, 11 (1976), 119-45.

Provides an etymological classification of the poem's
vocabulary. In Japanese.

884. Hirose, Taizo. "Synonyms for 'Man' and 'Woman' in
SGGK." *SBK*, no. 38 (1962), 1-13.

Analyzes nouns (and some substantive adjectives) meaning
"knight" and "lady"; considers the restrictions imposed
by alliteration. In Japanese. Cf. items 731, etc.

885. Hodgart, M.J.C. "In the Shade of the Golden Bough."
TC, 157 (1955), 111-19.

Includes an attack on item 1192 (pp. 116-17).

886. Holthausen, F. "Zu *SGGK.*" *AnglB*, 35 (1924), 32.

A note on lines 530-31.

887. Howard, Donald R. "Structure and Symmetry in *SG.*" *Speculum*, 39 (1964), 425-33. Rpt. in items 132, 827, and
891.

Discusses the juxtaposition of shield and girdle, suggesting that this symbolizes conflict between Christian-
ity and chivalry. Specifies parallels between Fitt IV
and Fitts II and III; endorses fourfold division. Cf.
items 1098, etc.

888.   ————. "Chivalry and the Pride of Life: *SGGK.*" *The
Three Temptations: Medieval Man in Search of the World.*
Princeton: UP; London: Oxford UP, 1966. Pp. 215-54.

The book discusses three poems in relation to the "three
temptations": Troilus to lust of the flesh, *Piers Plowman* to lust of the eyes, and G to the pride of life.
G's failure is analyzed in terms of the conflict, inherent in chivalry, between worldly and Christian values.
Emphasizes, however, that the hero's dilemma is presented in a comic spirit.

Reviews: R.T. Davies, *RES*, NS 18 (1967), 236-37.
        John Gardner, *JEGP*, 66 (1967), 249-54.

889.   ————. "*SGGK.*" *Recent ME Scholarship and Criticism:
Survey and Desiderata.* Ed. J. Burke Severs. Pittsburgh:
Duquesne UP, 1971. Pp. 29-54.

Provides a comprehensive review of writings since Bloomfield's survey (item 716) in 1961; suggests some areas
and approaches still relatively neglected. Cf. also
item 682.

890.   ————. "Renaissance World-Alienation." *The Darker Vi-
sion of the Renaissance: Beyond the Fields of Reason.*
Ed. Robert S. Kinsman. U.C.L.A. Center for Medieval
and Renaissance Studies Contributions, 6. Berkeley, Los
Angeles, and London: Univ. of California Press, 1974.
Pp. 47-76.

Suggests that the account of G's journey exemplifies
world-alienation (pp. 63-69).

891.   ————, and Christian Zacher, ed. *Critical Studies of
"SGGK."* Notre Dame and London: Univ. of Notre Dame
Press, 1968.

Contains items 707, 716, 721, 740, 749, 787, 820, 887,
932, 957, 967, 992, 993, 1026, 1109, 1171, 1188, 1258;
extracts from items 706, 719, 1191; Gardner's review of
item 706.

Reviews: S.S. Hussey, *N&Q*, 215 (1970), 471-72.
        P.B. Taylor, *ES*, 53 (1972), 154-56.

892. Hughes, Derek W. "The Problem of Reality in *SGGK*."
      UTQ, 40 (1971), 217-35.

      Argues that the poet explores the contrast between arti-
      ficial customs and false values (Camelot) on the one
      hand, and Christian natural law on the other. Cf. items
      840, etc.

893. Hulbert, J[ames] R. "*Syr Gawayn and the Grene Knyȝt*."
      MP, 13 (1915-16), 433-62, 689-730.

      1. Compares the Beheading Game in *G* with the versions in
         various analogues.

      2. Argues that the poet changed *G* from a story of the
         "fairy mistress" type into a test of loyalty.

      3. Specifies that the Green Chapel is a place haunted by
         evil spirits.

      4. Suggests that *G* may be associated with the founding
         of the Order of the Collar by Amedeo VI of Savoy, the
         "Green Count." (Cf. items 700, 776).

      5. Discusses the pentangle, pointing out that it may be
         an amulet.

      Conclusions: that *G* is derived from a single primitive
      tale and is not associated with the foundation of the
      Order of the Garter. Cf. items 934, etc.

894. ————. "The Name of the GK: Bercilak or Bertilak."
      The Manly Anniversary Studies in Language and Literature.
      Chicago: UP, 1923. Pp. 12-19.

      Suggests that the poet derived the name *Bertilak* from
      the Vulgate Cycle. Considers MS *Bercilak* a scribal mis-
      reading.

895. ————, James R. "A Hypothesis Concerning the Allitera-
      tive Revival." *MP*, 28 (1931), 405-22.

      Mentions parallels to *G* in Northern chronicles; suggests
      ꞏthat *Hautdesert* could be derived from the Castle Beau-
      desert, Warwickshire (pp. 417-20).

896. Hunt, Tony. "G's fault and the moral perspectives of
      SGGK." *Trivium*, 10 (1975), 1-18.

      Endorses Field's view (item 821) of G's sin and empha-
      sizes the mitigating circumstances of the acceptance of
      the girdle. Cf. items 810, etc.

897. ————. "Irony and Ambiguity in *SGGK*." *FMLS*, 12
      (1976), 1-16.

      Discusses the use of irony in comment and ambiguity in
      treatment of character and situation; suggests that this
      inhibits the reader from making simple or absolute judg-
      ments. (Cf. items 835, 845).

898. Hussey, S.S. "*SG* and Romance Writing." *SN*, 40 (1968),
      161-74.

      Illustrates the subtlety and restraint with which the
      poet handles the stock material and language of romance.
      Emphasizes the poem's seriousness.

899. Ikegami, Tadahiro. "G and the Arthurian Legend." *Lit-
      erature: Keio University Centennial Essays*. Ed. the
      Department of Literature, Keio Univ. Tokyo: Keio Univ.,
      1958. Pp. 143-70. English sum. on p. 171.

      Discusses the treatment of the life of G in medieval
      Arthurian literature.

900. ————. "The GK and the Beheading Game." *GeibunK*, no.
      11 (1960), 1-14.

      Considers the beheading game in relation to its ana-
      logues; discusses the role of the GK. In Japanese. Cf.
      items 934, etc.

901. ————. "On the 'temptation' in *SGGK*." *GeibunK*, nos.
      14-15 (Studies in Honour of Professor Junzaburo Nishi-
      waki), (1962), 62-75.

      An analysis of the function of the temptation scenes.
      In Japanese. Cf. items 1024, etc.

902. ————. "Nature in *SGGK*." *SEL*, 40 (1964), 1-15. Eng-
      lish sum. in *SEL*, English No., 1964, pp. 100-01.

      Praises the originality of the nature descriptions;
      suggests that nature functions both to test G and to
      reflect his state of mind. Cf. items 166, etc.

903. ————. "Courtesy in *SGGK*." *EBS*, 3, viii (1968), 38-
      41.

      Considers G's courtesy in the temptation scenes. In
      Japanese.

*   Isaacs, Neil D. See item 104.

904. Ito, Eiko. "'More Like a Passive' or 'Not Quite a Pas-
      sive': A Study of the Periphrastic Construction 'Be +
      the Past Participle' in SGGK." BKK, no. 10 (1971), 143-
      59.

      A description of syntactic elements used in G to imply
      agency or immediacy. In English.

905. Ito, Masayoshi. "Color and Nature in SGGK." Shiron,
      no. 6 (1964), 1-16.

      Discusses color imagery with reference to the poet's
      view of nature. In English. Cf. items 714, 802.

906. J., G.P. "The Author of SGGK." N&Q, 201 (1956), 53-54.

      Speculates that the poet may have been associated with
      Whalley Abbey.

907. Jackson, Isaac. "SGGK. Considered as a 'Garter' Poem."
      Anglia, 37 (1913), 393-423.

      Gives 1362 as the date of composition. Identifies the
      castle as Castle Beeston (Cheshire), the feast at Came-
      lot as a Garter feast, G as the Black Prince, and the
      girdle as the wedding favor of his wife Joan. Cf. items
      103, 893, 1136.

908. ———, I[saac]. "SG's Coat of Arms." MLR, 15 (1920),
      77-79.

      Suggests an Irish source for the portrayal of the Virgin
      in G's shield.

909. ———. "SG's Coat of Arms." MLR, 17 (1922), 289-90.

      Expresses reservations about the suggestion in item 908.

910. ———, Isaac. "GGK (A Note on fade, line 149)." N&Q,
      195 (1950), 24.

      Glosses "elvish."

911. Jacobs, Nicolas. "G's False Confession." ES, 51 (1970),
      433-35.

      Considers the confession in the light of conflict be-
      tween courtly and Christian values. Cf. items 739, etc.

912. Jahrmann, Gertrud. "Syr Gawayne and the Grene Knyght
      und Stuckens Gawân." NS, 26 (1919), 405-23.

Compares the form, content, and ideas of *G* with those of the 1902 stage adaptation by Eduard Stucken. Cf. item 961.

913. Jambeck, Thomas J. "The Syntax of Petition in *Beowulf* and *SGGK*." *Style*, 7 (1973), 21-29.

A comparative analysis of the speeches of petition of Beowulf to Hrothgar (*Beowulf* 407-32) and of G to Arthur (*G* 343-61).

914. Innes, Bridget   "*Pernyng* in *SGGK*, Line 611." *N&Q*, 206 (1961), 9.

Relates the word to *pirn* "reel, bobbin," and glosses "flitting."

915. Johnston, Everett C. "The Significance of the Pronoun of Address in *SGGK*." *LangQ*, 5, iii-iv (1967), 34-36.

Reviews the use of second-person pronouns, emphasizing the correctness of G's usage. Cf. items 816, etc.

*   Johnston, R.C. See item 1081.

916. Jones, Edward Trostle. "The Sound of Laughter in *SGGK*." *MS*, 31 (1969), 343-45.

Considers the human and social function of the laughter in *G* 2514. Cf. items 758, 1201.

917. Jones, Gwyn. *Kings [,] Beasts [,] and Heroes*. London, New York, and Toronto: Oxford UP, 1972.

Discusses the boar-hunt (pp. 103-05, 110).

*   ————. See also item 720.

918. Jones, Shirley Jean. "*SGGK*: Its Magic, Myth, and Ritual." Diss., Oklahoma, 1966. Abst.: *DA*, 26 (1966), 6696-97.

919. Käsmann, Hans. "Numerical Structure in Fitt III of *SGGK*." *Robbins*, pp. 131-39.

Suggests patterning in the proportion of lines describing hunts to those describing scenes in the castle. Cf. items 206, etc.

920. Kane, George. *ME Literature: A Critical Study of the Romances, the Religious Lyrics and "Piers Plowman."* London: Methuen, 1951.

Comments on the poet's descriptive powers and on his
mingling of everyday and supernatural elements (pp. 73-
76).

921. Kaske, R.E. "G's Green Chapel and the Cave at Wetton
      Mill." *Medieval Literature and Folklore Studies: Es-
      says in Honor of Francis Lee Utley.* Ed. Jerome Mandel
      and Bruce A. Rosenberg. New Brunswick: Rutgers UP,
      1970. Pp. 111-21.

      Provides detailed support for Day's identification (item
      88) of Wetton Mill as the Green Chapel. Includes four
      photographs. Also cf. items 805, etc.

922. Kee, Kenneth Orville. "G--A Study in Epic Degeneration."
      Diss., Toronto, 1956.

923. Kelley, Gerald Baptiste. "Graphemic Theory and Its Ap-
      plication to a ME text: *SGGK.*" Diss., Wisconsin (Madi-
      son), 1955. Abst.: *Summaries of Doctoral Dissertations,
      Univ. of Wisconsin,* 16 (1956), 542-43.

924. Kellogg, Alfred L. "The Location of the Green Chapel in
      SGGK." *YAPS,* 1966, pp. 652-54. Rpt. in Alfred L. Kel-
      logg, *Chaucer, Langland, Arthur: Essays in ME Litera-
      ture.* New Brunswick: Rutgers UP, 1972.

      Supports Madden's identification of "Chapel of the
      Grune," Skinburness, Cumberland. Cf. items 805, etc.

925. Kennedy, Sally Pitts. "Vestiges of Rule Ritual in
      SGGK." Diss., Tennessee, 1968. Abst.: *DA,* 29 (1968),
      1513A.

926. Kindrick, Robert LeRoy. "The Unknightly Knight: Anti-
      Chivalric Satire in Fourteenth and Fifteenth Century
      English Literature." Diss., Texas (Austin), 1971.
      Abst.: *DAI,* 32 (1972), 5742A.

      Includes material on *G.*

927. King, R.W. "Notes on *SGGK.*" *RES,* 5 (1929), 449-52.

      Notes on the following lines: 806, 839, 918, 943-44,
      955, 987, 999, 1112, 2126, 2301, 2318, 2339-40, 2345-47,
      2376, 2385.

928. ———. "A Note on *Sir Gawayn and the Green Knight,*
      2414ff." *MLR,* 29 (1934), 435-36.

Specifies parallels to G's anti-feminist statement (cf. item 796).

929. Kirkpatrick, Hugh. "The Bob-Wheel and Allied Stanza Forms in ME and Middle Scots Poetry." Diss., North Texas State, 1976. Abst.: *DAI*, 37 (1976), 3608A.

Contains material on *G*.

930. Kiteley, J[ohn] F. "Characterization in *SGGK*." B.Litt. thesis, Oxford, 1959.

931. ————. "The *De Arto Honeste Amandi* of Andreas Capellanus and the Concept of Courtesy in *SGGK*." *Anglia*, 79 (1961), 7-16.

Argues that the Lady's conception of "courtesy" coincides with views expressed in Andreas Capellanus's treatise. Cf. item 1091.

932. ————. "The Knight who cared for his Life." *Anglia*, 79 (1961), 131-37. Rpt. in item 891.

Finds parallels to G's fault, that he *lufed* his *lyf* (2368), in other romances; suggests that this may be an ancient tradition. Cf. items 1259, etc.

933. ————, John F. "'The Endless Knot': Magical Aspects of the Pentangle in *SGGK*." *SLitI*, 4, ii (1971), 41-50.

Emphasizes that in popular superstition the pentangle was a sign to ward off evil (cf. item 893); connects this with G's acceptance of the girdle.

934. Kittredge, George Lyman. *A Study of "SGGK."* Cambridge, Mass.: Harvard UP, 1916. Rpt. Gloucester, Mass.: Smith, 1960.

I.   A study of the relationships of sources and analogues of *G*. (Cf. items 706, 730, 893, 961, 1151).

    1. Suggests that the immediate source is a French poem. Divides the plot into Challenge and Temptation.

    2. Challenge: Summarizes and reviews versions in *The Champion's Bargain* and the Terror story from *Fled Bricrend*, *Le Livre de Caradoc*, *La Mule sanz Frain*, *Perlesvaus*, and *Hunbaut*. Reconstructs lost OF and AN romances of the Challenge. Recapitulates a theory of the relationships of these versions (pp. 74-76).

3. Temptation: Discusses folk-tale origins; summarizes and reviews versions in *Ider*, *The Carl
of Carlisle*, *Le Chevalier* à *l'Epée*, various minor analogues, and *Humbaut*.
4. Argues that the author of the putative French *G*
fused the two plot elements. Discusses the origin of *The Turk and G* and *The GK*. Suggests
which parts of *G* were added by the English poet.

II.   Illustrative material. Specifies and discusses
parallels from a wide range of sources under the
following heads: The Returning or Surviving Head;
The Demon of Vegetation; Disenchantment by De-
capitation; Duelling by Alternation; *The Book of
Caradoc*; *La Mule sanz Frain*; *The Carl of Carlisle*; *The Turk and G*; *The GK*.

Ends with a bibliographical note.

Reviews: Eilert Ekwall, *EStn*, 51 (1917), 121-24.
Kirby Flower Smith, *MLN*, 33 (1918), 45-46.

935. Knapp, Peggy A. "G's Quest: Social Conflict and Symbolic Meditation." *ClioI*, 6 (1977), 289-306.

Argues that the poem itself acts as a mediator between
the Arthurian tale of chivalric nationalism and the
Christian penitential meditation.

936. Knott, Thomas A. "The Text of *Sir Gawayne and the Green
Knight*." *MLN*, 30 (1915), 102-08.

A review article on items 97 and 100 (including revisions). Provides restoration of the text of the following lines from offsets: 1433, 1442-45, 1706, 1745, 2178-
79, 2329. Discusses various dubious readings in the
1912 revision of item 100 (comments on the following
lines: 51, 137, 461, 518, 646, 663, 718, 815, 910, 1063,
1230, 1369, 1447, 1719, 1720, 2027, 2523). Other comments and suggestions on the following lines: 43, 81,
264, 286, 427, 438, 591, 660, 683, 734, 795, 822, 825,
881, 884, 956, 984, 992, 1112, 1213, 1214, 1256, 1386,
1441, 1466-67, 1514, 1540, 1591, 1729, 1769, 2053,
2205, 2290, 2344, 2440.

937. Kobayashi, Atsuo. "Traits of Medieval Romances and the
Formative Grace of *SGGK*." *ARFAL*, 2 (1951), 110-50.
English sum. on pp. 5-6.

Discusses *G* in relation to the essential traits of medieval romance, considering the hero's character, the su-

pernatural elements, and the splendor of the courtly
settings. Praises the poem's "formative grace," emphasizing narrative patterning and the integration of the
beheading and temptation plots.

938.   ————. "*SGGK*: Its Traits as a Medieval Romance and
Formative Grace." *Medieval English Romance*. Tokyo:
Nan'undo, 1977. Pp. 1-76.

A modified version of item 937. Also includes analysis
of foreign words and some figures of speech. In Japanese.

939. Kökeritz, Helge. "*SGGK* 1954." *MLN*, 58 (1943), 373-74.

Glosses *bordes* (1954) "maidens, young ladies."

940.   ————. "Two Interpretations." *SN*, 14 (1945), 277-80.

Glosses *bordes* (1954) "maidens."

941. Krappe, A.H. "Who *Was* the GK?" *Speculum*, 13 (1938),
206-15.

Reviews interpretations and analogues of the GK. Identifies him as the "Lord of Hades." Cf. items 1099,
1118.

*   Kreuzer, James R. See item 107.

942. Kuhnke, Bruno. *Die alliterierenden Langzeile in der
Mittelenglischen Romance "Sir Gawayn and the Green
Knight."* Studien zum Germanischen Alliterationsvers, 4.
Berlin: Felber, 1900. Diss., Königsberg, 1899.

Reviews theories of two- and four-stress half-lines,
favoring the latter. Sets out to demonstrate, from an
examination of *G*, that the ME alliterative long line
consists of two half-lines, the first half having four
stresses and the second half three. Analyzes these in
turn, using Kaluza's types A, B, C, and D; systematical-
ly shows the distribution of each type in the text of *G*.

Reviews: Joseph Fischer, *AnglB*, 12 (1901), 65-76.
        Karl Luick, *AnglB*, 12 (1901), 33-49.

943. Kullnick, Max. *Studien über den Wortschatz in "Sir
Gawayne and the grene knyʒt."* Berlin: Mayer und Müller,
1902. Diss., Berlin, 1902.

A study of words used in *G* but obsolete by the late
nineteenth century.

I. Groups words according to origin:
    1. AS (including Latin borrowings established by
       the time of AElfric);
    2. ON;
    3. other Germanic origins;
    4. OF, and Latin words first used in ME;
    5. Celtic.

II. Specifies the use of these words elsewhere in ME
    writings:
    1. early secular poetry;
    2. fourteenth-century metrical romances;
    3. fourteenth-century alliterative verse;
    4. Chaucer;
    5. Northern religious verse;
    6. prose.

Review: P.G. Thomas, *EStn*, 47 (1913), 250-56.

944. L, O.E. "The Inner Side of the Shield." *N&Q*, 170
      (1938), 8.

      Asks whether it was customary for the Virgin to be de-
      picted on shields.

945. Lamba, B.P., and R. Jeet Lamba. "*SGGK*, 800-802." *Expl*,
      27 (1969), item 47.

      Argue that these lines suggest a moral warning, com-
      paring the *Parson's Tale* (*CT*, X.444--misnumbered 44) and
      Cl 1407-08 (misnumbered 1498-99). Cf. items 119, 1162.

946. Lanham, Margaret M. "Chastity: A Study of Sexual Moral-
      ity in the English Medieval Romances." Diss., Vander-
      bilt Univ., 1947. Sum., pub. separately with the same
      title, Nashville, Tenn.: privately printed, 1947.

      Singles out *G* as the one English medieval romance in
      which Christian and chivalric values are successfully
      blended (summary, p. 49).

947. Lass, Roger George. "*G*'s Apprenticeship: Myth and the
      Spiritual Process in *GGK*." Diss., Yale, 1965. Abst.:
      DA, 26 (1965), 2185.

948. ———, Roger [George]. "'Man's Heaven: The Symbolism
      of *G*'s shield." *MS*, 28 (1966), 354-60.

Considers that the pentangle suggests the weakness of
body and matter.

949.   Lavers, Norman.   "How G Beat the GK."   *PAPA*, 3, iii
(1977), 17-23.

Not seen.

950.   Leavis, Q.D.   "*SGGK* again."   *Scrutiny*, 17 (1950), 253-
55.

Cites Loomis in support of item 1192.

951.   Lehman, Anne Kernan.   "Thematic Patterning and Narrative
Continuity in Four ME Alliterative Poems."   Diss., Cornell, 1970.   Abst.: *DAI*, 31 (1971), 6558A.

Includes material on *G*.

952.   Leible, Arthur Bray.   "The Character of G in English
Literature."   Diss., Missouri (Columbia), 1961.   Abst.:
DA, 22 (1962), 3648.

953.   Leighton, J.M.   "Christian and Pagan Symbolism and Ritual in *SGGK*."   *Theoria*, 43 (1974), 49-62.

Discusses the significance of ritual in *G*; suggests that
the poet added new ritualistic symbolism to his source
material.   Cf. items 1192, etc.

954.   Lester, G.A.   "G's Fault in Terms of Contemporary Law
of Arms."   *N&Q*, 221 (1976), 392-93.

States that by wearing the girdle, G contravened contemporary rules for single combat (cf. item 850).

955.   Levitsky, Steven Eric.   "The Discovery of *SGGK*."   Diss.,
Johns Hopkins Univ., 1972.   Abst.: *DAI*, 33 (1972),
1689A.

956.   Levy, Bernard S.   "G's Spiritual Journey: *Imitatio
Christi* in *SGGK*."   *AnM*, 6 (1965), 65-106.

An interpretation of the poem as a spiritual journey in
imitation of Christ, through which G progresses from
pride to humility.   Suggests that G undergoes spiritual
circumcision, and that his temptation reflects the pattern of the world, the flesh, and the devil.   Argues
that the GK symbolizes the Devil; and that the two ladies
are manifestations of one figure, symbolizing Sin.   Cf.
items 965, 1159.

957. Lewis, C.S. "The Anthropological Approach." *English
      and Medieval Studies Presented to J.R.R. Tolkien on the
      Occasion of His Seventieth Birthday*. Ed. Norman Davis
      and C.L. Wrenn. London: Allen and Unwin, 1962. Pp.
      219-30. Rpt. in item 891 and in *Selected Literary Es-
      says by C.S. Lewis*, ed. Walter Hooper. Cambridge: UP,
      1969. Extract rpt. in item 827.

      Discusses the treatment of romance by "anthropological"
      critics; specific comment on Bertilak (pp. 222-23). Cf.
      items 1192, etc.

958. Lewis, John S. "*GGK*." *CE*, 21 (1959), 50-51.

      Points out that green and gold traditionally symbolize
      vanishing youth (cf. item 840).

959. Leyerle, John. "The Game and Play of Hero." *Concepts
      of the Hero in the Middle Ages and the Renaissance*. Ed.
      Norman T. Burns and Christopher Reagan. New York:
      State Univ. Press, 1975; London, etc.: Hodder, 1976.
      Pp. 49-82.

      Argues that at the heart of *G* is *gomnez* "games," under-
      stood in all the senses specified in the *MED* (in sum-
      mary: 1. mirth; 2 (a) festivity, (b) polite accomplish-
      ment, (c) hunting, (d) love-making; 3. tournament; 4.
      jest; 5. plan, trick; 6. quarry). Suggests that the
      "game and play of hero" may be seen as a literary para-
      digm. Cf. items 769, etc.

960. Lippmann, Kurt. *Das ritterliche Persönlichkeitsideal in
      der mittelenglischen Literatur des 13. und 14. Jahrhun-
      derts*. Meerane: Herzog, 1933.

      Includes comments on the poet's treatment of knightly
      virtues (pp. 119-23) and on tensions between courtly and
      Christian values in the temptation scenes (pp. 64-65).
      Cf. items 686, etc.

961. Löhmann, Otto. *Die Sage von "Gawain und dem Grünen Rit-
      ter."* Schriften der Albertus-Universität: Geisteswissen-
      schaftliche Reihe, 17. Königsberg und Berlin: Ost-
      Europa Verlag, 1938.

      Discusses the origins and history of the *G* story. (Cf.
      items 934, etc.).

      1. Introductory.
      2. Considers parallels in other works to (a) the behead-
         ing game; (b) the seduction scenes; (c) the story of
         the obedient guest.

3. Compares *G* with *The GK*, and argues for a common English source.
4. Discusses various versions of the beheading game and tabulates their relationship.
5. Compares versions of the seduction scene and the exchange of winnings motif.
6. Considers the relation of *G* to Celtic folktale motifs, in particular the journey to the otherworld. (Cf. items 969, etc.).
7. Provides a speculative account of the development of the story.
8. Considers modern use of the material in Yeats's *The Green Helmet* and Stucken's *Gawan*.

Reviews: Karl Brunner, *AnglB*, 49 (1938), 336-37.
Albert Eichler, *LfGRP*, 61 (1940), 95-96.
Henry L. Savage, *JEGP*, 38 (1939), 445-50.

962. Loganbill, Dean. "The Medieval Mind in *SGGK*." *BRMMLA*, 26 (1972), 119-26.

Considers Irish analogues. Argues that *G* represents a blend of mythical and modern elements. Cf. items 969, etc.

963. Long, Charles. "Arthur's Role in Morgan La Fay's Plan in *SGGK*." *TPB*, 7 (1970), 3-10.

Suggests that Morgan was motivated by the wish to regain Arthur as her lover.

964. ————. "Was the GK Really Merlin?" *Interpretations*, 7 (1975), 1-7.

Not seen.

965. Longo, Joseph A. "*SGGK*: The Christian Quest for Perfection." *NMS*, 11 (1967), 57-85.

Argues that *G* is about the Christian quest for perfection, and that this is emphasized by the metaphors of pilgrimage and knightly battle. Associated symbolism is seen to inform the accounts of the hunts and temptations, and the letting of *G*'s blood. (Cf. items 956, 1159).

966. Loomis, Laura Hibbard. "Foreword" to item 77 rpt. in *Loomis/Loomis*, pp. 324-28.

Reviews the themes of romance.

967.   ————. *"GGK." Arthurian Literature in the Middle
        Ages: A Collaborative History.* Ed. Roger Sherman Loomis.
        London: Oxford UP, 1959. Pp. 528-40. Rpt. in item 891;
        Newstead; and Laura Hibbard Loomis, *Adventures in the
        Middle Ages: A Memorial Collection of Essays and Studies*,
        New York: Franklin, 1962.

        Discusses sources, analogues, and style; regards the
        Lady as Morgan's "other self and agent" (cf. items 696,
        etc.).

968.   Loomis, Roger Sherman. "The Story of the Modena Archi-
        volt and its Mythological Roots." *RR*, 15 (1924), 266-
        84.

        Includes discussion of the origin of the name *Bercilak*.

969.   ————. *Celtic Myth and Arthurian Romance.* New York:
        Columbia UP, 1927.

        Reviews analogues (pp. 59-60). Proposes equivalents in
        Celtic myth to various characters and events in *G* (pp.
        69-83). Also various passing references. Cf. items
        736, 962, 970-72, 1182.

970.   ————. "G, Gwri, and Cuchulinn." *PMLA*, 43 (1928), 384-
        96.

        Further elucidation of the theory advanced in item 969;
        includes comments on the GK (p. 393).

971.   ————. "The Visit to the Perilous Castle: A Study of
        the Arthurian Modifications of an Irish Theme." *PMLA*,
        48 (1933), 1000-35.

        Includes endorsement of the views of Buchanan (item
        736) on the relationship between *G* and its Irish ana-
        logues (pp. 1004, 1023-24, 1027).

972.   ————. "More Celtic Elements in *GGK*." *JEGP*, 42 (1943),
        149-84. Rpt. in *Studies in Medieval Literature: A Mem-
        orial Collection of Essays by Roger Sherman Loomis*. New
        York: Franklin, 1970.

        1. Proposes Irish sources (in tales from the Cúchulainn
           cycle) for the girdle and the pentangle.
        2. Proposes a Welsh source (*Pwyll*) for various details
           in the plot of *G*, and suggests that the influence of
           Celtic mythology is reflected in the designation of
           Morgan (2452). (Cf. items 969, etc.).

973.   ————. *Arthurian Tradition and Chrétien de Troyes.*
       New York: Columbia UP, 1949.

       Discusses parallels between *G* and Chrétien's *Yvain* and
       Conte del Graal (pp. 278-84, 418-20). Cf. items 1061,
       1197.

974.   ————. "Welsh Elements in *GGK.*" *Wales and the Arthur-*
       ian Legend. Cardiff: Univ. of Wales Press, 1956. Pp.
       77-90. Rpt., Folcroft, Pa.: Folcroft Press, 1969.

       A revised version of the second part of item 972.

975.   ————. *The Development of Arthurian Romance.* Hutchin-
       son Univ. Lib. London: Hutchinson, 1963. New York:
       Harper, Torchbooks, 1964.

       Contains a general account of *G*, including discussion of
       plot strands, Celtic sources, descriptive technique,
       character, and theme (pp. 152-65).

976.   Lovecy, Ian Charles. "A study of the supernatural in
       some selected mediaeval romances." Ph.D. thesis, Cam-
       bridge, 1973/74.

       Includes a section on *G*.

977.   Lucas, Peter J. "G's Anti-Feminism." *N&Q*, 213 (1968),
       324-25.

       Argues (in response to item 741) that G's "anti-femi-
       nism" is appropriate to the situation. Cf. items 1025,
       etc.

978.   Lupack, Alan C. "Structure and Tradition in the Poems
       of the Alliterative Revival." Diss., Pennsylvania, 1974.
       Abst.: *DAI*, 36 (1975), 323A.

       Includes discussion of *G*.

 *   M., W. See item 747.

979.   McAlindon, Thomas Edward. "The Treatment of the Super-
       natural in ME Legend and Romance, 1200-1400." Ph.D.
       thesis, Cambridge, 1960/61.

       Includes a section on *G*.

980.   ————, T[homas Edward]. "Comedy and Terror in ME Lit-
       erature: The Diabolical Game." *MLR*, 60 (1965), 323-32.

       Includes discussion of the GK as a terrifying jester.

981. ————. "Magic, Fate, and Providence in Medieval Nar-
      rative and *SGGK*." *RES*, NS 16 (1965), 121-39.

      Relates *G* to the medieval Christian reorientation of in-
      herited pagan material, observing that G is shown not
      to be the victim of omnipotent magic or unalterable
      fate.

982. McClure, Peter. "G's *Mesure* and the Significance of The
      Three Hunts in *SGGK*." *Neophil*, 57 (1973), 375-87.

      Argues that G's adventure is a test of *mesure*, and that
      the hunted animals symbolize the human weakness he must
      master. Cf. item 1188; items 1127, etc.

983. Macdonald, Angus. "*SGGK*, 11. 14ff." *MLR*, 30 (1935),
      343-44.

      A discussion of *G* 14-19; suggests glossing *wonder* "de-
      struction."

984. ————, A[ngus]. "A Note on *SGGK*." *ES*, 35 (1954), 15.

      A note on lines 385 and 395.

985. McIntosh, Angus. "ME *upon schore* and Some Related Mat-
      ters." *Schlauch*, pp. 255-60.

      Glosses *vpon schore* (*G* 2332) "at a slant."

*   ————. See also item 247.

986. Mckee, John DeWitt. "Three Uses of the Arming Scene."
      MTJ, 12, iv (1965), 18-19, 21.

      Compares the arming scenes in *G*, Chaucer's *Tale of Sir
      Thopas*, and Twain's *A Connecticut Yankee*.

987. McKeehan, Irene Pettit. "St. Edmund of East Anglia: the
      Development of a Romantic Legend." *UCS*, 15 (1925), 13-
      74.

      Connects the motif of the severed head speaking in *G*
      with the legend of St. Edmund (pp. 18-20).

988. Magoun, Francis P., Jr. "Anmerkungen zum Glosser des
      Tolkien-Gordonschen *SGGK*." *Anglia*, 52 (1928), 79-82.

      Lists errors and omissions in the glossary of item 111.
      Adds specific suggestions on the following lines: 160,
      659, 892, 1021, 1049, 1155, 1750.

989.   ————, Francis P. [Jr.]. "Kleine Beiträge zu *SG*."
        Anglia, 61 (1937), 129-35.

        Further comments on item 111. Deals with the interpre-
        tation of scribal abbreviations, punctuation, the glos-
        sary, and the list of names.

990.   ————, Francis P., Jr. "*SG* and Medieval Fottball." *ES*,
        19 (1937), 208-09.

        Suggests that the members of Arthur's court play foot-
        ball with the GK's head.

991.   ————, F[rancis] P., Jr. "Chaucer's SG and the OF Ro-
        man de la Rose." *MLN*, 67 (1952), 183-85.

        In response to item 1259 suggests that Chaucer's refer-
        ence to G could have been inspired by the *Roman*.

992.   Malarkey, Stoddard, and J. Barre Toelken. "G and the
        Green Girdle." *JEGP*, 63 (1964), 14-20. Rpt. in item
        891.

        Argue that *lace* (2226) signifies the girdle that G has
        received from the Lady. Cf. item 830.

993.   Manning, Stephen. "A Psychological Interpretation of
        SGGK." *Criticism*, 6 (1964), 165-77. Rpt. in item 891.

        An analysis of the poem in archetypal terms as a story
        of the ego's encounter with the shadow. Cf. item 795.

994.   Margeson, Robert W. "Structure and Meaning in *SGGK*."
        PLL, 13 (1977), 16-24.

        Discusses the tensions between circular and linear pat-
        terns as they reflect the moral theme. Cf. items 1098,
        etc.

995.   Marino, James Gerard Americus. "Game and Romance."
        Diss., Pittsburgh, 1975. Abst.: *DAI*, 37 (1976), 1538A-
        39A.

        Includes material on *G*.

996.   Markman, Alan Mouns. "SG of Britain: A Study of the
        Romance Elements in the British G Literature." Diss.,
        Michigan, 1955. Abst.: *DA*, 15 (1955), 1613.

997.   ————, Alan M[ouns]. "The Meaning of *SGGK*." *PMLA*, 72
        (1957), 574-86. Rpt. in item 132.

Emphasizes that *G* should be read as a romance; argues that its purpose is to show "what a splendid man G is."

998. Markus, Manfred. "Some Examples of Ambiguity in *SGGK*." *NM*, 75 (1974), 625-29.

Discusses ambiguity arising from the relation between words and contexts in lines 237, 955, 968, 1236-67, and 1273.

999. Martin, John Wiley. "*La Mule Sans Frein*: A New Approach to *SGGK*." Diss., Rochester, 1972. Abst.: *DAI*, 33 (1972), 319A.

1000. ————, John W[iley]. "The Knight who Stayed Silent through Courtesy." *Archiv*, 210 (1973), 53-57.

Suggests that *sum* (247) means "one" and that the line refers to G. Cf. item 1021.

1001. Mathew, Gervase. "Ideals of Knighthood in Late-Fourteenth-Century England." *Studies in Medieval History Presented to F.M. Powicke*. Ed. R.W. Hunt, W.A. Pantin, R.W. Southern. Oxford: Clarendon, 1948. Pp. 354-62. Rpt. in item 827.

Considers the knightly virtues symbolized by the pentangle. Repeats the suggestions about composition made in item 255. Cf. items 686, etc.

1002. Mathews, J.C. "*SG*, Line 133: An Emendation." *PQ*, 9 (1930), 215-16.

Suggests inserting *ne* before *myȝt*.

1003. Mathewson, Jeanne Thompson. "*SGGK* and the Medieval Comic Tradition." Diss., Stanford, 1968. Abst.: *DA*, 29 (1969), 2678A-79A.

1004. Matonis, Ann Therese. "*SGGK*: Characterization and Structural Motifs." Diss., Pennsylvania, 1966. Abst.: *DA*, 27 (1967), 4259A.

1005. ————, Ann [Therese]. "*GGK*: Flux and the *Fayntyse of the Flesche*." *JNT*, 1 (1971), 43-48.

Argues that the theme of cyclical change is introduced at critical moments in *G* (lines 491-531, 1998-2008).

*   Matsui, Noriko. See item 1313.

1006. Matsumoto, Hiroyuki. "An Essay on *SGGK*--from the Sty-
       listic Point of View." *BHB*, 6 (1972), 29-38.

       Discusses the treatment of the relationship between
       the ideal and the actual in *G*. In Japanese.

1007. ————. "An Analysis of Dialogue in *SGGK*." *BHB*, 9
       (1975), 27-40.

       Emphasizes the dramatic function of dialogue, particu-
       larly in the temptation scenes. In Japanese.

1008. ————. "The Pronoun + Preposition Word-Order in ME
       Alliterative Poems." *BHB*, 10 (1975), 1-26.

       Includes material on *G*. In Japanese.

1009. Matthews, William. *The Tragedy of Arthur: A Study of
       the Alliterative "Morte Arthure."* Berkeley and Los
       Angeles: Univ. of California Press, 1960.

       In addition to many passing references, comments on
       the contrast between G and Arthur in the challenge
       scene (pp. 162-63), and enumerates parallels between
       G and the *Awntyrs* (pp. 208-09). Cf. items 197, 504.

1010. ————. *"bi lag mon*: A Crux in *Sir Gawayn and the Grene
       Kny3t*. *M&H*, NS 6 (1975), 151-55.

       Discusses interpretations of *lad bi lagmon*, and glosses
       "cunningly led astray."

 *   ————. See also item 747.

1011. Mehl, Dieter. "Zu *SGGK*." *GRM*, 43 (1962), 414-17.

       Emphasizes the ambiguity of lines 1237-38; discusses
       parallels in *Pe* 399, *Cl* 683, *G* 252, etc.

1012. ————. "'Point of View' in mittelenglischen Romanzen."
       GRM, 45 (1964), 35-46.

       Includes discussion of the poet's subtle handling of
       point-of-view in *G* (pp. 38-41, 44). Cf. items 254,
       706, 719.

1013. ————. *Die mittelenglischen Romanzen des 13. und 14.
       Jahrhunderts*. Heidelberg: Winter, Universitätsverlag,
       1967. Tr., in expanded and rev. form, as *The ME Ro-
       mances of the Thirteenth and Fourteenth Centuries*, Lon-
       don: Routledge, 1969.

Emphasizes the moral seriousness of *G*, and suggests
that the two plot strands are linked by the theme of
contract. Discusses structure and narrative technique
(pp. 193-206 in English ed.).

1014.   Meier, Hans Heinrich. "ME Styles in Action." *ES*, 55
        (1974), 193-204.

        Provides a stylistic analysis of lines 1719-32 and
        three other ME passages describing vivid action.

1015.   Menner, Robert J. "*SGGK* and the West Midland." *PMLA*,
        37 (1922), 503-26.

        In response to item 211 provides evidence to justify
        assigning the dialect of *G* (and, by implication, the
        other three poems) to the NW Midlands.

1016.   ———. "Notes on *SGGK*." *MLR*, 19 (1924), 204-08.

        Notes on *sturtes* (MS, 171), *ver* (866), and lines 1264-
        67.

1017.   ———. Review of item 111. *MLN*, 41 (1926), 397-400.

        Contains specific suggestions on the following lines:
        646, 660, 1441, 1442, 1444, 2208-09, 2329, 2511.

1018.   ———. "ME *Lagmon* (*G* 1729) and ModE 'Lag.'" *PQ*, 10
        (1931), 163-68.

        Provides evidence that *lagmon* existed in ME; discusses
        the etymology of *lag*.

1019.   Mertens-Fonck, Paule. "Morgan, Fée et Déesse." *Mé-
        langes offerts à Rita Lejeune, Professeur à Universi-
        té de Liège*. Gembloux: Duculot, 1969. II, 1067-76.

        Considers the significance of Morgan's being referred
        to as both *la Fee* (2446) and *þe goddes* (2452). Cf.
        items 696, etc.

1020.   Metcalf, Allan A. "*SG* and 'You.'" *ChauR*, 5 (1971),
        165-78.

        Analyzes the poet's use of "you" as a formal second-
        person singular pronoun; suggests ways in which this
        reflects social status and setting. Cf. items 816, etc.

1021.   ———. "Silent Knight: *Sum for Cortaysye*?" *Archiv*,
        213 (1976), 338-42.

        Replies to item 1000, arguing that *sum* (247) is plural.

1022.   Michiyuki, Sukehiro. "On the Subjunctive Mood in
        SGGK." *OSR*, 7 (1972), 175-90.

        Describes the use of the subjunctive in independent
        and dependent clauses; also specifies form and tense.
        In English.

1023.   Miller, J. Furman. "The *G* Poet's Possible Indebted-
        ness to Jesus' Temptation." *C&L*, 21, i-ii (1971-2),
        27-29.

        Suggests that the temptation of Jesus influenced the
        poet's account of the temptation of *G*.

1024.   Mills, David. "An Analysis of the Temptation Scenes
        in *SGGK.*" *JEGP*, 67 (1968), 612-30.

        A closely argued analysis of the temptation scenes;
        pays particular attention to vocabulary; emphasizes
        that the conflict becomes progressively less comic and
        more morally charged day by day. Cf. items 786, 833,
        1210.

1025.   ————. "The Rhetorical Function of G's Antifeminism?"
        NM, 71 (1970), 635-40.

        Suggests that G's anti-feminist comments are made in a
        "semi-humorous tone." Cf. items 796, 823, 928, 977.

1026.   Mills, M. "Christian Significance and Romance Tradi-
        tion in *SGGK.*" *MLR*, 60 (1956), 483-93. Rpt. in item
        891.

        Argues that a fully allegorical reading of *G* is not
        justified, contrasting the *Queste del Saint Graal*.
        Considers the effect of G's reputation as a philanderer.
        Cf. items 1185; 1259, etc.

1027.   Mizutori, Yoshitaka. "Historical Present in *SGGK.*"
        SHumO, 19, vii (1968), 1-26.

        Points out that in scenes of exciting action, attention
        is constantly directed to the events of the moment, and
        tenses are often inconsistent. In Japanese.

1028.   ————. "SG's Journey to Wirral." *SHumO*, 27, x (1975),
        35-51.

        Interprets *fordez* (699) as referring to the fords of
        rivers through which G has waded before reaching the
        Wirral. In Japanese. Cf. items 753, etc.

1029.   Moody, Patricia A.   "The *Childgered* Arthur of *SGGK*."
        SMC, 8-9 (1976), 173-80.

        Reviews interpretations of *childgered* (86); emphasizes
        ambivalence and ambiguity in the poet's treatment of
        Arthur.

1030.   Moody, Philippa.   "The Problems of Medieval Criticism."
        MCR, 3 (1960), 94-103.

        Appeals for better critical writing on *G* as a poem;
        discusses the inadequacies of items 170, 967, and 1192.

1031.   Moon, Douglas M.   "Clothing Symbolism in *SGGK*."   *NM*,
        66 (1965), 334-47.

        Suggests that mantles and hoods are used to symbolize
        chastity, and that *capados* (186, etc.) is a corruption
        of *carados*.

1032.   ————.   "The Role of Morgain la Fée in *SGGK*."   *NM*, 67
        (1966), 31-57.

        Stresses the importance of Morgan.   Denies that she is
        benevolent (contrast item 696); discusses the idea that
        she is both the young lady and the old (cf. items 748,
        967, etc.).   Concludes that Morgan is mistaken about
        the morality of Camelot.   Cf. items 696, etc.

1033.   Moorman, Charles.   "Myth and Mediaeval Literature:
        SGGK."   *MS*, 18 (1956), 158-72.   Rpt. in item 132.   Rpt.,
        in abbreviated form, as "The Stained Knight: *SGGK*."
        *A Knyght There Was: The Evolution of the Knight in
        Literature*.   Lexington: Univ. of Kentucky Press, 1967.

        Expresses reservations about "mythic" interpretations,
        but accepts that G's experiences may be seen as a *rite
        de passage* (cf. item 729).   Suggests that the chivalric
        morality of Camelot is tested through exposure to Ber-
        tilak's court.   Cf. items 1192, etc.

1034.   Morgan, H.E.   "An analysis of the methods and presumed
        functions of characterization in the three ME romances
        of *Yvain and Gawain*, *Morte Arthure*, and *GGK*."   B.Litt.
        thesis, Oxford, 1969.

1035.   Mori, Yoshinobu.   "Notes on the Interpretation of Some
        ME Poems."   *StLit*, no. 58 (1958), [pp. unknown].

        Includes notes on lines 1283-87.   In Japanese.

1036. Morton, A.L. "The Matter of Britain: The Arthurian
      Cycle and the Development of Feudal Society." *ZAA*, 8
      (1960), 5-28.

      Mentions the mingling of English and French elements
      in *G* (pp. 14, 17).

1037. Musker, Francis. "*SGGK.*" *PMLC*, 70 (1955-7), 7-19.

      A general critical reading, which includes a plot sum-
      mary, and comments on sources, dialect, local refer-
      ences, dating, descriptive technique, and the charac-
      ter of C.

1038. Nagano, Yoshio. "Old Icelandic Loan-Words in *SGGK.*"
      SELL, no. 12 (1962), 56-66; no. 16 (1966), 51-70.

      Considers the form, sound, and meaning of these words.
      In English.

1039. Nakao, Sr. Bernadette Setsuko, A.C.J. "SG's Confes-
      sions Reconsidered--A Catholic View." *SELit*, 53 (1976),
      3-25. English sum. in English No., 1977, 215-16.

      Argues that G's confession is valid, since he is un-
      aware of any transgression in accepting the girdle,
      but that he is guilty of insincerity toward his host.
      Cf. items 739, etc.

1040. Nakao, Toshio. "Alliterative Patterns in *SGGK.*" *SDAP*,
      1 (1961), 58-66.

      Investigates alliterative patterns in the poem. In
      English.

1041. ————. "Word-Order in *SGGK*: V-S." *BFLA*, no. 11
      (1961), 1-11.

      A description of the various conditions which cause
      the inverted order, verb-subject. In English.

1042. ————. "Word-Order in *SGGK*: Double Complement Con-
      struction." *BFLA*, no. 12 (1962), 1-5.

      Discusses the occurrence of this construction. In Eng-
      lish.

1043. ————. "Structure of Nominal Modification in *SGGK.*"
      BFLA, no. 13 (1964), 1-7.

Considers both prenominal and postnominal modifiers;
investigates what brings about the latter structure.
In English.

1044.   ———. "Word-Order in *SG*: V-Comp." *BFLA*, no. 14
         (1964), 1-4.

         Discusses the verb-complement construction. In Eng-
         lish.

1045.   ———. "Word Order in *SG*: V-Obj." *BFLA*, no. 14
         (1964), 5-8.

         A linguistic description of object-verb and verb-object
         structures. In English.

1046.   ———. "Alliteration in *SG*." *ForL*, no. 14 (1965),
         67-70.

         A graphemic description of consonant clusters. In
         English.

1047.   ———. "Alliterative Patterning in *SG*: Stress and
         Alliteration." *BFLA*, no. 15 (1965), 1-9.

         Proposes four degrees of significant stress. (In con-
         trast to the widely accepted four-stress theory, in
         which only two degrees of significant stress are dis-
         tinguished). In English.

1048.   ———. "Metrics of Bob and Wheel in *SGGK*." *SELing*,
         no. 2 (1973), 61-70.

         A metrical analysis of the bob and wheel lines in *G*.
         Proposes some modifications to the generally accepted
         metrical rules. In English.

1049.   Napier, Arthur S. "Old and ME Notes." *MLQ* (Lon), 1
         (1897), 51-53.

         Includes notes on *G* 427, 1281, 1399, 1451.

1050.   ———. "Notes on *Sir Gawayne and the Green Knight*."
         MLN, 17 (1902), 85-87.

         Suggests the following emendations: MS *bot* to *both*
         (144), *gedereʒ* to *gerdeʒ* (777), and *sleʒeʒ* to *sleʒe*
         (893). Also comments on the following lines: 228-29,
         681, 893, 1009, 1284, 1331, 1444, 1999.

1051.   Naruse, Masaiku. "On the Interpretation of ll. 1020-
         1028 in *SGGK*." *ShoR*, no. 23 (1958), 13-23.

Maintains that *þe last of þe layk* should be interpreted as "the last of the festivities held at Bertilak's castle." In Japanese.

1052.   ———. "A Study of the ME Alliterative Poem *SGGK*." *ShoR*, no. 27 (1958), 97-129; no. 28 (1959), 147-92.

Provides a detailed analysis of the temptation scenes, which the author considers the heart of the poem. Goes on to discuss the ways in which the implications of the temptation are explored in the fourth fitt. Concludes that the poet's intention is to depict the Christian recognition of human weakness. In Japanese.

1053.   ———. "Manuscription, Edition and Interpretation: *SGGK*, 11. 1282-1289." *ShoR*, no. 36 (1960), 17-45.

On the punctuation and interpretation of lines 1282-89. Glosses *lode* (1282) "burden." In Japanese.

1054.   ———. "The Interpretation of a Medieval Poem and its Text: on the lines 1046-1067 of *SGGK*." *ShoR*, no. 53 (1962), 1-36.

Deals with the punctuation and interpretation of these lines. Suggests that *kynqez kourt* (1048) refers to Bertilak's court (cf. item 1055). In Japanese.

1055.   ———. "Manuscript, Edition and Interpretation." *EigoS*, 108 (1962), 618-19.

Argues that *kynqez kourt* (1048) refers to the lord's castle (cf. item 1054), and that *kyng* (992) should be retained. In Japanese.

1056.   Neale, Robert. "*SGGK*." *UE*, 20 (1968), 41-46.

A general critical account; includes comments on sources, structure, theme, and the translations in items 107 and 110.

1057.   Neaman, Judith S. "SG's Covenant: Truth and *Timor Mortis*." *PQ*, 55 (1976), 30-42.

Urges a liturgical reading; concludes that *G* is a "*timor mortis* poem" commemorating the Feast of the Circumcision.

1058.   Newstead, Helaine. "Recent Perspectives on Arthurian Literature." *Frappier*, II, 877-83.

Includes discussion of the contrasting approach to *G* in items 957 and 1192.

1059. Nickel, Gerhard. "Die Begleiterepisode in *SGGK*." *GRM*, 46 (1965), 355-65.

Argues that the temptation of the guide is more significant than that of the lady (cf. item 787).

1060. Nitze, William A. "Is the GK Story a Vegetation Myth?" *MP*, 33 (1936), 351-66.

Compares versions of the beheading game in *Perlesvaus* and various other works including *G*. Concludes that the GK story is a vegetation ritual. Cf. items 1192, etc.

1061. ———. "The Character of Gauvain in the Romances of Chrétien de Troyes." *MP*, 50 (1953), 219-25.

Suggests that the characterization in *G* reflects the influence of Chrétien (cf. items 973, 1197).

1062. Noguchi, Shun'ichi. "The Language of *SGGK*: An Interpretation of the Poem." *HSELL*, 8 (1961), 76-91.

Considers the symbolic meaning of some adjectives. Concludes that G, associated with gold and pearl, is an image of human perfection. In English.

1063. Nossel, Margaret Anne. "Christian Commitment and Romance Ideals in *SGGK*." Diss., Cornell, 1968. Abst.: *DA*, 29 (1969), 4464A.

1064. Oakden, J[ames] P. "The Continuity of Alliterative Tradition." *MLR*, 28 (1933), 233-34.

Discusses metrical evidence in support of the theory of continuity, mentioning alliterative enjambment in *G* 509-10.

1065. Ogura, Michiko. "Formulas and Systems in *SGGK*." *BR*, no. 2 (1977), 17-53.

A classification of formulaic systems in the poem. In English.

1066. Oiji, Takero. "Catholicism in SGGK." *SELit*, 51 (1974), 5-21. English sum. in *SELit*, English No., 1975, 161-62.

Considers G's piety (as shown by his devotion to the Virgin, etc.); emphasizes the poem's penitential nature (cf. items 681, 739, 741). Rpt. in item 284.

1067.   Olszewska, E.S. "Illustrations of Norse formulas in English." *LeedsSE*, 2 (1933), 76-84.

Includes notes on lines 1255, 1480, 1881.

1068.   ———, "*Wylyde werke*: *SGGK* 2367." *N&Q*, 211 (1966), 451-52.

Reviews interpretations and quotes contemporary usage.

1069.   Ong, Walter J. "The GK's Harts and Bucks." *MLN*, 65 (1950), 536-39.

Demonstrates the precision of the poet's use of terminology referring to deer.

1070.   Onions, C.T. "*SGGK*." *TLS*, 16 Aug. 1923, p. 545.

Suggests emending MS *sage* (531) to *fage*, attributing the idea to Bradley. (Cf. items 864, 1071, 1073, 1076).

1071.   ———. "*SGGK*." *TLS*, 20 Sept. 1923, p. 620.

Further support for the suggestion in item 1070.

1072.   ———. "Notes on *SGGK*." *N&Q*, 146 (1924), 203-04, 244-45, 285-86.

Notes on the following lines: 28, 69, 110, 155, 155-57, 184, 194, 262, 290, 319, 440, 670, 774, 822, 841 (cf. 890), 958, 1015, 1174, 1533, 1696, 1708, 1710, 2018, 2102.

1073.   ———. "*No Fage*." *TLS*, 11 Feb. 1926, p. 99.

Further evidence in support of the suggestion in item 1070.

1074.   ———. "*Fade* in *SGGK*." *TLS*, 20 Jan. 1927, p. 44.

Identifies this word (149) with the provincial *fade* "mould on cheese" (cf. items 1075, 1176, 1177).

1075.   ———. "*Fade* in *SGGK*." *TLS*, 3 Feb. 1927, p. 76.

Answers item 1176; cf. item 1074.

1076. ———. "*No Fage.*" *TLS*, 5 Feb. 1931, p. 99.

Further evidence in support of the suggestion made in item 1070.

1077. ———. "ME *gawne*: a correction, with some notes." *MAE*, 22 (1955), 111-13.

Includes discussion of the derivation of *gayne* (2349).

1078. Oppel, Ingeborg. "The Endless Knot: An Interpretation of *SGGK* through its Myth." Diss., Washington, 1960. Abst.: *DA*, 21 (1961), 3092-93.

  *   Osberg, Richard H. See item 830.

1079. Owen, D.D.R. "Burlesque Tradition and *SGGK*." *FMLS*, 4 (1968), 125-45.

Argues that *G* reflects a burlesque tradition which grew up around G from the earliest romances; and that *Le Chevalier à l'epée* and *La Mule sans frein* are the poet's "chief and immediate sources" (cf. items 1080, 1081).

1080. ———. "The *G*-Poet." *FMLS*, 8 (1972), 79-84.

A review article on item 330. Considers the relation between G and *Le chevalier à l'epée* and *La Mule sans frein*. Cf. items 1079, 1081.

1081. ———. "Parallel Readings with *SGGK*." *Two Old French Gauvain Romances*, pt. 2. Ed. R.C. Johnston and D.D.R. Owen. Edinburgh and London: Scottish Academic Press, 1972.

Divided into: 1. introduction; 2. commentary; 3. conclusion.

1. Discusses the relationship between *G* and *Le Chevalier à l'epée* and *La Mule sans frein*, arguing that the English poet made systematic use of both French poems.
2. Provides a detailed examination of the poet's treatment of these sources, working through *G* and considering each episode or passage in turn.
3. Comments on the poet's manipulation and restructuring of his source material.

Cf. items 934, etc.; 1079-80.

*   P., G.   See Paris, Gaston.

1082.   Pace, George B.   "Physiognomy and *SGGK*." *ELN*, 4
        (1967), 161-65.

        Discusses the physiognomy of Morgan, with particular
        emphasis on her *blake broȝes* (961).

1083.   ———.   "G and Michaelmas." *Traditio*, 25 (1969),
        404-11.

        Suggests the relevance of the fact that Michaelmas is
        a quarter day, and thus associated with the settling
        of accounts, to lines 532-35.

1084.   Paganoni, Matilde. *"Sir Gawayn and the Green Knight."*
        Diss., Milano, 1960.

1085.   Palazzi, Annalisa. *"SGGK* in rapporto alla tradizione
        celtica e alla letteratura medievale." Diss., Bolo-
        gna, 1977.

1086.   P[aris], G[aston]. *Histoire Littéraire de la France*,
        XXX.   Paris: Imprimerie Nationale, 1888.

        Includes a section on *G*, consisting mainly of plot
        summary and discussion of the poem's relation with its
        sources (pp. 71-78).

1087.   Patrick, Michael.   "Racy Relevance in *SG* and *The Grad-
        uate*." *MEB*, 29 (1972), 30-32.

        Compares Benjamin's refusal of Mrs. Robinson's ad-
        vances to *G*'s refusal of the Lady's.

1088.   Pearce, T.M.   "SG and the Hostess." *AN&Q*, 1 (1963),
        70-71.

        Discusses the Lady's fox-like guile.

1089.   Pearsall, D[erek] A.   "The Style of *SGGK* and its Po-
        etic Relations."   M.A. thesis, Birmingham, 1952/3.

1090.   ———, Derek A.   "Rhetorical *Descriptio* in *SGGK*."
        MLR, 50 (1955), 129-34.

        Argues that critical assessments of the poet's de-
        scriptive technique have underestimated the influence
        of rhetorical convention.

1091. Perényi, Erzsébet. "*SGGK* and the Traditions of Medi-
       eval Art." *AUSB*, 1 (1969-70), 101-07.

       Sees *G* as a parody of romance. Line 1515 is inter-
       preted as a reference to Andreas Capellanus. (Cf.
       item 931).

1092. Perry, L.M. "*SGGK*." *MLR*, 32 (1937), 80-81.

       Suggests emending MS *non* (2511) to *mon*.

1093. Pierle, Robert C. "*SGGK*: A Study in Moral Complex-
       ity." *SoQ*, 6 (1968), 203-11.

       Summarizes critical views; argues that the central
       theme is the conflict between the flesh and the spirit.

1094. Plessow, Gustav. *Gotische Tektonik im Wortkunstwerk.*
       Künstlerisches im Bau der mittelenglischen Romanze
       von "Gawain und dem Grünen Ritter": Eine eidologische
       Literaturbetrachtung. München: Hueber, 1931.

       1. The first chapter establishes a system of gothic
          principles applicable to the creative arts. The
          following two chapters consider *G* mainly in rela-
          tion to architectural and musical concepts.
       2. Discusses the organization of the poem, emphasizing
          the function of the bobs and wheels. Relates the
          poetic structure of *G* to composition and perspec-
          tive in gothic art and architecture. Pronounces
          G a typically gothic artefact, and contrasts *The*
          GK.
       3. Discusses the patterns created by variations in
          emphasis and intensity, and by the rhythm of the
          poetry. Considers the effect of the different epi-
          sodes and of the use of description.

       Review: Kurt Herbert Halbach, *LfGRP*, 57 (1936), 314-
            18.

1095. Pollard, William Frank, Jr. "Franciscan Exemplarism
       in *GGK*." Diss., Duke Univ., 1976. Abst.: *DAI*, 37
       (1977), 7766A.

1096. Pons, E. "Y a-t-il une psychologie proprement ang-
       laise du caractère de Gauvain?" *BBSIA*, 3 (1951), 103.
       (Sum. of a paper read at the 3rd Arthurian Congress,
       Winchester).

       Suggests that G has a specifically English character.

*   ————. See also item 295.

1097. R. "The Five Wounds." *N&Q*, 171 (1936), 227, 336.

Queries the sense of line 642. Cf. items 697 and 1203.

1098. Randall, Dale B.J. "A Note on Structure in *SGGK*."
MLN, 72 (1957), 161-63.

Illustrates the balanced structure of *G* diagrammatical-
ly, and compares *Pe*. Cf. items 693, 715, 876, 887,
994, 1102.

1099. ————. "Was the GK a Fiend?" *SP*, 57 (1960), 479-91.

Suggests that *G* is about the testing of a Christian
knight by a fiend. Cf. items 941, 1118.

1100. Ray, B.K. "The Character of G." *DUB*, 11 (1926), 1-
13. Also pub. separately: London: Oxford UP, 1926.

Reviews the treatment of G from the *Mabinogion* to
Tennyson. Emphasizes the nobility of his character
in *G*. Cf. items 1259, etc.; 1100.

1101. Reeves, James. *A Short History of English Poetry
1340-1940*. London, Melbourne, and Toronto: Heinemann,
1961; New York: Dutton, 1962.

A brief summary with critical comments (pp. 5-7).

1102. Reichardt, Paul F. "A Note on the Structural Symmetry
in *GGK*." *NM*, 72 (1971), 276-82.

Endorses the account of structure in item 887. Suggests, in addition, that the Virgin is balanced against
Morgan. Cf. items 1098, etc.

1103. Reicke, Curt. *Untersuchungen über den Stil der mittel-
englischen alliterierenden Gedichte "Morte Arthure,"
"The Destruction of Troy," "The Wars of Alexander,"
"The Seige of Jerusalem," "Sir Gawayn and the Green
Knight": Ein Beitrag zur Lösung der Huchown-Frage*.
Königsberg: Hartung, 1906. Diss., Königsberg, 1906.

Reviews the Huchown controversy. Supports the theory
of common authorship for *Pe*, *Cl*, *Pat*, and *G*. After
considering evidence of phraseology and vocabulary,
concludes that Neilson's ascription (item 274) of the
four romances specified in the title of this book to
the poet of *G* is unconvincing. Cf. items 274, etc.

1104.   Reid, Margaret J.C. *The Arthurian Legend: Comparison
        of Treatment in Modern and Mediaeval Literature: A
        Study in the Literary Value of Myth and Legend.* Edin-
        burgh and London: Oliver and Boyd, 1938; 2nd ed., 1960.
        Ph.D. thesis, Aberdeen, 1937.

        Relates *G* to other English G romances; summarizes plot
        (pp. 60-62). Cf. item 1100.

1105.   Renoir, Alain. "Descriptive Technique in *SGGK*." *OL*,
        13 (1958), 126-32.

        Suggests that the frequently praised vividness of *G*
        owes much to the poet's use of detail for psychological
        effect.

1106.   ────. "*G* and *Parzival*." *SN*, 31 (1959), 155-58.

        Compares lines 740-62 with a passage in the *Parzival*
        of Wolfram von Eschenbach.

1107.   ────. "A Minor Analogue of *SGGK*." *Neophil*, 44
        (1960), 37-38.

        Suggests *Miles Gloriosus* as an analogue.

1108.   ────. "The Progressive Magnification: an Instance
        of Psychological Description in *SGGK*." *MSpr*, 54
        (1960), 245-53.

        Examines the technique by which surroundings are mag-
        nified (and thus made more threatening) in direct pro-
        portion to G's anxiety.

1109.   ────. "An Echo to the Sense: The Patterns of Sound
        in *SGGK*." *EM*, 13 (1962), 9-23. Rpt. in item 891.

        Discusses the effectiveness of the poet's use of lan-
        guage to persuade the audience to imagine significant
        sounds.

1110.   Rice, Nancy Hall. "Beauty and the Beast and the Little
        Boy: Clues about the Origins of Sexism and Racism from
        Folklore and Literature: Chaucer's 'The Prioress's Tale,'
        SGGK, the Alliterative *Morte Arthure*, Webster's *The
        Duchess of Malfi*, Shakespeare's *Othello*, Hawthorne's
        'Rappaccini's Daughter,' Melville's 'Benito Cereno.'"
        Diss., Massachusetts, 1975. Abst.: *DAI*, 36 (1975),
        875A.

1111. Richardson, M.E. "A note on *SGGK*, l. 877." *N&Q*, 180
       (1941), 96-97.

       Glosses *koynt* "of subtle or curious workmanship."

1112. Richter, Marcelle T. "The Allegory of Love's Hunt. A
       Medieval Genre." Diss., Columbia, 1962.

       Includes material on *G*. Cf. item 1228.

1113. Rigby, Marjory. "The GK Shoeless Again." *RES*, NS 7
       (1956), 173-74.

       Provides further support for the gloss in item 760 of
       scholes (160).

1114. Rix, Michael M. "A Re-Examination of the Castleton
       Garlanding." *F-L*, 64 (1953), 342-44.

       A parallel to the GK.

1115. Robbins, Rossell Hope. "A *G* Epigone." *MLN*, 58 (1943),
       361-66.

       Specifies parallels between a poem by Humfrey Newton
       and *G*. Cf. items 775 and 1116.

1116. ————. "The Poems of Humfrey Newton, Esquire, 1466-
       1536." *PMLA*, 65 (1950), 249-81.

       Mentions the parallels noted in item 1115 (pp. 258-59).

1117. ————. "ME Misunderstood: Mr. Speirs and the Goblins."
       Anglia, 85 (1967), 270-81.

       A destructive analysis of Speirs's writings on ME, in-
       cluding his essay on *G* (item 1192).

1118. Robertson, D.W., Jr. "Why the Devil Wears Green."
       MLN, 69 (1954), 470-72.

       Mainly on the *Friar's Tale*. Provides evidence that
       the Devil was thought to wear green (as a hunter). Cf.
       item 1099.

1119. Robinson, Ian. "Chaucer's Contemporaries: 2, *SGGK*."
       Chaucer and the English Tradition. Cambridge: UP,
       1972. Pp. 219-33.

       Considers a number of issues, including the signifi-
       cance of the challenge and temptation. Sees G as an
       example of patience. Appends a note on line 1770.

1120. Rosenthal, F. "Die alliterierende englische langzeile im 14. Jahrhundert." *Anglia*, 1 (1878), 414-59.

Discusses the characteristics of the alliterative long line, illustrating his argument from eight poems, including *G*. Summarizes information on editions, date, and dialect of *G* (p. 417).

1121. Ryan, J.S. "The *Ubi Sunt* Theme in *SGGK*." *JFA*, 3 (1967), 211-13.

Suggests that this theme implies Camelot's decline from an earlier ideal.

1122. Sakai, Tsuneo. "On Conjunctive Particles Introducing Subordinate Clauses in *SGGK*." *Shiron*, no. 1 (1958), 74-103.

A structural and descriptive analysis of conjunctive particles introducing subordinate clauses. In Japanese.

1123. ————. "On Some Aspects of the Infinitives in *SGGK*." *BK*, 11, vii (1962), 1-15.

A descriptive analysis of infinitive phrases. In English.

1124. Samson, Anne. "*SG*." *EIC*, 18 (1968), 343-47.

Makes a number of points in response to item 139, emphasizing in particular the structural unity of *G*. Cf. items 1098, etc.

1125. Sanderlin, George. "*Thagh I were burde bryghtest--GGK*, 1283-1287." *ChauR*, 8 (1973), 60-64.

Argues against emending 1283, and against some editorial punctuation of 1283-84.

1126. Saperstein, J. "Some Observations on *SGGK*." *ESA*, 5 (1962), 29-36.

Praises the poet's descriptive technique, and the delicate irony of his criticism of the chivalric ideal. Cf. items 707, etc.

1127. Savage, Henry L[yttleton]. "The Significance of the Hunting Scenes in *SGGK*." *JEGP*, 27 (1928), 1-15.

Suggests that there are symbolic connections between
equivalent hunting and temptation scenes; provides evidence of prevailing attitudes to the deer, boar, and
fox from manuals on hunting and heraldry. Cf. items
738, 834, 872, 982, 1228; also 1148.

1128. ————. "*SGGK*, l. 1704." *MLN*, 44 (1929), 249-50.

Discusses the meaning of *fyske₃* and the antecedent of
he.

1129. ————. "*Fnasted* in *SG*, 1702." *PQ*, 9 (1930), 209-10.

Argues for glossing "sniffed."

1130. ————. "A Note on *SGGK*, 700-2." *MLN*, 46 (1931), 455-
57.

Provides evidence that the Wirral was considered law-
less during the Middle Ages.

1131. ————. "Notes on *SGGK*." *PMLA*, 46 (1931), 169-76.

Notes on the following lines: 296, 310, 493, 722, 1006,
1028, 1147, 1154-59, 1161, 1320, 1324, 1380, 1423, 1467,
1563, 1595, 1602, 1603, 1604, 1701, 1714, 1726, 1913,
2251.

1132. ————. "A Note on *SGGK* 2035." *MLN*, 49 (1934), 232-
34.

Parses *gay* (2035) as an adverb "rather."

1133. ————, Henry [Lyttleton]. "A Note on *SGGK*, l. 1700."
MAE, 4 (1935), 199-202.

Glosses *traylez* (1700) "search a wood for game."

1134. ————. "*Scrape* in *SG*." *TLS*, 26 Sept. 1936, p. 768;
31 Oct. 1936, p. 887.

Glosses *scrape* (1571) "sharpen," and compares *scraped*
"inscribed" in *Cl* 1546. The second note corrects a mis-
print.

1135. ————. "*Brow* or *Brawn*." *MLN*, 52 (1937), 36-38.

Disputes the emendation of MS *browe* (1457) to *browen* in
item 111. Glosses "brow."

1136. ————. "SG and the Order of the Garter." ELH, 5
       (1938), 146-49.

       A brief statement of the author's theory about Enguer-
       rand de Coucy (developed in item 1148).

1137. ————. "The historical background of the 14th cen-
       tury English poem SGGK." YAPS, 1939, pp. 281-82.

       Outlines plans for the research which later appeared
       in item 1148.

1138. ————. "A Note on SG 1795." MLN, 55 (1940), 604.

       Discusses the gloss "woman" for the second may in this
       line.

1139. ————. "Methles in SGGK 2106." MLN, 58 (1943), 46-
       47.

       Glosses "without principle."

1140. ————. Review of item 88. MLN, 59 (1944), 342-50.

       Sepcific comments and suggestions on the following
       lines: 98, 123, 143, 306, 336, 409, 447, 452, 743, 820,
       832, 992, 1020-29, 1077, 1124, 1159, 1176, 1238, 1266,
       1343, 1396, 1429, 1460, 1466, 1467, 1511-12, 1569, 1573,
       1621, 1700, 1706, 1726, 1728, 1736, 1743, 1751, 1795,
       1863, 1999, 2002, 2022, 2026, 2055, 2076, 2082, 2098,
       2226, 2232, 2318, 2409, 2420, 2450, 2467, 2482.

1141. ————. "Lote, Loteȝ in SGGK." MLN, 60 (1945), 492-
       93.

       Discusses the sense of lote in G 639. Lists suggested
       glosses for all occurrences of lote(ȝ) in G, Pe, and
       Pat.

1142. ————, H[enry] L[yttleton]. "SGGK, lines 875-77."
       Expl, 3 (1945), item 58.

       Comments on the chair and cushions.

1143. ————, Henry L[yttleton]. "SGGK, lines 206-7." Expl,
       4 (1946), item 41.

       On the description of holly.

1144. ————. "SG fer ouer þe French flod." JEGP, 47 (1948),
       44-52.

A review article on item 103. Includes comments on sources, authorship, and hunting terms.

1145.   ————. "The GK's *Molaynes*." *Philologica: The Malone Anniversary Studies.* Ed. Thomas A. Kirby and Henry Bosley Woolf. Baltimore: Johns Hopkins Press; London: Cumberledge, 1949. Pp. 167-78.

Reviews interpretations of *molaynes* (169); suggests that it signifies the bosses on the end of the bit.

1146.   ————. "Hunting Terms in ME." *MLN*, 66 (1951), 216.

Offers a minor correction to item 1069.

1147.   ————. "The Feast of Fools in *SGGK*." *JEGP*, 51 (1952), 537-44.

Suggests that lines 63-65 describe the noisy and irreverent behavior associated with the Feast of Fools.

1148.   ————, Henry Lyttleton. *The "G"-Poet: Studies in His Personality and Background.* Chapel Hill: Univ. of North Carolina Press; London: Oxford UP, 1956.

1. Provides a general account of the poet's work (taken to include *Erk*), discussion of the experience it reflects, and speculation that he belonged to a great household in the NW.
2. A modified version of item 1127.
3. A summary of the life of the French nobleman Enguerrand de Coucy, a Guines. (He married Isabella, eldest daughter of Edward III, took over estates in NW England, and became a Knight of the Garter; on the renewal of war in 1377, he abandoned his wife and returned to France.) Draws parallels between *G* and the life of Coucy, suggesting that these are deliberate allusions.
Appendixes: A. The English estates of the Coucy-Guines; B. linguistic data for the localization of *G*; C. evidence for dating; D. potential patrons among the Garter knights; E. connections between the pentangle and the French Order of the Star; F. the life of Philippa (Coucy's daughter); G. hypothesis that *G* 862-71 alludes to the Coucy or Guines arms (illustrated); H. hypothesis that *G* 642-50 refers to a Coucy *cri de guerre*; J. hypothesis that *G* 2515-20 alludes to the foundation of the (French) Order of the Crown (associated with Coucy's

return); K. suggestion that the poet had legal training; L. text of Coucy's letter of resignation from the
Order of the Garter.

Reviews: Anon., *TLS*, 31 May 1957, p. 337.
John Conley, *Speculum*, 32 (1957), 858-61.
N[orman] D[avis], *RES*, NS 9 (1958), 426-28.
George J. Engelhardt, *CE*, 18 (1956), 128.
R. Highfield, *MAE*, 28 (1959), 129-31.
Thomas A. Kirby, *MLN*, 72 (1957), 212-14.
William McColly, *JEGP*, 57 (1958), 119-21.
Charles Moorman, *MP*, 54 (1957), 271-73.
B.J. Timmer, *YWES*, 37 (1956), 80.

1149. ―――――, Henry L[yttleton]. "'Hang Up Thine Axe.'"
N&Q, 210 (1965), 375-76.

Comments on the proverbial expression in line 477.

1150. ―――――. "*Fare*, Line 694 of *SGGK*." *Schlauch*, pp. 373-
74.

Glosses "state of things," or, more likely, "food."

1151. Schaubert, E[lse] v[on]. "Der englische Ursprung von
Syr Gawayn and the Grene Knyȝht." *EStn*, 57 (1923),
331-446.

1. A plot summary.
2. Summarizes the views of Hulbert (item 893) and Kittredge (item 934) on the relationship between *G* and
   its sources.
3. A discussion of the theories of Hulbert and Kittredge. Rejects Hulbert; endorses Kittredge on the
   beheading game, but questions his views on the temptation theme, the combined plot, and the artistic
   merit of *G*.
4. Suggests that in view of the characteristics of
   French Arthurian literature, it is unlikely that *G*
   is based on a French original.
5. Argues that the combination of an Arthurian story
   and a strong moral theme is typical of the English
   tradition (drawing parallels with various other alliterative poems), but not of the French.
6. A brief summary.
Cf. items 934, etc.

1152. Schelp, Hanspeter. "*Nurture*: Ein mittelenglischer
Statusbegriff." *Anglia*, 83 (1965), 253-70.

Argues that *nurture* is the key concept in the adulation
of G at the castle (pp. 253-54).

1153. Schiller, Andrew. "The *G* Rhythm." *Lang&S*, 1 (1968),
268-94.

A metrical analysis of *G* as isochronic verse, illustrated by part of the text (lines 60-84) annotated with
musical notation. Draws parallels with other alliterative verse (both OE and ME) and with stylistic devel-
opments in contemporary music.

1154. Schlauch, Margaret. "*SG* as Society Romance." *Anteced-
ents of the English Novel 1400-1600 (from Chaucer to
Deloney)*. Warszawa: Panstwowe Wydawnictwo Naukowe;
London: Oxford UP, 1963. Pp. 23-28.

Summarizes the plot and discusses narrative technique.

1155. ————. "Arthurian Material in Some Late Icelandic
Sagas." *BBSIA*, 17 (1965), 87-91.

Mentions parallels between *G* and *Vilhjálms saga sjóds*.
Cf. items 837, etc.

1156. Schmittbetz, Karl Roland. *Das Adjectiv im Vers von
"Syr Gawayn and þe Grene Knyȝt."* Bonn: Eisele, 1908.
Diss., Bonn, 1908.

The fourth part of the author's investigation into the
adjective in *G*; the first three parts form item 1157.

Analyzes the adjective's function in the verse under
the following headings: 1. alliteration and rhyme in
long and short lines; 2. relationship between alliteration and stress; 3. position of the adjective in relation to alliteration and rhyme; 4. syntactical uses of
the adjective.

1157. Schmittbetz, K[arl Roland]. "Das Adjectiv in *Syr Gawayn and the Grene Knyȝt.*" *Anglia*, 32 (1909), 1-60,
163-89, 359-83.

A study of the adjectives in *G*.

A. Formal aspects of the adjective.
B. 1. The adjective considered as a vehicle for meaning.
     Lists all adjectives, and deals with them in sub-
     sections (according to derivation; those with
     prefixes and suffixes; composite adjectives; sub-
     stantive adjectives; uncertain derivations).

2. Considered stylistically. Groups adjectives according to their descriptive function, and with regard to the object described.
C. The function of the adjective in the clause: 1. attributive; 2. appositive; 3. predicative; 4. substantive; 5. affecting addition or completion; 6. introducing a clause.

See item 1156.

1158. Schnyder, Hans. "Aspects of Kingship in *SGGK*." *ES*, 40 (1959), 289-94.

Suggests that Arthur's kingship is vitiated by pride; compares him to Belshazzar in *Cl*. Cf. item 1159.

1159. ————. *"SGGK": An Essay in Interpretation*. Cooper Monographs on English and American Literature, 6. Bern: Francke, 1961.

1. Reviews trends in criticism on *G*.
2. Argues for the allegorical interpretation of all medieval fiction.
3. Fitt 1: Interprets Arthur as a proud king (cf. item 1158), the GK as the Word of God (or, anagogically, Christ), and the beheading as the cutting away of the Old Law.
4. G's journey: Sees this as an inward journey (cf. item 1217), associating G's opponents with the seven deadly sins.
5. Lines 763-1997: Interprets the arrival at the castle as G's discovery of Jerusalem within himself; the temptations as (respectively) greed, vainglory, and covetousness; and the hunted animals as (respectively) the flesh, the world, and the devil.
6. Interprets the journey to the Green Chapel tropologically, as a descent into hell.

Reviews: Guy Bourquin, *EA*, 16 (1963), 70.
        Basil Cottle, *JEGP*, 61 (1962), 913-15.
        K.H. Göller, *Anglia*, 79 (1961), 473-75.
        Werner Habicht, *Archiv*, 199 (1962), 51-52.
        A. Macdonald and Betty Hill, *YWES*, 42 (1961), 66-67.
        R.M. Wilson, *MLR*, 57 (1962), 298-99.

1160. Schroeder, Henry Alfred, Jr. "*SGGK*: An Essay in Criticism." Diss., Yale, 1964.

1161.   Schutt, J.H. *An Introduction to English Literature*, I.
         Groningen: Wolters, 1928; 2nd ed., 1935.

         A summary of the plot with brief comments. Reproduces
         one MS illustration (pp. 28-30 in 2nd ed.).

1162.   Scott, P.G. "A Note on the Paper Castle in *SGGK*."
         N&Q, 211 (1966), 125-26.

         Argues that *G* 800-02 implies a moral warning, and com-
         pares *Cl* 1407-08 and the *Parson's Tale* (*CT* X.444, mis-
         numbered 445) Cf. items 119, 945.

1163.   Scudder, Vida D. *"Le Morte Darthur" of Sir Thomas
         Malory: A Study of the Book and its Sources*. London:
         Dent; New York: Dutton, 1921.

         Briefly compares the story in *G* with other versions.

1164.   Self-Weeks, W. *"Gawayne and the Green Knight: Harled."*
         N&Q, 148 (1925), 122.

         Glosses "knotted, entangled" (line 744).

*   Serjeantson, Mary S. See item 88.

1165.   Shedd, Gordon M. "Knight in Tanished Armour: The Mean-
         ing of *SGGK*." *MLR*, 62 (1967), 3-13.

         Analyzes the nature of G's failure, and argues for its
         thematic importance in a romance which explores man's
         weaknesses as well as his strengths.

1166.   Shepherd, Geoffrey. "The Nature of Alliterative Poetry
         in Late Medieval England." Sir Israel Gollancz Memo-
         rial Lecture, 1970. *PBA*, 56 (1970), 57-76. Also pub.
         separately, London: Oxford UP, 1971.

         Comments on the function of the hunting scenes (pp. 58-
         59).

1167.   Shibata, Shozo. "On the Construction of the Third Fitt
         in *SGGK*." *EngS*, no. 5 (1973), 61-66.

         An analysis of the subtle structure of the third fitt.
         In Japanese.

1168.   Shimizu, Aya. "Approaches to *SGGK*." *BTGU*, ser. II, 19
         (1968), 83-110.

         A general study of the poem. Emphasizes and praises
         its artistic unity. In Japanese.

1169.   Shippey, T.A.   "The Uses of Chivalry: *Erec* and *G.*"
        MLR, 66 (1971), 241-50.

        Argues that the evaluation of *joie* as an ethical abso-
        lute in chivalric society is reflected in the creation
        of *joie* through voluntary risk-taking in *Erec* and *G.*

1170.   Shuttleworth, Jack M.   "On *G*'s Hagiology." *Discourse*,
        10 (1967), 348-51.

        Discusses references to Saints Peter, Julian, Giles,
        and John. Cf. item 1218.

1171.   Silverstein, Theodore.   "The Art of *SGGK*." *UTQ*, 33
        (1964), 258-78. Rpt. in item 891.

        A critical reading of the description of the seasons
        (491-535). Discusses the use of rhetorical devices,
        and the function of aphorisms and the *de contemptu
        mundi* theme; emphasizes the passage's energy and rele-
        vance to the narrative. Also comments on lines 713-23
        and 1998-2005.

1172.   ————.   "*SG*, Dear Brutus, and Britain's Fortunate
        Founding: A Study in Comedy and Convention." *MP*, 62
        (1965), 189-206.

        Discusses the traditions on which the poet draws in
        lines 1-26, and suggests that the motif of *blysse and
        blunder* informs the tone and matter of the whole poem.
        Cf. item 1221.

1173.   ————.   "Allegory and Literary Form." *PMLA*, 82 (1967),
        28-32.

        Argues that *G* should not be read as an allegory (pp.
        31-32).

1174.   ————.   "SG in a Dilemma, or Keeping Faith with Marcus
        Tullius Cicero." *MP*, 75 (1977), 1-17.

        Identifies the virtues specified in lines 651-55 as
        the components of justice in a traditional formula
        which goes back to Cicero; stresses their relevance to
        the theme of keeping one's promise. Cf. item 1195.

1175.   Sims, James H.   "Gawayne's Fortunate Fall in *Sir Ga-
        wayne and the Grene Knight*." *OL*, 30 (1975), 28-39.

        Argues that the poem conforms to the pattern of the
        felix culpa in that G achieves true perfection through

succumbing to temptations which destroy his assumed perfection. Cf. item 855.

1176. Sisam, Kenneth. "*Fade* in *G*, line 149." *TLS*, 27 Jan. 1927, p. 60.

Glosses "valiant, bold"; cf. items 1074, 1075, 1177.

1177. ————. "*Fade* in *G*, line 149." *TLS*, 17 Mar. 1927, pp. 193-94.

Further support for the interpretation in item 1176.

1178. ————. "*SG*, lines 147-50." *N&Q*, 195 (1950), 239.

Glosses *fade* "valiant." Cf. items 910, 1183.

1179. Skinner, Veronica L. "The Concept of *Traw þe* in *SGGK*." *MSE*, 2 (1969), 49-58.

Examines the use of *traw þe*, arguing that it embodies the central moral theme of *G*. Cf. item 741.

1180. Sklute, Larry Martin. "The Ethical Structure of Courtly Romance: Chrétien de Troyes' *Yvain* and *SGGK*." Diss., Indiana, 1967. Abst.: *DA*, 28 (1968), 3648A.

1181. Smith, John Harrington. "*G*'s Leap: *GGK* l. 2316." *MLN*, 49 (1934), 462-63.

Glosses *spenne-fote* "with feet together."

1182. Smith, Roland M. "Guinganbresil and the GK." *JEGP*, 45 (1946), 1-25.

Includes the suggestions that a green knight occurs in the Irish source for *G*, and that *Bercilak* is derived from Irish *Bresalach* "contentious." Cf. items 969, etc.

1183. Smithers, G.V. "A Crux in *SGGK*." *N&Q*, 195 (1950), 134-36.

Glosses *fade* "supernatural being, fairy"; cf. items 910, 1178.

1184. ————. "Story-patterns in some Breton lays." *MAE*, 22 (1953), 61-92.

Includes discussion of what lines 30-36 may suggest about the genesis of *G* (pp. 89-92). Cf. item 836.

1185. ————. "What *SGGK* is About." *MAE*, 32 (1963), 171-89.

Argues that the poet was influenced by *La Queste del Saint Graal*, and that his concern is with the values of spiritual rather than secular knighthood. Cf. item 1026.

1186. Snell, Beatrice Saxon. "Four Notes on *SGGK*." *N&Q*, 148 (1925), 75.

Discusses lines 11, 19, 171, 744, and 1292-1301.

1187. Snell, F.J. *The Fourteenth Century*. *Periods of European Literature*, III. Ed. George Saintsbury. Edinburgh and London: Blackwood, 1899.

Summarizes the plot (pp. 50-52).

1188. Soloman, Jan. "The Lesson of *SG*." *PMASAL*, 48 (1963), 599-608. Rpt. in item 891.

Argues that G learns *mesure* through the undermining of his pride. Cf. item 982.

1189. Sosnoski, James Joseph. "The Methodology of Kenneth Burke's Literary Criticism as Applied to *SGGK*." Diss., Pennsylvania State, 1967. Abst.: *DA*, 29 (1968), 275A.

1190. Soucy, Arnold Francis. "Linear Pattern within the Cyclical Patterns of *SGGK*." Diss., Minnesota, 1972. Abst.: *DAI*, 33 (1973), 3613A-14A.

1191. Spearing, A.C. "*SGGK*." *Criticism and Medieval Poetry*. London: Arnold; New York: Barnes and Noble, 1964. Pp. 26-45. Extract rpt. in item 891 as "G's Speeches and the Poetry of *Cortaysye*."

Maintains that the focus of interest is G (rather than the GK), discusses the significance of *cortaysye*, and analyzes G's *cortayse* style of speech (lines 343-61 and 1535-45). Passing references elsewhere in the book. Cf. item 761.

1192. Speirs, John. "*SGGK*." *Scrutiny*, 16 (1949), 274-300. Rpt. in item 827. Rpt., with some revisions, in his *Medieval English Poetry: The Non-Chaucerian Tradition*. London: Faber, 1957.

Dismisses existing scholarship. Goes on to provide a reading of G as a "midwinter festival poem," interpret-

ing the GK as a vegetation god (cf. item 1060) and the
winter landscape as a wasteland, and pointing out that
chastity is a requirement of fertility ceremonies.
Cf. items 698, 885, 950, 1117, 1193-94, 1246. On
"mythic" criticism, see items 708, 709, 767, 953, 957,
1033, 1060, 1117, 1237, 1272, 1273.

1193.   ————. Untitled reply to item 698. *Scrutiny*, 17
         (1950), 130-32.

         Defendo his reading of G (item 1192).

1194.   ————. Untitled reply to item 1246. *Scrutiny*, 18
         (1951-2), 193-96.

         Rejects Watson's criticisms.

1195.   Spendal, R.J. "The Fifth Pentad in *SGGK*." *N&Q*, 221
         (1976), 147-48.

         Suggests that the five virtues (651-55) are components
         of justice. Cf. item 1174.

1196.   Steele, Peter. "*SGGK*: The Fairy Kind of Writing."
         SoRA, 3 (1969), 258-65.

         Argues that G is essentially a fairy story; considers
         the role of game and ambiguity.

1197.   Steinbach, Paul. *Der einfluss des Crestien de Troies
         auf die altenglische Literatur*. Leipzig: Fock, 1886.

         Includes brief general comments on possible influence
         on the English G romances (pp. 48-50). Cf. items 973,
         1061.

1198.   Stephany, William Alexander. "A Study of Four ME Ar-
         thurian Romances." Diss., Delaware, 1969. Abst.: *DAI*,
         30 (1969), 1537A.

         One of the four is G.

1199.   Stevens, John. *Music and Poetry in the Early Tudor
         Court*. London: Methuen, 1961.

         Comments on *dalyaunce* (1012), *luf-talkyng* (927), and
         the New Year's gifts (66-70), on pp. 158-59, 176-77.

1200.   ————. *Medieval Romance: Themes and Approaches*.
         Hutchinson Univ. Lib. London: Hutchinson, 1973.

Analyzes G's first speech (pp. 172-74) and the first
temptation scene (pp. 188-90). Numerous passing comments.

1201. Stevens, Martin. "Laughter and Game in *SGGK*." *Speculum*, 47 (1972), 65-78.

Arguing that the festival spirit of the poem has been
neglected, discusses the function of play, games (including contests), laughter, and holidays. Cf. items
758, etc; 769, etc.

1202. Stillings, Justine T. "A Generative Metrical Analysis
of *SGGK*." *Lang&S*, 9 (1976), 219-46.

Maintains that *G* is written in syllabotonic metre, and
that the poet had a set of five metrical base rules
which permitted variation. Sees the metre of *G* as representative of a transitional phase between OE and modern verse.

   *   Stone, Brian. See item 110.

1203. Strachan, L.R.M. "The Five Wounds." *N&Q*, 171 (1936),
266.

Comments on *G* 642. Cf. items 697, 818, 1097.

1204. Sudo, Jun. "Some French Adjectives in the language of
SGGK." *HSELL*, 8 (1961), 66-75.

Considers the contribution of French loan-words to the
romantic atmosphere. In English.

1205. Sundén, K. "Några förbisedda skandinaviska lånord i
Sir Gawayne and the Grene Knyзt." *GHÅ*, 26 (1920
[Minneskrift utgift av Filologiska samfundet]), 140-53.

Discusses the meaning and etymology of the following
words: *for* (2173), *nirt* (2498), *snyrt* (2312), *skayued/
skayned* (2167), *spenne* (1076), *spenne-fote* (2316).

1206. Suzuki, Eiichi. "The Green Knight As Enigma." *ESELL*,
51-2 (1967), 99-116. Japanese tr. rpt. in *Oiji*, pp.
161-83.

Surveys interpretations of the GK, emphasizing their
mutually contradictory nature; concludes that he is essentially enigmatic. Cf. items 723, 867.

1207.   ————. "The Aesthetic Functions of Synonyms for 'Man,
        Knight' in *SGGK*." *ESELL*, nos. 53-4 (1968), 1-14.

        Takes issue with Benson's suggestion (item 706) that
        the variation of synonyms for "man" and "knight" be-
        comes a mode for defining character, arguing that its
        function is more local and limited. In English.

1208.   ————. "The Character of SG." *Oiji*, pp. 184-200.

        Suggests that the diction and plot of the poem present
        a dual view of G--realistic and idealistic. In Japa-
        nese.

1209.   ————. "Some Notes on *SGGK*." *ESELL*, no. 55 (1969),
        63-79.

        Glosses *of hyghe eldee* (844) "advanced in years," and
        argues that G's use of *hende* in 2330 suggests an ambi-
        valent attitude to the GK. (Cf. item 1213). In Japa-
        nese.

1210.   ————. "The Temptation Episode in *SGGK*." *JEI*, 1
        (1969), 1-31.

        Summarizes various interpretations of the temptation
        scenes. Discusses the significance of the temptation
        in the context of medieval value structures, and the
        nature of G's loyalty. In Japanese. Cf. items 1024,
        etc.

1211.   ————. "Morgan le Fay in *SGGK*." *ESELL*, no. 59 (1972),
        1-29.

        Argues that though she is a minor character, Morgan has
        a significant relationship to the central theme of the
        poem, in that she symbolizes the evil in G's blood. In
        Japanese. Cf. items 696, etc.

1212.   ————. "Oral-Formulaic Theme Survival: Two Possible
        Instances and Their Significance in *SGGK*." *SELit*, Eng-
        lish Number, 1972, 15-31.

        Considers lines 687-739 and 2069-90 in the light of the
        oral-formulaic themes of "exile" and "the hero on the
        beach" respectively.

1213.   ————. "A Note on the Age of the GK." *NM*, 78 (1977),
        27-30.

Argues that *of hyghe eldee* (844) should be glossed "old, advanced in age." Cf. item 1209.

1214.   Sveinsson, Einar Ól. "Herra Valvin og Karlinn grái." *StI*, 34 (1975), 117-69.

Includes discussion of parallels between the third section of *Sveins-rímur Máksssonar* and *G* (pp. 128-39). Cf. items 837, etc.

1215.   Szücs, Clara Anna Ilonka de Becze. "Visual Experience in *SG*: A Method of Discovering Depictive Techniques." Diss., Michigan, 1974. Abst.: *DAI*, 35 (1975), 4470A-71A.

1216.   Taitt, Peter Stewart. "The Quest Theme in Representative English Works of the Thirteenth and Fourteenth Centuries." Diss., British Columbia, 1974. Abst.: *DAI*, 35 (1974), 3703A.

Includes material on *G*.

1217.   ————, Peter [Stewart]. "SG's Double Quest." *RUO*, 45 (1975), 508-17.

Sees G's quest as simultaneously exterior (chivalric adventure) and interior (self-discovery).

1218.   Tamplin, Ronald. "The Saints in *SGGK*." *Speculum*, 44 (1969), 403-20.

Emphasizes the aptness of the poet's references to saints (the Virgin, St. John, St. Peter, St. Giles, and St. Julian) in view of the traditions associated with each of them. Cf. item 1170.

1219.   Taylor, A[lbert] B. *An Introduction to Medieval Romance*. London: Heath Cranton, 1930.

Contains specific discussion of Morgan (p. 77), G's character (pp. 82-84), the poet's skill (pp. 164-65), and supernatural elements (pp. 216, 220). Also various passing references.

1220.   Taylor, Andrew. "*SGGK*." *MCR*, 5 (1962), 66-75.

A general critical reading. Emphasizes the contrast between courtly civilization and the amoral energy of nature. Cf. items 840, etc.

1221.   Taylor, P[aul] B[eekman]. "*Blysse and blunder*: Nature
        and Ritual in *SGGK*." *ES*, 50 (1969), 165-75.

        Suggests that *G* portrays the confrontation between
        blysse (human conformity to the laws of nature and
        God), and *blunder* (human deviation from these laws).
        Cf. item 1172.

1222.   ————, Paul Beekman. "Icelandic Analogues to the
        Northern English G Cycle." *JPC*, 4 (1970), 93-106.

        Mentions parallels to the shape-shifter and some de-
        tails in *G*. Cf. items 837, etc.

1223.   ————, P[aul] B[eekman]. "Commerce and Comedy in *SG*."
        PQ, 50 (1971), 1-15.

        Discusses the comic effect of the poet's use of the
        language of commerce; suggests that G's commercial and
        courtly debts represent spiritual penury.

1224.   ————. "G's Garland of Girdle and Name." *ES*, 55
        (1974), 6-14.

        Argues that the questioning of G's name and identity
        symbolizes the testing of his moral identity.

1225.   Tegethoff, Ernst von. *Märchen, Schwänke, und Fabeln.*
        Bücher des Mittelalters, IV. Ed. Friedrich von der
        Leyen. München: Bruckmann, 1925.

        A summary of *G* in German, with a brief introductory
        note.

1226.   Tester, Sue K. "The Use of the Word *Lee* in *SGGK*."
        Neophil, 54 (1970), 184-90.

        Discusses the origin and meaning of this word, and its
        significance in *G* 849 and 1893.

1227.   Thiébaux, Marcelle. "SG, the Fox Hunt, and Henry of
        Lancaster." *NM*, 71 (1970), 469-79.

        Draws parallels between Bertilak (as hunter and con-
        fessor/corrector) and Henry of Lancaster, and between
        the symbolism of the fox hunt in *G* and Henry's *Livre de*
        Seyntz Medicines.

1228.   ————. "The Instructive Chase." *The Stag of Love:*
        The Chase in Medieval Literature. Ithaca and London:
        Cornell UP, 1974. Pp. 71-88. (Cf. item 1112).

Brings evidence from hunting manuals and moral writings
to illustrate the various moral implications of the
contrast between the activity of the hunts and the in-
activity of G. Cf. items 1127, etc.

1229.   Thomas, Martha Carey. *"Sir Gawayne and the Green
        Knight":* a *Comparison with the French "Perceval,"* pre-
        ceded by an *Investigation of the Author's other works,*
        and followed by a *Characterization of G in English po-
        ems.* Zurich: Füssli, 1883. Diss., Zurich, 1883.

        Supports common authorship, suggesting the sequence *Pe-
        G-Cl-Pat,* and arguing that *Cl* and *Pat* were written af-
        ter the B-text of *Piers Plowman.*

        Compares episodes in *G* to the Carados and Guigambresil
        stories in the French *Perceval;* also mentions parallels
        in the prose *Perceval* and some English poems. Reviews
        the treatment of G in English romances.

        Review: G[aston] P[aris], *Romania,* 12 (1883), 376-80.

1230.   Thomas, P.G. "The ME Alliterative Poem *Sir Gawayne
        and the Green Knight.*" *EStn,* 47 (1913), 311-13.

        Comments on the following lines: 28, 153-55, 160, 267,
        795, 1097, 1238, 1296, 1623, 1663, 1764, 2175, 2438.

1231.   Thompson, Raymond Henry. "SG and Heroic Tradition: A
        Study of the Influence of changing Heroic Ideals upon
        the Reputation of G in the Medieval Literature of
        France and Britain." Diss., Alberta, 1970.

1232.   Thomson, E. "An Analysis of the Character and Role of
        SG in ME Arthurian Romances." M.A. thesis, Manchester,
        1973/5.

*   Toelken, J. Barre. See item 992.

1233.   Toyota, Masanori. "Structure and Technique of *SGGK.*"
        EQ, 8 (1971), 94-110.

        Considers the poet's contrastive technique in the var-
        iation of expressions denoting G. In Japanese.

1234.   Trautmann, Moritz. "Zur kenntniss und geschichte der
        mittelenglischen stabzeile." *Anglia,* 18 (1896), 83-100.

        Argues that the alliterative long line has seven stress-
        es, using lines 37-54 as one of the illustrative pas-
        sages.

1235. Turville-Petre, Joan. "The Metre of *SGGK*." *ES*, 57 (1976), 310-28.

Suggests the need for modification of the views of Luick (item 241). Analyzes the metre of *G* under the following heads: 1. the structure of the statement; 2. accentual patterns; 3. alliteration and accentuation.

1236. Tuttleton, James W. "The Manuscript Divisions of *SGGK*." *Speculum*, 41 (1966), 304-10.

Argues that all nine large capitals are significant, dividing *G* into major and minor parts analogous to acts and scenes. Cf. items 715, 880.

1237. Utley, Francis Lee. "Folklore, Myth, and Ritual." *Critical Approaches to Medieval Literature: Selected Papers from the English Institute, 1958-1959.* Ed. Dorothy Bethurum. New York and London: Columbia UP, 1960. Pp. 83-109.

Includes a review of "mythic" critiques of *G* (pp. 86-92). Cf. items 1192, etc.

1238. ———. "The Strategies of Translation." *JAE*, 3 (1969), 137-48.

Mainly concerned with Constance Hieatt's version of *G* for children (omitted from this bibliography: see introduction, p. x). Also makes some more general observations on the problems of translating *G*. Cf. item 879.

1239. Valaitis, Kristina Anne. "The Narrator of *SGGK*." Diss., Northern Illinois, 1974. Abst.: *DAI*, 35 (1974), 2957A.

1240. Veitch, John. *The Feeling for Nature in Scottish Poetry*, I. Edinburgh and London: Blackwood, 1887.

Considers *G* a Scottish poem. Praises the nature descriptions, quoting at length (pp. 134-39, 144-45). Cf. items 166, etc.

1241. Ven-Ten Bensel, Elise Francisca Wilhelmina Maria van der. *The Character of King Arthur in English Literature*. Amsterdam: Paris, 1925. Diss., Amsterdam, 1925.

Includes a brief discussion of the youthfulness and courtesy of Arthur in *G* (pp. 136-37). Cf. items 746, etc.

1242. Waldron, R[onald] A. "The Diction of English Romances
       of the Fourteenth Century in the Alliterative Long
       Line without Rhyme: Some Studies in the Conventional
       Elements, with Special Reference to Use of the Recur-
       ring Formulae." M.A. thesis, London, 1953/4.

       Contains material on *G*. Cf. item 352.

1243. ————. "*SGGK*, 1046-51." *N&Q*, 207 (1962), 366-67.

       Suggests an ironic interpretation of these lines.

1244. Walsh, Edward Michael. "The Meaning of Rhythmic
       Changes in Fourteenth-Century English Poetry." Diss.,
       Southern Illinois, 1974. Abst.: *DAI*, 35 (1975),
       7883A.

       Includes material on *G*.

1245. Waswo, Richard. "Parables of Civilization: *SGGK* and
       The Tempest." *Genre*, 6 (1973), 448-61.

       Argues that both works are parables affirming the value
       of a civilization which can acknowledge human limita-
       tions.

1246. Watson, John Gillard. Letter. *Scrutiny*, 18 (1951-2),
       191-93.

       Expresses reservations about the attitude to scholar-
       ship in item 1192. Cf. item 1194.

1247. Watson, Melvin R. "The Chronology of *SGGK*." *MLN*, 64
       (1949), 85-86.

       Suggests that the poet telescoped the third and fourth
       days of the period between Christmas and New Year's
       Day. Cf. item 854.

1248. Webb, P.H. "*SGGK*." *UES*, 1 (1967), 29-42.

       Not seen.

1249. Weidhorn, Manfred. "The Anxiety Dream in Literature
       from Homer to Milton." *SP*, 64 (1967), 65-82.

       Includes brief discussion of *G* 1750-54 (p. 79).

1250. Weiss, Victoria L[ouise]. "G's First Failure: the Be-
       heading Scene in *SGGK*." *ChauR*, 10 (1976), 361-66.

Argues that in beheading the GK, G responds to the challenge with unnecessary violence.

1251. ———, Victoria Louise. "Knightly Conventions in *SGGK*." Diss., Lehigh Univ., 1977. Abst.: *DAI*, 38 (1977), 2110A.

1252. Weston, Jessie L. "*SGGK*." *The Legend of SG: Studies upon its Original Scope and Significance.* Grimm Lib., 7. London: Nutt, 1897. Pp. 85-102.

Provides a plot summary, and a discussion of the relationship of analogues to G and to each other.

1253. Whaley, Helen R. "*SGGK* and Biblical Tradition: The Scriptural Pattern of the Work of the G-poet." Diss., New York State (Buffalo), 1972. Abst.: *DAI*, 33 (1973), 4370A-71A.

1254. Whitbread, L. "A Reading in *Sir Gawayne*." *N&Q*, 189 (1945), 189-90.

Suggests transposing *þaʒ* (350) and *þat* (352).

1255. White, Beatrice. "*Chevisaunce* as a Flower Name." *RES*, 21 (1945), 317-19.

Mentions the use of this word in G.

1256. ———. "Two Notes on ME." *Neophil*, 37 (1953), 113-15.

The second note discusses *barlay* (296).

1257. ———. "The GK's Classical Forbears." *NM*, 66 (1965), 112-19.

Provides evidence that the motif of the continuing life of the severed head is found in classical literature as well as folk-lore.

1258. White, Robert B., Jr. "A Note on the GK's Red Eyes (*GGK*, 304)." *ELN*, 2 (1965), 250-52. Rpt. in item 891.

Argues that the red eyes would have been taken to signify courage and ferocity.

1259. Whiting, B.J. "G: His Reputation, His Courtesy, and His Appearance in Chaucer's *Squire's Tale*." *MS*, 9 (1947), 189-234. Rpt. in item 827.

Provides an extensive review of the treatment of G in literature written in various periods and languages. In the final section, suggests that the *Squire's Tale* reflects familiarity with *G*. Cf. items 932, 991, 1026, 1079, 1096, 1100, 1104.

1260. Whiting, Ella Keats. "Introduction" to her ed. of *The Poems of John Audelay*. EETS, OS 184. London: Milford, Oxford UP, 1931. Rpt., New York: Kraus, 1971.

Lists words which occur in both Audelay's poem 54 and *G* (pp. xxiv-xxv).

1261. Wilson, Anne. "*SGGK*." *Traditional Romance and Tale: How Stories Mean*. [Cambridge]: Brewer; [Totowa, N.J.]: Rowman and Littlefield, 1976. Pp. 96-108.

Suggests that the poem consists of events and situations which G dreams, thus revealing his psychological make-up. Elsewhere in the book, discusses, in passing, non-naturalistic elements (pp. 1-6) and the hunting and temptation scenes (pp. 80-82). Cf. items 729, 795, 993.

1262. Wilson, Janet. "A Note on the Use of the Word *knyȝt* in Fitt 4 of *SGGK*." *Parergon*, no. 13 (Dec. 1975), 49.

Not seen.

1263. Woods, William Forrester. "The Hero in Search of Himself: the Ethical Development of the Hero in *Yvain*, *Parzival* and *SGGK*." Diss., Indiana, 1975. Abst.: *DAI*, 36 (1975), 2803A.

1264. Wright, Elizabeth Mary. "Notes on *Sir Gawayne and the Green Knight*." *EStn*, 36 (1906), 209-27.

Notes on the following lines: 169, 186, 191, 211, 296, 412, 420, 630, 717, 745, 752, 789, 795, 958, 1026, 1160, 1169, 1421, 1427, 1466, 1497, 1514, 1663, 1698, 1700, 1710, 1726, 1896, 1972, 2003, 2018, 2076, 2080, 2081, 2137, 2167, 2182, 2189, 2199, 2274, 2303, 2316, 2337, 2370, 2424, 2498.

1265. ————, Elizabeth M[ary]. "The Word *Abloy* in *Sir Gawayne and the Green Knight*." *MLR*, 18 (1923), 86-87.

Glosses "dazed, transported, reckless."

1266. ————. "*SGGK*." *JEGP*, 34 (1935), 157-79, 339-50.

Sees the GK's appearances as a kind of "play-acting."
Comments on the following lines: 16, 39, 48, 91, 98,
104, 112, 229, 235, 274, 277, 308, 349, 412, 432, 447,
465, 483, 506, 521, 554, 572, 601, 617, 660, 683, 723,
750, 752, 792, 863, 896, 946, 979, 983, 984, 1004, 1006,
1114, 1116, 1124, 1139, 1143, 1161, 1202, 1247, 1283,
1312, 1319, 1377, 1390, 1409, 1421, 1427, 1460, 1474,
1486, 1513, 1562, 1606, 1621, 1637, 1647, 1663, 1698,
1713, 1743, 1748, 1751, 1822, 1895, 1939, 1940, 1968,
1972, 1983, 1986, 2012, 2022, 2041, 2048, 2051, 2054,
2075, 2083, 2084, 2111, 2126, 2140, 2173, 2181, 2205,
2211, 2219, 2230, 2232, 2342, 2370, 2387, 2400, 2420,
2424, 2511.

1267. ————. "*SGGK*." *JEGP*, 35 (1936), 313-20.

Notes on the following lines: 91, 143, 167, 384, 409,
694, 889, 918, 1108, 1109, 1128, 1129, 1250, 1266,
1479, 1499, 1696, 1811, 1861, 1889, 1999, 2076, 2300,
2506.

*   ————. "Additional Notes on *SGGK*." *JEGP*, 38 (1939),
1-22. See item 583.

1268. Wright, Thomas L. "SG *in vayres*." *PQ*, 53 (1974), 427-
28.

Suggests that these words (1015) may refer to a heral-
dic design.

1269. Yamaguchi, Hideo. "A Lexical Note on the Language of
SGGK." *PP*, 8 (1965), 372-80.

Discusses OF and ON influence on the poet's language;
tabulates synonyms with these respective origins. In
Japanese.

1270. Yamanouchi, Kazuyoshi. "Alliterative Words for 'Man,
Warrior' in *SGGK*." *SHumS*, no. 20 (1969), 1-30.

An investigation of the ten synonyms for "man, warrior"
which occur in the poem. In Japanese. Cf. items 731,
etc.

1271. Yerkes, David. "*SGGK* 211: *Grayn*." *N&Q*, 220 (1975), 4.

Provides another instance of *grayn* meaning "spike."

*   Zacher, Christian. See item 891.

1272.   Zimmer, Heinrich. *The King and the Corpse: Tales of the Soul's Conquest of Evil.* Ed. Joseph Campbell. Bollingen ser., 11. New York: Pantheon, 1948; 2nd ed., 1956. Extract rpt. in item 827.

Provides a detailed plot summary. Relates *G* to cyclical myths and Eastern stories; interprets the GK as Death and the Lady as Life. Goes on to discuss various other stories associated with G (pp. 67-95). Cf. items 1192, etc.

1273.   ———. *"Gawan beim grünen Ritter."* *DBGÜ*, 7 (1953), 46-56.

A "mythic" interpretation of *G*, as a story of death and rebirth. Cf. items 1192, etc.

1274.   Zimmerman, Rüdiger. "Verbal Syntax and Style in *SGGK*." *ES*, 54 (1973), 533-43.

Provides an analysis of the stylistic implications of the poet's use of tense, voice, and mood.

1275.   Zucchi, M.R. *"Sir Gawain e il Cavaliere Verde."* Diss., Torino, 1976.

III. REFERENCE

1276. Ackerman, Robert W., comp. *An Index of Arthurian Names in ME*. Stanford Univ. Pubs., Univ. ser.: Language and Literature, 10. Stanford: UP; London: Cumberlege, Oxford UP, 1952. Rpt. New York: AMS Press, 1967.

Includes all personal and place names in *G*; provides notes on sources and traditions.

1277. Bateson, F.W., comp. *600-1660*. *The Cambridge Bibliography of English Literature*, I. Cambridge: UP, 1940.

Contains sections on *G* (pp. 135-36) and the other three poems (pp. 201-03). See also item 1289.

1278. Beale, Walter H., comp. "The *Pe*-Poet (fourteenth century): *Pat*, *Pe*, *Pur*, *StE*, *SGGK*." *Old and ME Poetry to 1500: A Guide to Information Sources*. Detroit: Gale, 1976.

A selective, annotated bibliography of editions, translations, and critical writings.

* Billings, Anna Hunt. See item 710.

1279. Chapman, Coolidge Otis, comp. "A Lexical Concordance of the ME *Pe*, *Clannesse*, *Pat* and *Sir Gawayne and the Grene Knight*." Diss., Cornell, 1927.

Cf. item 1280.

1280. ————. *An Index of Names in "Pe," "Pur," "Pat," and "G."* Cornell Studies in English, 38. Cornell: UP; London: Oxford UP, 1951.

An index which lists every occurrence of names and proper nouns, and provides notes on references, sources, and traditions. Includes (for example) a list of periphrases for *God* (under *Gode*) and for *Christ* (under

Kryst), and references for all quotations from the Bible (under *Holy Wryt*). Cf. item 1279.

Reviews: Robert W. Ackerman, *JEGP*, 50 (1951), 538-39.
Thomas A. Kirby, *MLN*, 68 (1953), 582.
A. Macdonald, *RES*, NS 4 (1953), 276-78.
Henry Savage, *Speculum*, 27 (1952), 364-66.

1281. Courtney, Charles Russell, comp. "The *Pe* Poet: An Annotated International Bibliography, 1955-1970." Diss.,
Arizona, 1975. Abst.: *DAI*, 37 (1976), 327A.

1282. Foley, Michael M., comp. "A Bibliography of *Pur* (*Cl*),
1864-1972." *ChauR*, 8 (1974), 324-34.

Aims at comprehensiveness; not annotated. Cf. item
1286.

1283. Greenfield, Stanley B., comp. "A ME Bibliographical
Guide." *Zesmer*.

Includes annotated entries on the four poems, with emphasis on *G* and *Pe* (pp. 342-46, 350).

1284. Hambridge, Roger A., comp. "*SGGK*: An Annotated Bibliography, 1950-1972." *Comitatus*, 4 (1973), 49-84.

Items are listed chronologically; includes an alphabetical index of authors. Aims at comprehensiveness.

1285. Hamilton, Marie P., comp. "The *Pe* Poet." *Severs/Har-
tung*, II.

Summarizes the plots of *Pe*, *Pat*, and *Cl*, and the major
trends in scholarly writings on them (pp. 339-53).
Provides an extensive list of bibliographical references (pp. 503-16). Cf. items 1287, 1291.

1286. Metcalf, Allan A., comp. "Supplement to a Bibliography
of *Pur* (*Cl*)." *ChauR*, 10 (1976), 367-72.

An annotated supplement to item 1282.

1287. Newstead, Helaine, comp. "Arthurian Legends." *Severs/
Hartung*, I.

Summarizes the plot, sources, and major characteristics
of *G* (pp. 54-57). Provides an extensive list of bibliographical references (pp. 238-43). Cf. items 1285,
1291.

* Page, Charles. See item 1288.

1288. Tubb, Margaret, comp. "Appendix." *Ford*. Rev. Charles Page, 1969.

Provides brief bibliographies of *Pe* and *G* (pp. 488-89 in rev. ed.).

1289. Watson, George, comp. *Supplement: A.D. 600-1900. The Cambridge Bibliography of English Literature*, V. Cambridge: UP, 1957.

Includes sections on *G* (pp. 111-13) and the other three poems (pp. 128-29). Cf. item 1277.

1290. ————. *600-1600. The New Cambridge Bibliography of English Literature*, I. Cambridge: UP, 1974.

Contains sections on *G* (cols. 401-06) and the other three poems (cols. 547-54). Cf. items 1277, 1289.

1291. Wells, John Edwin, comp. *A Manual of Writings in ME 1050-1400*. 2 vols. and 9 supps. New Haven: Yale UP, 1916; 1919-51.

The *Manual* provides basic information and plot summaries (*G*, pp. 54-57; other poems, pp. 578-85), and bibliographies (*G*, p. 770; other poems, pp. 863-65). Each supplement offers a review of critical trends and supplies additions to the bibliographies. The page-numbering sequence begun in the *Manual* continues throughout the supplements. Relevant material is contained on the following pages: *G*: criticism: 953-54, 1050, 1168, 1260, 1344, 1562, 1664, 1789; bibliography: 1004, 1102, 1206, 1298, 1385-86, 1487, 1604, 1701-02, 1895. Other poems: criticism: 993-94, 1082-83, 1185, 1283, 1370, 1469, 1586-87, 1682, 1853; bibliography: 1026, 1138-39, 1229, 1319-20, 1418, 1525, 1638, 1729, 1923.

Superseded by *Severs/Hartung* (see items 1285, 1287).

SUPPLEMENTARY LIST

I.D. Editions and Translations of Pearl

1292. Miyata, Takeshi, tr. *"Shiratama": A Japanese Transla-*
tion of "Pe." Kobe: Konan Univ. Bungakukai, 1954.

A complete Japanese translation.

1293. Naruse, Masaiku, ed. and tr. "A Study of the ME *Pe.*
Part I: A Text Newly Edited with Japanese Translation."
JCulS, 6 (1971), 133-85, 221-88.

Provides a ME text, Japanese translation, and textual
notes. See item 502.

1294. Sekigawa, Sakyo, tr. *"Akoyadama*: A Japanese Translation of *Pe* (Extracts)." *An Anthology of English Lyrics.* Ed. Konosuke Hinatsu. Tokyo: Kawadeshobo, 1952.
Pp. 6-12.

Translates stanzas 1-4 and 100-01.

1295. Terasawa, Yoshio, tr. *"Shinju*: A Japanese Translation
of *Pe."* *Ancient and Medieval. Anthology of Great Poetry of the World*, I. Tokyo: Heibon-sha, 1960. Pp.
316-33.

A complete Japanese translation.

II.A. Critical Writings on more than one poem

1296. Kuriyagawa, Fumio. *English Language and Literature in
the Middle Ages.* Tokyo: Kenkusha, 1951.

211

Suggests that the theme of *G* is the victory of chastity (pp. 205-10). Provides general critical comments on *Pe* and *Cl* (pp. 266-71). In Japanese.

1297. Kuruma, Norio. "Notes on the Phonology and Spelling of MS Cotton Nero A.x." *JFLit*, no. 5 (1969), 53-66.

Deals with spellings which present problems when reading aloud. In Japanese.

1298. Matsunami, Tamotsu, and Kazuzo Ogoshi. *The Middle Ages and the Renaissance. History of English and American Literature: Poetry*, I. Tokyo: Taishukan, 1977.

Contains general comments on all four poems (pp. 251-60). In Japanese.

1299. Nakao, Toshio. "Word Order in Three Alliterative Poems, *SG*, *Cl*, *Pat*: Object-Preposition." *ForL*, no. 11 (1962), 52-58.

Concludes that word-order is almost always subservient to the demands of alliteration. In English.

1300. Naruse, Masaiku. "On the Illustrations Found in the MS. of the *G*-Group." *JCulS*, 1 (1965), 1-40, 125-66.

A detailed discussion of the relationship between the illustrations and the passages which they represent. Concludes that the illustrator did not have a good understanding of the poems; that he often provides a naively literal portrayal of points in the texts; and that he does not reflect the influence of Gothic iconography. In Japanese.

1301. ————. "On *Glode* in the *G*-Poet's Works." *Essays and Studies in Celebration of the Fiftieth Anniversary of Kobe Univ. of Commerce*. 1975. Pp. 577-612.

States that *glode* is derived from OE *gloed*, *gled*; that it originally meant "burning coal, live coal, gleed, ember, fire, flame"; and that figuratively it suggests brightness or brilliance. Goes on to discuss occurrences of this word in *Pe* 79 and 1111, and in *G* 2181 and 2266. In Japanese.

1302. ————. "The *G*-Poet: Man and Life." *JCulS*, 13 (1977), 1-50.

Reviews and rejects the theories which identify the poet as Huchoun of the Awle Ryale, Strode, John Donne or

John Pratt, and Hugo de Masci (see items 274, etc.; 185, etc.; 147; 275, etc.). Goes on to provide an imaginary reconstruction of the poet's life. In Japanese.

* Ogoshi, Kazuzo. See item 1298.

1303. Sakai, Tsuneo. "On the Future Expressions in the *SG*-Poet's Works." *BTIT*, no. 3 (1967), 63-80; no. 4 (1968), 18-37.

A descriptive and syntactical analysis of the future expression systems in the four poems. In English.

1304. Shibata, Shozo. "On the *G* Poet's certain Mannerism." *EngS*, no. 4 (1972), 10-19.

Suggests that the use of an adjective ending in -*ande* as the first alliterating word in a line is a common feature of the four poems. In Japanese.

1305. Soeda, Hiroshi. "On Color Words in *SGGK* and *Pe*." *BDENU*, no. 16 (1967), pp. unknown.

Not seen.

1306. Tajima, Matsuji. "On the Use of the Participle in the Works of the *G*-Poet." *SHumF*, no. 34 (1970), 49-70.

An investigation of the use of the participle in the four poems. In English.

1307. ————. "On the Use of the Gerund in the Works of the *G*-Poet." *SHumF*, no. 35 (1971), 1-24.

An account of the use of the gerund in the four poems. Considers a total of 123 examples. In English.

1308. ————. "On the Use of the Infinitive in the Works of the *G*-Poet." *SHumF*, no. 36 (1972), 1-56.

Provides a detailed survey of the use of the infinitive in the four poems. In English. Cf. item 362.

1309. ————. "The Neuter Pronoun *Hit* in the Works of the *G*-Poet." *LingS*, 11-12 (1976), 23-36; English sum., 89-90.

Reviews the use of *hit*. Suggests that variations in usage between the poems may be seen as evidence against the theory of common authorship.

1310. Yamanouchi, Kazuyoshi. "Some Notes on Stylistic
       Differences between *SGGK* and *Cl*." *SHumS*, no. 21 (1970),
       1-19.

       A comparative study of the vocabulary of the two poems;
       questions the theory of common authorship. In Japanese.

II.B. Critical Writings on *Pearl*

1311. Oyama, Toshiko. *Women in English Literature*. Tokyo:
       Shinozakishorin, 1955.

       Discusses the use of symbolism, parable, and romance
       tradition in the description of the Maiden (pp. 30-36).
       In Japanese.

II.E. Critical Writings on *Sir Gawain and the Green Knight*

1312. Enomoto, Tsuneya. "The English Language in *SGGK*."
       *Studies in English Language and Literature in Honor of
       Prof. Tadao Yamamoto on the Occasion of his Being
       Awarded the Japan Academy Prize*. Tokyo: Kenkyusha,
       1957. Pp. 253-63.

       Deals with phonology and accidence. Assigns the poem
       to an area comprising SE Lancashire, NE Cheshire, and
       NW Derbyshire.

1313. Matsui, Noriko. "*SGGK*: A Consideration with Special
       Reference to its Religious Elements." *Essays and Stud-
       ies in English and American Literature Presented to
       Prof. Kyoko Ohara on the Occasion of her Retirement*.
       Tokyo: Nihon Women's Univ., 1969. Pp. 107-22.

       Emphasizes the co-existence of earthly and heavenly
       values.

INDEXES

Note to the Indexes

1. Line-number index

The purpose of this index is to juxtapose the numbers of particular lines or groups of lines with the numbers of items which comment specifically on them. Though complete objectivity and consistency in the compilation of such an index is no doubt impossible, the criteria on which I have intended to work are as follows.

Items included fall into two groups: those which provide (a) textual commentary (suggested emendations, interpretation of particular words, etc.), and (b) specific comments on ideas or traditions alluded to in the line(s) in question. Items offering observations of a literary critical nature are not included. Also excluded are notes to editions and translations, and items 703 and 1081--since (a) inclusion of such material would have greatly increased the bulk of the index, and (b) such items do not present the reader with any difficulties in locating the notes relevant to particular lines.

2. Alphabetical index of authors

This is a straightforward alphabetical list of the names of authors, editors, and translators, juxtaposed with the appropriate item numbers. Reviewers are not included. As in the main bibliographical list, the letters ä, ö, ø, and ü are treated as *ae*, *oe*, *oe*, and *ue*.

Line Index: *Pearl*

Line(s)	*Item(s)*	*Line(s)*	*Item(s)*
1	165, 348, 1280	31-32	374
		32	415
1-2	375	37-38	472
1-8	373	39	262, 374, 426, 431, 443, 513, 1280
1-12	133, 193, 330, 374, 377, 550		
1-60	468	40	471
2	583	41	443, 510
3	1280	43	374, 577, 579
8	414, 423, 437, 457	43-44	510
9-10	443	44	534
9-62	413, 478	49	444, 583
10	414, 423, 437, 444, 472	49-60	457
		51	437, 461, 583
11	370, 457, 461, 472, 541, 568, 600	51-56	422
		52	374
		52-56	531
		53	414, 444, 461
13-14	444		
14-16	415	54	415, 461
17	584	55-56	532
18	478, 567	56	415, 437, 584
19	584		
19-20	444	57	415, 806
19-22	404	58-59	159
21	408, 472	59	531
22	583	61	133
23	423, 472	61-62	437
24	414, 423	61-64	468
25-36	571	62-63	432
29	159, 414	65-160	413
30	337	66	414, 415, 583

Line Index: *Cleanness*

Line Index: *Patience*

Line Index: *Gawain*

Line(s)	Item(s)	Line(s)	Item(s)
1	165, 348, 715, 880, 1236, 1276, 1280	37-59	719
		39	1266, 1276, 1280
1-2	259	40	741, 746, 897
1-19	855	43	752, 936
1-26	1172	46	726, 809, 1067
2	346		
3-4	780, 897	48	1266
3-7	738, 1280	51	936
5	1276, 1280	54	1201
7	1280	55	809
8	1276, 1280	58-59	165
10	269	60	689, 809
11	150, 755, 1186, 1276, 1280	62	809
		63	809
12	1276, 1280	63-65	1147
13	150, 1276, 1280	64	348
		66-70	1190
13-14	165	67	809
14	1276, 1280	67-70	726
14-19	983	68	809
16	717, 1266	72	809
18-19	1159	74	1276, 1280
19	1186	74-80	809
25	316	76-77	689
26	1276, 1280	77	1280
28	809, 1230	81	936
30-31	165	86	245, 741, 897, 1029
30-36	1184	88	809
33	809	91	1266, 1267
33-36	146, 775	93	689
35	119, 828, 967	95	719
		98	809, 1140, 1266
37	1276, 1280		

Line(s)	Item(s)	Line(s)	Item(s)
1215	809	1328	809
1223	689	1328-38	733
1224	809	1329	809
1228	1024	1331	1050
1230	936	1333	809
1236	133	1336	809
1236-67	998	1342-43	733
1237	269, 741,	1343	1140
	762, 786,	1345	809
	1024	1347	321, 324
1237-38	1011	1351	689
1238	809, 1140,	1355-61	733
	1230	1356	809
1240	136	1358	809
1247	1266	1360	809
1250	809, 1267	1368	843
1256	154, 809,	1369	936
	936	1372	689
1264	1024	1377	726, 1266
1264-67	1016	1379	1223
1265	689	1380	1131
1265-66	809	1381	809
1266	1140, 1267	1386	809, 936
1273	998	1390	689, 1255,
1281	1049		1266
1281-89	159	1395-97	726
1282-89	1053	1396	1140
1283	1266	1399	809, 1049
1283-84	1125	1403	809
1283-87	809, 1035	1407	809
1284	706, 1050	1409	1266
1284-85	1080	1421	323, 324,
1292	154		325, 715,
1292-1301	1186		806, 809,
1293	689, 809		880, 1236,
1296	1230		1264, 1266
1298	931	1422	689, 809
1301	809	1423	809, 1131
1304	689, 742,	1426	809
	809	1427	1264, 1266
1312	1266	1429	244, 1140
1315	809	1430	806, 1159
1319	1266	1431	346, 726,
1319-22	1069		806
1320	1131	1433	936
1324	1131	1438	1159

Author Index